# Tools for Dreamers

## Strategies for Creativity and the Structure of Innovation

by

### Robert B. Dilts

Meta Publications Inc.
P. 0. Box 1910, Capitola, CA 95010
(408) 464-0254  Fax (408) 464-0517

Library of Congress Card Number 91-061373
I.S.B.N. 0-916990-26-5

# Contents

# Dedication

We dedicate this book with deepest respect
and affection to our co-author Robert W. Dilts.
He approached this project as he did
everything else in life—"loaded for bear."

Robert B. Dilts
Todd Epstein

# Acknowledgements

We would like to acknowledge Richard Bandler and John Grinder for providing the basic tools of Neuro-Linguistic Programming, along with their dreams and their support to us as mentors and colleagues. We would also like to acknowledge George Miller, Eugene Galanter and Karl Pribram for formulating the T.O.T.E. model which serves as a fundamental organizing principle for this work; Gregory Bateson for inspiring the development of the logical levels model; and Walt Disney, whose process of Dreamer, Realist and Critic serves as the meta program for this book.

We would also like to thank our three role models: Michael Colgrass, Lowell Nobel and Bjorn Rorholt for sharing their creative insights with us. Finally, we want to extend our thanks to the participants in the seminar from which this book was drawn, and the U.S. patent system which provided the context within which we could express our own creativity.

Robert B. Dilts
Todd Epstein
Robert W. Dilts

# Introduction

*Imagination is more important than knowledge.*
—Albert Einstein

*Every animal leaves traces of what it was; man alone
leaves traces of what he created.*
—J. Bronowski, *The Ascent of Man*

Look around you and chances are that most of what you see
will in some way be the product of human creativity: books,
buildings, computers, furniture, roads, televisions, telephones,
light bulbs, airplanes, music... The list could go on forever. All
of these things were at one time just a dream in someone's
mind. Now they are a reality. That is something truly magical. What makes it possible? How does it happen? This book
is about some of the tools that turn dreams into reality.

As Einstein's comment above implies, knowledge without
imagination is useless. Imagination is what brings knowledge to life. Imagination and creativity are the driving force
behind change, adaptation and evolution. Human creativity
is the source of new possibilities and hope; of dreams, action
and accomplishment. It is also the source of uncertainty and
insecurity. Imagination and creativity can cause as many
problems as they solve if they are not managed appropriately.

On a very practical level, managing the process of creativity is one of the most important elements for success and survival, as individuals and organizations strive to adapt to the accelerating changes that are occurring in technology and society on a global level.

Thomas Edison is widely quoted as having said that the process of invention is, *"1% inspiration and 99% perspiration."* The implication of this statement is that most creative activity is in fact an incremental process that has a structure and requires organization and constant effort to maintain. In many ways, however, creativity has remained elusive—a seemingly mysterious *gift* that you either have or don't have—rather than a set of skills that can be transferred and managed systematically and explicitly.

Certainly, the development and management of the creative process has its own unique problems and issues. Creativity tends to be an individual thing. It is something we tend to learn on our own, in our own way and, in most cases, we are not quite sure how we do what we do when we *are* being creative. Creative people are largely unaware of the strategies they use to create. It is a well-known fact that the things we do best we do unconsciously. We are not aware of all of the sophisticated computations and programs we go through to drive a car, choose what to eat from a menu, or even keep our balance as we walk down the street. We know that we have learned something well when we no longer have to consciously think about it while we are doing it.

For example, as you are reading this you are making meaning out of the words on this page but are probably unaware of exactly how you are doing it. As we speak and write, we make up sentences of our own that follow sophisticated syntactic rules with no consciousness of the process we are going through. Similarly, most of us are not conscious of the rules and strategies which influence our ability to think creatively. The consequence of this limitation of consciousness has been that our creative ability has been a function of such things as our level of inspiration, mood, the number of hours we slept the previous night, etc., rather than being available to us at will. As a result, the explicit management of creativity has been hampered in the following areas:

1. There is a lack of vocabulary about our internal creative processes, making it difficult to discuss creativity with others, even peers;
2. It is difficult to explicitly teach others what we have learned about creativity and how to apply it to their own problems;
3. In some situations we can find ourselves "stuck," without a clue as to what to do about it;
4. It is difficult to identify others who have the potential and/or the ability to contribute what is needed for a particular task.

*Neuro-Linguistic Programming* (NLP) provides a set of tools that can allow us to take major steps toward the overcoming of these limitations. The mission of NLP has been to define and extend the leading edge of human knowledge—and in particular the leading edge of human knowledge about humans. One of the great contributions of NLP is that it gives us a way to look past the behavioral content of what people do to the more invisible forces behind those behaviors; to the structures of thought that allow people to perform effectively. NLP provides a structure and a language to be able to put into a set of chunks or steps the relevant mental processes used by creative and innovative people so that those mental processes can be communicated about, stimulated and managed in a systemic way.

The field of Neuro-Linguistic Programming has developed out of the modeling of human thinking skills. The NLP modeling process involves finding out about how the brain

("Neuro") is operating by analyzing language patterns ("Linguistic") and non-verbal communication. The results of this analysis are then put into step-by-step strategies or programs ("Programming") that may be used to transfer the skill to other people and content areas.

The purpose of this book is to examine the structure and principles of creativity in order to enhance and supplement the creativity and productivity of individuals, teams and organizations. Using the behavioral technology provided by Neuro-Linguistic Programming we can make the strategies and steps involved in the creative process more explicit on a number of different levels. Our goals are:

1. To define the creative process on an individual, group and organizational level.

2. To create a vocabulary that will support and enhance the creative process.

3. To provide specific ways people can more effectively support, enhance and direct creativity in individuals and teams.

4. To determine ways to identify different types of creative people.

These principles, models and skills may then be applied to:

1. Stimulating Personal Creativity: enhancing day-to-day creativity and flexibility on a personal level.

2. Managing Group Creativity: stimulating innovation within the dynamic patterns of groups and teams.

3. Promoting Entrepreneurial Beliefs and Attitudes.

A major portion of this book will be drawn from a seminar entitled *Strategies for Creativity and The Structure of Invention* which was conducted by the three authors, Robert B. Dilts, Todd Epstein and Robert W. Dilts, in San Francisco, California in May of 1983. We feel that it is quite appropriate that there are three of us presenting this material on creativity. Creativity is a multi-faceted process that involves the combination of different perspectives. We each have a different angle on the subject that will help to give you an overview of the key elements involved in the many expressions of creativity.

While not all of the material will be in the form of transcripts, we think that it is appropriate for a book on creativity to preserve the spontaneity, humor and feel of a live seminar. We have indicated the names of the individual authors in relationship to their personal contributions in order to maintain the sense of diversity and dynamic interaction. We will also be using transcripts of interviews of exceptionally creative people to further bring to life and illustrate the principles and elements of creativity that we will be covering in the book.

We would like to begin by introducing ourselves and giving you an idea of the particular perspectives that each of us are going to bring to this exploration of creativity.

### Robert B. Dilts (RBD):

I've been involved with NLP since 1975. I studied with the founders of NLP, John Grinder and Richard Bandler, when they were first formulating the core concepts that make up the foundation of NLP. I co-wrote the book *Neuro-Linguistic Programming Volume I* with them and have written a number of other books, articles and monographs on various applications and developments in NLP, including a series of studies of famous creative people such as Albert Einstein, Leonardo da Vinci, Mozart, Walt Disney and a number of others, entitled *Strategies of Genius*. I have also designed computer software based on principles of NLP. They help people to develop effective states and strategies for particular kinds of productive thinking.

My orientation in this exploration of creativity will be to uncover the specific mental events that take place inside of somebody's mind as they are being creative. This is called a *strategy* in NLP (*see* Strategy Overview in Appendix A). For example, I was once involved in a modeling project for Activision, a successful video game company. They had made 50 million dollars in one year with five software designers and were interested in continuing the trend. The goal was to take their five top game designers, and find out what their mental strategies were for creating video games.

As a function of that, we could:

1. Make a distillation of what types of thought processes went into the types of creativity that characterized the designers that they had and already liked. Then when they were hiring people or screening people, they could check for these strategies—they could find out: "Do they share the same types of thinking processes as our current designers?" When you have to interview hundreds of people it is useful to know how to tell if a particular person has the kind of creativity you are looking for.

2. Help to optimize and add to the creativity strategies of the people that already worked for the company. Each person has strengths in certain areas and weaknesses in others. For instance, some people might be creative about coming up with new ideas, but when it comes to getting a game done, six months down the road, they are still only halfway through. As one of the designers there said, "When you are totally sick and tired of the game you are working on, that means that you are about halfway through." I think this is a very insightful statement about the creative process. So, some designers have flashes of brilliance. Others have ferocious tenacity. How can we transfer what one person has to his or her colleagues who need it?

I will be talking about developing a technology for generalizing creative processes between different people and between different contexts. For instance, something that struck me about these video game designers was that very few of them took the strategies they had for being creative and applied them to other areas where they got stuck. Instead of stepping back and applying their creativity about how to resolve software problems to help with personal or relational issues, they limited their creativity to a certain narrow scope. They didn't know how to apply it to themselves.

I was involved in a similar project with Xerox. They were interested in the creativity strategy of Chester Carlson, the man who invented xerography. It was a pretty neat idea—one that personally made Carlson millions of dollars, and created a 9 billion dollar-a-year company at the same time. They were interested in how they could take his strategy and develop it in somebody else. They showed us video tapes of interviews with him to see what we could learn about his thinking process.

One of the things that NLP allows us to do is to look beyond the conscious content of someone's response to the deeper unconscious cognitive structure behind it. Most of the time, if you ask somebody what was going on in their mind when they did something creative, they are going to look back at you and say, "I don't know, it just happened." Few people are familiar enough with their own brain to be able to answer questions like that based on their own introspection. In fact, for some people, the workings of their brain are so unfamiliar, it is as if their brain belongs to somebody else. If your brain was really yours, why would it show you pictures of desserts when you are trying to diet? Why would that voice come in and tell you you are going to blow it again when you are trying to do something that you want to do? Richard Bandler has a theory that since the earth is slightly tilted on its axis, everybody actually has a brain like the person next to them. And it is unhappy being in the wrong person. And so it is constantly trying to get back at you.

A lot of people experience that; it's like your thoughts are in control of you instead of you being in control of them. One of things that I want you to take with you from this book is the ability to recognize and change the way that you are thinking if it's not suiting you, especially if it's not getting you to the outcomes that you want.

One of the interesting issues that I want to address in reference to the creative process, for instance, is the difference between 'gestation', when you are preparing to be creative, and 'procrastination', when you have actually stopped working on something and are indeed stuck. Sometimes there is a good reason for putting things off; other times it is destructive. When you are not being creative and want to be, is it because you have got a "block" or is it because there is something vital that you are actually waiting for before you can ecologically continue?

I once did a consultation with a woman who had written the first draft of a novel, and had put it in a drawer in 1977, and it was still there eight years later! She wanted to finish it, but she never had. So this procrastination/gestation problem was a very critical issue to resolve.

One analogy might be that there are certain strategies that operate like telephone numbers for different parts of our mind. If you want a pizza, you dial a certain number. If you want a haircut, you dial a different one. Sometimes you get confused and you dial the hairdresser and order a pizza with anchovies. And they don't know what you are talking about. And you wait and wait and nothing happens, and it never gets delivered. And sometimes, you might dial the pizza company by mistake, and ask for the piano tuner, and you might get a singing pizza. Then you have done something creative. One thing that is useful to do is to find out the telephone numbers used by very creative people like Albert

Einstein. What did he do in his mind that enabled him to come up with the theory of relativity? Of course, most people have their inner telephone numbers unlisted. So it's difficult to simply look them up in the phone book. Although, by the time we finish, I hope we have a telephone book of strategies that you all can use.

In summary, my particular orientation will be: How do we uncover the specific events that go on in your mind when you are creative versus when you are not? Then you can do more of what you want when you want, and have creativity at your fingertips rather than waiting for it to magically happen.


## Todd Epstein (TE):

I've been involved with NLP since 1979. I was a co-developer with Richard Bandler of a number of applications of what are called 'submodalities' in NLP. Robert was talking about a strategy as being similar to dialing the right number. What I'm going to talk about is what you do after you get someone to answer the phone. If you've connected with somebody's phone, how do you get the person you want to speak with on the other end of the line. You may have dialed the right number, but after you get that far, there are a lot of things that can happen. Just think about the creation of the hold button or answer machines.

I am going to be teaching you about some of the small chunk distinctions in the creative process. For instance, creativity is often associated with the ability to visualize and manipulate visual images. Often it's not enough to just have any picture in your mind. For instance think about the difference between having a picture in your mind that is lifelike with movement, and one that is more like a picture on a wall, flat and still. Think about the difference between having a picture in your mind that is in color as opposed to being black and white? These are some of the small chunk differences that you may need to add to that dialing sequence of creativity. You might think of it in terms of zip codes. You add five numbers to the end of the address that gets your mail to the right place. It is sort of a fine tuning device. That is one of the areas that I am going to be talking about.

I was also involved in the music business for twenty years. I have worked as a creative consultant for production, writing and engineering. And if there is one place that you hear a lot about creativity, it is in the arts. Whether it's music, dance, or theater, artists are constantly saying, "Let's be creative!" Or, "This doesn't sound very creative to me, can't we come up with something different?"

One of the things that interests me is the phenomena of unconscious creativity. It's one thing to uncover a particular thought process, and know specifically when you are being creative, and it's another thing to have the capability to make it happen that way whenever you choose. Developing the skills of creativity is a lot like when you ride a bicycle—you do it unconsciously. You don't get on and think, "Well, what foot goes on first, and how do I balance it, and where do I put this, and how do I see where I'm going while I'm pedaling, and steering at the same time?" You just get on the bicycle and go.

After you uncover some of the specific processes that Robert was referring to, the next step is to find out how to turn them into naturally occurring phenomena. As Robert said, there is a difference between when you are being creative and when you are not. What interests me, however, is how do you know *when* to be creative? Knowing how to be creative doesn't necessarily help you make the decisions about when to be creative, and when to be unconsciously creative.

For example, we had a big storm come along and devastate the coastline here in California, beyond recognition. Most of the people who live here said, "This is disaster!" Not many people ran down to the coastline and said, "Gosh that was creative, did you see what the storm did?" Often people don't even notice their most creative times or the creativity in certain types of events. They are looking for "the right answer," and all this other stuff they come up with on the way to get to the right answer, isn't considered creative. That's not the creative part.

To me, everything you do, whether it's what you wanted to do, or whether it's not what you wanted to do, is creativity.

You may go out to accomplish point A and get to point B instead and consider yourself a total failure. However, the way in which you got to point B may have been quite creative, even though the outcome is not what you wanted. As an NLP person, I would want to know how I got to be that far off creatively from where I was going. Because someday I might *want* to be that far off the mark, sort of like throwing caution to the winds. Mostly it's about the individual's beliefs and equivalency for creativity. Sometimes you get to the end of the line, you get stuck, and you ask, "What can I possibly do now?" And you throw your hands up and you say, "Anything! Anything is a better choice than what I've been doing." And all of a sudden you find yourself being creative. That's another part of the creative process that I'm interested in: getting people through what they believe to be blocks to creativity.

What happens when you come up against a stone wall? What happens when you're blocked? What are the effects of stress? Some people, for example, believe that they can only be creative under stress: People can be extremely creative about how they manage to produce stressful context. "When the going gets tough, the tough get going." Some people certainly seem to be really much more creative when they're under a lot of pressure. Other people can only be creative when they are really relaxed. One of the things that I'm going to be dealing with is how different states of consciousness effect creativity. Once we find out what it is that allows us to be creative, what's going on, what are the mental processes, then the question is: "How do we get ourselves back into that state of consciousness when we are creative?" "Where's our on-and-off switch?" "What do we have to do to put ourselves in the right "frame of mind" to be able to utilize the strategies that we've elicited and revealed?"

So that's generally what I'm going to be covering: unconscious phenomena, breaking blocks, dealing with stress, having fun. My belief is, "Have fun, and if you make money and learn something, you've got to be engaging in the process of creativity somewhere along the line." And even if you don't know you're being creative, others might. You might as well be creative about believing them when they tell you you're being creative.

### Robert W. Dilts (RWD):

I've been practicing patent law for some thirty years so I'm familiar with the social and legal aspects of creativity.

In my years of practice, I've come into contact with a lot of inventors and highly creative people. The difficulty is that these people have already been creative before they come to me. I used to talk to people and they would say, "Gee, it must be great to work with all those inventors," as if these people were different from everybody else: "You're working with *inventors*." And the longer I was in the practice of patent law, the more confused I got. Because at first I felt the same way: "You ought to be able to tell an inventor when you see him on the street, or when he comes into your office. You ought to be able to recognize if this man is an inventor or not. There must be something special about an inventor." But I've never been able to pin down any specific characteristics.

I've seen more creative effort put into trying to identify creative people and inventors. They've tried to do it by age, by nationality, by personality, but have never found a pattern.

My experience is that inventors come in all sizes, all nationalities, all ages. The only thing I'm sure of is that inventors are always stubborn.

One of the things that caused me to look into NLP is the belief that it is an approach to answer the question of how people invent. I know why they do. I know where they do. I know when they do. I know what the result of it is. But the how has always escaped me until I began to realize everybody is creative.

I think people are born creative. I think that during the period from the time a child is six months old until they're two years old they've gone through one of the most tremendously creative times of their life. They get to be two years old, big enough to get up and move on their own, and from that time on they begin to be "educated." And to my way of thinking, education in many cases is little more than suppressing the natural creativity of the individual. "You can't do it that way." "You don't spell cat with a 'k'." "You don't do this, you don't do that." Most of education is antithetical to creativity. The strategies that were learned and enabled this being that couldn't walk, couldn't talk, couldn't feed himself to grow in an incredibly short period of time, one or two years, into a human being who can walk, talk, communicate, feed himself, are slowly suppressed—or beaten out of him, in some cases.

Now we've begun to realize that processes like NLP offer a way for unlocking or going back and reconstructing these earlier strategies. There are some fortunate people who have received encouragement at the right time, in their growing period, when their creative strategy has been encouraged and they hung on to it despite all of the inhibiting factors that are imposed on them by society.

Society is kind of a two-headed monster. There are many parts of society that encourage invention and creativity, but there are an awful lot of parts of society—government, even our own attitudes—that discourage invention and creativity.

Creativity brings change, and change brings insecurity. Everybody likes things to be nice and comfortable and normal. That can be threatened by change.

Look at what has happened in the field of electronics. God I loved the old electronics. I started out at RCA when vacuum tubes were the state of the art. And it was a beautiful art. Glass envelope tubes with cathodes and anodes. You could see the electrodes—I mean you could actually see what was going on. Then some damn fool invented the transistor. Now you have all this "solid state" technology and nobody can see what is going on. It's too small. There is no bright cathode that lights up when the circuit is on. How do you know when the thing is working correctly? You can't see anything.

I resisted it. And there were big companies, like RCA, that did not get into transistors as soon as they should have for that same reason. They didn't jump on the bandwagon. They fought it, a lot of people fought it. In industry and in society there is this problem of inertia, the lack of desire to change.

These are some of the things that I am going to be talking about. Number one, what kind of legal encouragement is there for creativity? Number two, what kind of encouragement and what kind of discouragement does society give to creativity? If you are going to learn strategies that are going to enable you to be creative, then I think I should at least tell you that you should get some smattering of what you ought to do to protect the results of your creativity. You also ought to get some smattering of some of the pitfalls and problems that you might run into with your creativity. I am going to be approaching the topic from a point following the initial creative act.

All of this business of finding out how people are creative is like trying to figure out what's going on inside of a transistor when you can't see inside it. It shakes me up every time I think about. So I'll let my colleagues handle that part of it.

**RBD**: Now that you know a little bit about us, we'd like you to ask yourself the following question: *"If I got what I wanted from this material and my creativity had been significantly enhanced, what would I have? How would I know?"* That is, what would you be able to do better as a result of improved creativity? Would you be able to do things *faster*? Would you be able to do *more* things? What kind of experiences specifically would you have that would indicate to you that something had happened?" Think about that for a moment.

What are your goals in studying this material? There can be many, many benefits of creativity regardless of the professional field you are in.

Below are the responses to this question that were given by some of the participants in the creativity seminar that serves as the basis of this book. Perhaps they will reflect, stimulate or enrich some of your own ideas and goals for applying this material to your life.

Kathy:     I think I have a lot of creativity in some areas, like in music and writing. I'd like to be able to take that and put it into some other areas of my life. I'd like new ways to do things as easily as I do music—in other areas.

James:     I am studying the ministry at this time, and I'm a teacher. Now that I'm getting in touch with my power to create, I'd like to be able to focus it.

Bob:     I'm an industrial relations consultant, a computer analyst. And to answer your question about how to gauge this class: money. Will I make more money as a result of it?

Alan:     I work for Boeing. I'd like to look at the world and see things I've never seen before, so that I can use them.

Tom: I teach mathematics and writing at a university. I also write books and articles. I would like to be creative in a whole bunch of ways and get other people to be creative as well.

Betty: I'm a software manager for a computer company that deals with custom hardware and software. I'd like to have more creativity and be able to use it in the rest of my life. Everything at work for me is very creative. I'd like to have a more creative feeling in the rest of my life.

Mary: I'm in the field of communication. I am a specialist in the use of science, and so I'm specialized now in the philosophy of Science of Mind, and my talent is to take a very abstract concept and to be very creative in including it in the program, so that our minister out in the field can interpret what I write and be very successful with it.

Wayne: I'm a computer programmer. I'd like to learn how to be more creative in my programming, and come out in the field with more solutions to my problems, newer and better ways.

Chuck: I'm a chiropractor. Creativity is important in everything I do, but I have trouble bringing it to an end result. I'd like to be more creative in how I look at people.

Mark: I'm in small business. And the way I would judge the success would be if I could sell people better. And if I could run my business more effectively.

Frank:    I am a physical therapist. I have bursts of creativity. What I'd like to be is to have it in a more organized, effective and systematic way.

Clearly, our seminar participants were a diverse group with diverse goals: software engineers, therapists, ministers, musicians, teachers, sales people, consultants and managers. The goals they expressed have to do with many levels and facets of creativity—ranging from the *where* and *when* of creativity and innovation to the *what, how* and *why* of the creative process.

We expect our readers to be a diverse group as well. Creativity and innovation have a broad range of practical significance regardless of your profession. Obviously, we are not going to be focusing our exploration of creativity in any particular content area or field. We will be presenting principles, models and strategies for improving your ability to create and innovate in a way that is relevant to all of the areas mentioned above.

The ability to generalize creative processes from one area to another is going to be one by-product of understanding the underlying structures and strategies behind creative thinking. Furthermore, through understanding the strategies and creative processes of people from different fields, you will be learning more and more about how other people think. This can help you to widen your own creative thinking abilities and help you to communicate your ideas to others more effectively.

# 1

---

# Defining the Creative Process

What do we mean by the creative process?

**RWD**: I think a very important insight into the creative process is provided by a study that was done at RCA some years ago. I started out in patent law at RCA. Of course, RCA was interested only in the kind of creativity that led to patentable inventions. They were not much interested in other forms of creativity back in the early '50s. At that time, they decided to try to figure out and identify who was likely to be an inventor. When they hired people into the research and development laboratories, the David Sarnoff laboratories, they wanted to be able to pick the inventors from the general public. They began looking for certain attributes, identifying the inventors by personality, size, and age. The age criteria produced an interesting result. They had a well-established program where anybody who made an invention turned in a disclosure to the patent department. The invention was assigned a number so that there would be a record of how many inventions were made by a particular individual.

They began analyzing their backlog of disclosures. They wanted to see how many disclosures were turned in by the inventors at each age. They found, of course, that they didn't hire anybody before they were eighteen. Technical people were hired somewhere between the age of eighteen and twenty-two. Since they were there a few years before these people became accustomed to the company and were able to get their feet on the ground, they were thirty years old by the time they began turning in disclosures. The graph showed a sharp drop-off in the number of disclosures submitted by the older employees.

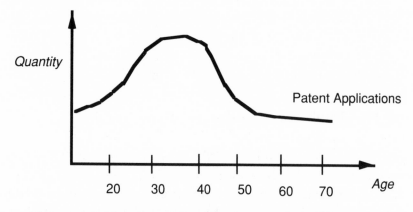

**Figure 1.1. Number of Patent Applications Filed According to Age.**

After the company had analyzed these results, they suppressed them. The indication from this kind of a graph is that substantially all invention is done between the ages of thirty to forty years old and that people's creativity abilities are seriously limited past that age. The idea that this was a truthful assessment of creative activity among human beings bothered them a good deal because the company had many valued employees who were older. Somebody finally pointed out that the results were based solely on the number of disclosures. Everyone knows that young people are very creative, but they are not skilled at filtering their ideas. The most creative period in your life is probably between the ages of two and four when you're learning all the things that you need to know to exist in the world as a human being. You are developing from a baby to an operating functional human being. Many of the attributes of youth are necessary in order to successfully engage in creative activity. One example is optimism. However, younger people do less evaluation, less filtering of their ideas.

Somebody once said that "Russell Varian (the inventor of the Kleistron) has an idea a minute and some of them are good." In creating, you have to first free-wheel, create, throw out a lot of ideas, and then go back and look at them. You can't be critical of your ideas and create them at the same time.

As a result, the people at RCA said, "We should not include all of the ideas submitted. Let's include only the good ones." Instead of looking at all of the disclosures, age was related only to the number of viable patent applications. Not all the disclosures that were received were viable patent applications. Presumably, the patent applications had been filed and evaluated. The results of this new analysis were very interesting.

The first finding remained the same: there was no data on anybody younger than eighteen or twenty. The new graph still reflected that more viable patent applications were filed by younger inventors. The curve on the graph became much smoother and broader overall, but the curve still dropped off rather sharply.

The results still suggested that people ceased to be creative at an older age. Many people at the time believed this to be true. They also thought that young people's ideas are not any good

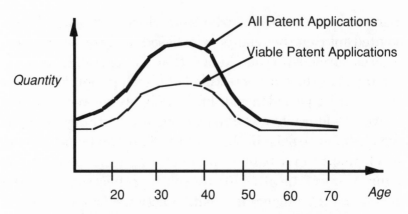

**Figure 1.2. Number of Patent Applications Granted According to Age.**

because they are not based on enough background experience. It appeared that inventions of any value were, in fact, made in that central age group of thirty to forty years old. Again, the people at RCA were not satisfied with the results. They decided to try something else.

Many patent applications are granted but never amount to anything. They decided to look at the most valuable inventions the company had and then at the age of the person responsible for the invention. The results proved better than before. The curve in this graph started a little earlier and lower than that of the last one. The curve was even broader than before. This new analysis was based on the economic value of patents during the life of the company.

They decided to conduct one final test. They said, "Let's not look only at patents. Let's throw in paintings and musical compositions. Let's look outside the company and use the same approach we used before in analyzing only valuable patents. Let's arbitrarily pick those musical compositions, poetry and so on that everybody would agree is something of importance. Let's look at the age of anybody who's a public figure well-known for his or her creativity." The results of this

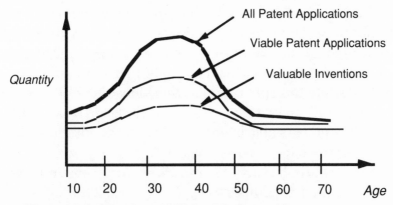

**Figure 1.3. Number of Valuable Inventions
According to Age.**

final test showed musical compositions of great importance
created by the age of ten and inventions made past the age of
eighty. They found that there was really no correlation when
you applied all the filters and tested all the ideas over a long
period against what everyone would agree was an important
creative contribution. They found that the hump that had
previously appeared in the graph at the age of thirty or forty
had disappeared and had become much longer, creating almost a level graph. These results tend to show that valuable
creativity is not age-related.

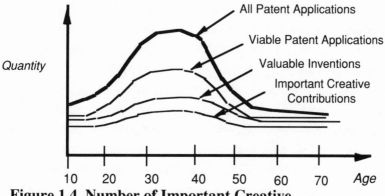

**Figure 1.4. Number of Important Creative
Contributions According to Age.**

The earlier charts showed what you might expect: Young people are more aggressive and are more likely to turn in disclosures. That's why there was a big hump in the initial disclosure charts. The earlier charts showed that young people are less likely to apply filters to their ideas. The reason the sixty-year-old doesn't have a lot of disclosures is that he knows better. He's able to go through and sift out those ideas that are not going to go anywhere. The thirty-year-old has more disclosures because his mind is working constantly and he doesn't have the filters to apply.

The fact that an idea arises in the mind of a young person does not necessarily mean that there is anything wrong with it. It's just that young people tend to be more like Russ Varian: They have an idea a minute and some of them are good.

Both RCA and the writers of the U.S. Constitution believed that creative effort was something special. They viewed inventive effort as something different than the effort required to manage people or to be ingenious in organizing a business. But the question still remains, "What is inventive effort?" Is inventing different from the kind of mental effort that is used in thinking about what you are going to have for dinner?

**RBD**: In my study on Strategies of Genius, one of the best descriptions of the creative process that I came across was in a statement someone made about Walt Disney. One of his animators claimed, "...there were actually three different Walts: the *dreamer*, the *realist*, and the *spoiler*. You never knew which one was coming into your meeting."

I think creativity involves all three of those processes. One of the implications of the RCA study is that the most valuable and important creative contributions are those which involve all three functions. The *dreamer* generates the initial conceptual formulation of the idea. The dreamer is the one who comes up with an idea a minute. The *realist* carries out the task of implementing the idea in a tangible form. The realist makes the dreams viable. The *spoiler*, who I choose to call the *critic'*, is the one that really turns something into a valuable contribution. The critic is the evaluator. If something can please the critics, it will probably be lasting.

All three of these processes are a function of what you do in your mind. And each one is composed of its own sub-components and skills that we will be exploring explicitly in the body of this book. In the course of this exploration we will be providing specific tools to enhance the range of creativity of all three of these faculties: dreamer, realist and critic.

The NLP view is that creativity is like spelling or reading. It is a set of steps that you go through mentally, and that can be learned and recapitulated by others. Of course, the results of creativity are a little different than something like spelling (although you might be surprised at how similar the process is sometimes). The goal of creativity, ideally, is to generate something unique, whereas the goal of spelling is to generate something that is the same. As my father (RWD) said, you don't get reinforced for creative spelling when you are a child. Creative writing is okay, but not creative spelling. That gets confusing sometimes when you're a child. I remember being slightly confused about why you should be creative about one thing and not another. Actually, I tend to agree with the American president Andrew Jackson, who said, "I just can't trust someone who only knows how to spell a word one way."

Yet, while the outcome of creativity is different than other mental processes the basic elements that go into producing it are the same. While creativity is something you're born with, it is not a function of a specific creativity gene. I don't think people have a spelling gene or a music gene or a physics gene. I think creativity is a function of the way that you use your neurology—the way that you organize the process of **how** you think about something. The goal of NLP is to help people develop all kinds of thinking abilities. And the ability to think, as far as NLP is concerned, is learnable.

Thomas Edison's comment that invention is 1% inspiration and 99% perspiration means it can be a lot of work. But the other implication is that it isn't magical or mystical, but rather a function of individual effort and ability. I think it doesn't necessarily have to be a lot of work, but it does take systematic thought. Of course, the next question then becomes, "What is thought?"

One of the most essential functions of the brain is to process sensory representations. In other words, you take all this information in through your sense organs and make maps of it in that lump of gray stuff up between your ears. You begin to create representations of the world around you. And it's the way in which you manage those representations that is going to determine your ability to be creative. How well you can direct and utilize your representational systems determines how rich your model of the world will be. The ability to be creative comes from learning how to use your sensory representational systems in a certain way—to develop and direct your imagination.

The thing that allowed Einstein to come up with his theory of relativity was not necessarily his skills in mathematics. In fact, he used the same equations that someone had come up with fifteen years earlier to describe relativity. Einstein's comment about mathematics was that, *"No really productive thinker could think in such a paper fashion."* The theory of relativity wasn't an innovation in mathematics. It was an innovation in how to think about reality from multiple perspectives. The theory of relativity is a description of how to use your imagination in a certain way. According to Einstein it started from a kind of a daydream he had in his childhood. Which, as I understand it, started when he got bored with math class. From about the age of sixteen, he used to wonder what would it look like to be riding on the end of a light beam. In his mind he would go riding around on light beams and, as you might imagine, the world looked very different. That is where the inspiration for the theory of relativity came from—trying to reconcile reality to what he saw in his imagination.

Einstein claimed, *"Imagination is more important than knowledge."* In fact, Einstein used to try to get all these physics professors to do 'thought experiments' in their minds. He would have them running around on light beams in their minds, or falling in an elevator through space looking out of a hole in the side of the elevator with a flashlight, or visualizing three dimensional shadows. Einstein's creativity came from a unique ability to use certain types of visual imagery. And according to NLP, this ability can be developed in others. How many of you reading this right now could visualize what it would look like to be passing through the room you are in at the speed of light?

The richness of our imagination comes from our ability to make maps in our minds through what we call *representational systems*, which basically correspond to your senses: *sight, sound, feeling, taste,* and *smell.* According to NLP we build our mental maps out of information from the five senses. Our senses constitute the form or structure of thinking as opposed to its content. Every thought that you have, regardless of its content, is going to be a function of pictures, sound, feelings, smells or tastes, and how those representations relate to one another.

**TE**: You are constantly linking together sensory representations to build and update your map of reality. It's like when you're a little kid, and you first confront a door, you might initially try to walk through it—and end up with a sore nose. You create a certain map of reality. Then you start noticing people doing something with a little round thing on the door and it magically opens. So you try fooling around with that little round thing with your hand, and suddenly it opens. You add that to the map. Pretty soon you learn to stick your hand out elegantly to twist the door knob and get through it, and you enrich your map even more. But then one day you come up to a door that doesn't have a knob. Now what do you do? You have to get creative and figure out how to get through that one, and add that to your map. You start to generalize to doors with handles, and doors with bars that you push, and revolving doors. I remember when I was a kid and I went to the supermarket and reached to open the door. As I stepped on a strange rubber mat, the door opened without me having to push anything. I immediately added that to my map of doors. We make these maps based on feedback from our sensory experience.

**RBD**: When you make a map, it allows you to do things—but it also starts to restrict your way of perceiving it. In the story of the Arabian Nights, for instance, the hero came up to the door and there wasn't any door knob. There wasn't any mat that he could step on. There wasn't anything he could do kinesthetically. He had to figure out that he needed to switch to his auditory representational system and say "Open sesame!" To get through that door he had to be really creative.

**TE**: That was the first security system, by the way.

**RBD**: On one hand, making maps allows us to be more efficient. On the other hand, existing maps can begin to limit your ability to perceive new choices. Familiarity with something can be a limitation as well as a resource. As soon as you think you've got doors figured out, people change the way doors work.

If you want to be creative in particle physics, there is a certain amount of background knowledge and information that is required before you can actually start to be creative in that field. But the paradox is that acquiring that knowledge might begin to shape your thinking about the subject and actually inhibit creativity. It's a well known fact that often the people who are most creative in a particular industry or field are people who were not trained in that industry or field. They were able to be creative because they had a fresh perspective. They just started from scratch.

**TE**: Many times I've been in a problem-solving situations and somebody with no background at all comes walking in and asks, "How come you can't just do that with it?" And the people that have been trained for twenty years go, "Funny, we never asked that question."

One of the creative processes we're going to be engaging in is something called *"not knowing."* Most of the time you look at something and you go, "I know what that is." Right away you have a map built on one of these representational systems that has the potential to limit you. Somebody asks, "Do you know what that is?" And you answer, "Yes, I know what that is." As soon as you know what that is, then you've put one of those existing maps up in your mind and you've matched it with something on the outside. You have met your criteria for "I know" and you often stop.

The question is, can you walk up to something that you think you know, and say, "No, I don't know what it is," "I have no idea what it is." Could you see a table and say "I don't know what that is." That's the kind of childlike, fresh perspective that allows you to make new maps, different kinds of maps, to engage in the activity of something I call "not knowing." As Robert (RWD) pointed out, children are very creative because they don't have a lot of maps. They are making new maps all the time. One of the things we want to explore is the ability to remake your maps.

**RBD**: Another way of saying it is that sometimes the biggest limitation to creativity is success. You do something and it works, so you decide to do more of it. So, if a 'pet rock' sells really well, you decide to have 'pet sand,' and 'pet bricks,' and 'pet clay.' Or you make big cars, and they sell really well. So you build a whole industry around selling big cars, and then there's a gas shortage that starts to change the way that industry works, and you're in big trouble.

One of the reasons that Xerox came to us to find out more about creativity was because they took a look ten years into the future and they didn't see a whole lot of paper, and thus Xerox machines, in business offices. Businesses are switching to electronic mail and computer terminals. Who'd want to sit there and open letters and push paper, when you can punch a button and everything you need comes up on your computer screen?

A man from Xerox corporate intelligence came and interviewed Richard Bandler and I about the office of the future. His first question was, "What do you think of the office of the future?" We both looked at each other for a moment and responded, "What office?" We both had international consulting and training practices that we essentially ran from our homes. Because we each had several computers, we had all the information we needed to run our businesses immediately available to us. I have immediate connections to almost anywhere in the world through my computer modem, fax machine and the telephone. You don't necessarily need to go to an office to work.

Xerox was aware of this kind of trend but was in a kind of a trap from their own past success. They were interested in getting into the area of personal computers. But if I said to you, "I need a Xerox," you would most likely think I was referring to a photocopy. To most people, Xerox was synonymous with photocopying, not with personal computers. People associate Apple with personal computers. And, as I understand it, that is who has ended up with most of Xerox's initial creative developments in the computer area.

My point is that success can sometimes be as much as a limitation as anything else if you don't keep some doors open.

It's difficult when you're really successful in one thing to step back and put all that success aside so you can stay open-minded, challenge your own presuppositions and continue to update your maps.

The same kind of pattern happens on an individual level as well. Often a strength in one representational ability is developed at the expense of another. For instance, while Einstein had a great imagination, he had a difficult time remembering his appointments, forgot to eat breakfast, etc. He had developed certain internal processes to a very strong extent and others had become a little weaker.

In NLP we distinguish between:

1. most highly *developed*,

2. most highly *valued*, and

3. most *conscious* representational systems.

The *development* of a representational system is determined by the capability to manipulate, organize, synthesize and distinguish information within that system.

How much a representational system is *valued* is determined by the impact it has on a person's behavior. Some people, for example, have a very highly developed ability to use language, yet what they say has very little to do with how they act. Other individuals may value feelings very highly, but do not possess much skill in distinguishing or changing them.

*Consciousness* of a representational system is a function of how much a person is aware of the information being processed through that system. Someone may be very conscious of feelings but not value them very highly or be unable to manipulate them very well-in fact, sometimes that is why they remain in consciousness so much. Conversely, a person may have a very well-developed ability to create and respond to visual imagery and yet have no conscious awareness of making internal images.

It is possible for someone to have one representational system which is the most developed, most valued *and* most conscious. It is also possible that these functions might each involve a different sensory system. For example, a person could be most able to manipulate words and sounds, respond most often to feelings, yet be most consciously aware of what he or she sees.

The point is that individuals differ in their abilities to use their senses. For example, some of the computer game designers I interviewed for the project I mentioned earlier, could not imagine what their game was going to look like until they actually started writing it. They had to invent the game before they knew what it was going to look like. Which makes a very interesting challenge. Other designers would have played the game two or three times in their minds before they ever wrote a word of computer code. In fact, one designer sat down and closed his eyes and played the game in his own mind without ever even seeing an actual video screen. I figure if we teach people that, we can really hit the market there. You can save a lot of money that way. You could maybe even make a few more Einsteins.

**TE**: You could put the video game industry out of business. You'd tell the kids, "Here play this in your head. You don't have to spend your allowance on all those games. Besides, your mother and your teachers won't know you're playing it. You won't even have to skip school. You could do it right during math class. You could even make it part of math class."

**RBD**: In any event, these fundamental representational skills play a key role in the development of creative ability. One of the primary goals of this book is to define the representational strategies that accompany creativity and help you to develop and enrich your own representational flexibility.

# The R.O.L.E. Model

One of the fundamental sets of tools we will be using to examine and capture the structure of the thought processes involved in creativity is what I call the R.O.L.E. Model. The goal of the R.O.L.E. modeling process is to identify the essential elements of thinking and behavior used to produce a particular response or outcome. This involves identifying the critical steps of the mental strategy and the role each step plays in the overall neurological "program." This role is determined by the following four factors which are indicated by the letters which make up the name of the **R.O.L.E.** Model: *R*epresentational systems, *O*rientation, *L*inks, *E*ffect. (For a detailed description of the R.O.L.E. Model distinctions refer to Appendices B and C.)

## Representational Systems

Representational Systems have to do with which of the five senses are most dominant for the particular mental step in the strategy: **V**isual (sight), **A**uditory (sound), **K**inesthetic (feeling), **O**lfactory (smell), **G**ustatory (taste).

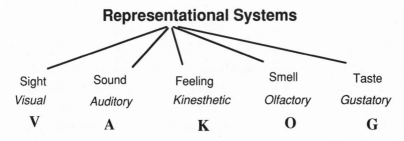

**Representational Systems**

| Sight | Sound | Feeling | Smell | Taste |
|-------|-------|---------|-------|-------|
| *Visual* | *Auditory* | *Kinesthetic* | *Olfactory* | *Gustatory* |
| **V** | **A** | **K** | **O** | **G** |

**Figure 1.5. Sensory Representational Systems.**

Each representational system is designed to perceive certain basic qualities of the experiences it senses. These include characteristics such as *color, brightness, tone, loudness, temperature, pressure,* etc. These qualities are called "sub-modalities" in NLP since they are sub-components of each of the representational systems.

## Orientation

Orientation has to do with whether a particular sensory representation is focused (**e**)xternally toward the outside world or (**i**)nternally toward either (**r**)emembered or (**c**)onstructed experiences. For instance, when you are seeing something, is it in the outside world, in memory or in your imagination?

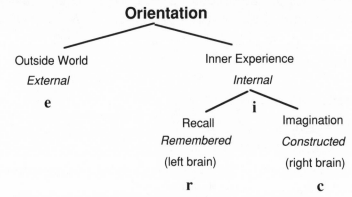

**Figure 1.6. Possible Orientations of the Senses.**

## Links

Links have to do with how a particular step or sensory representation is linked to the other representations. For example, is something seen in the external environment linked to internal feelings, remembered images, words? Is a particular feeling linked to constructed pictures, memories of sounds or other feelings?

There are two basic kinds of ways that representations can be linked together: sequentially and simultaneously. Sequential links act as *anchors* or triggers such that one representation follows another in a linear chain of events.

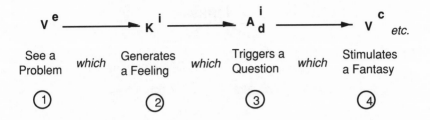

Figure 1.7. Sequential Links.

Simultaneous links occur as what are called *synesthesias*. Synesthesia links have to do with the ongoing overlap between sensory representations. Certain qualities of feelings may be linked to certain qualities of imagery-for example, visualizing the shape of a sound or hearing a color.

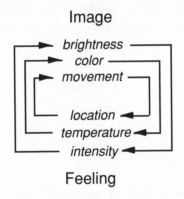

Figure 1.8. Synesthesia Links.

Certainly, both of these kinds of links are essential to the process of effective creativity and innovation.

## Effect

Effect has to do with the result, effect or purpose of each step in the thought process. For instance, the function of the step could be to generate or input a sensory representation, to test or evaluate a particular sensory representation, or to operate

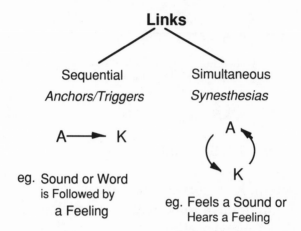

**Figure 1.9. Types of Links Between the Senses.**

to change some part of an experience or behavior in relationship to a sensory representation. The kinds of inputs, tests and operations we use will change as we shift from dreamer to realist to critic.

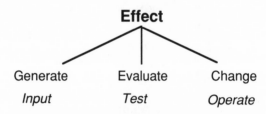

**Figure 1.10. Types of Effects.**

The first two elements of the R.O.L.E. Model—Representational systems and Orientation—have to do with the micro structure of the thinking processes behind creativity. Exploring the Links between and Effects of these elements at the micro level leads us to address the macro structure of the creative process.

The micro structure of a strategy has to do with the specific individual steps you take as you are thinking. You say a specific set of words to yourself, then you make a visual image or get some feeling, and you do each of these things in that order and in real time. It is like the instructions of a computer program. They are specific steps directed toward achieving specific results.

But these micro processes are generally sub-operations functioning inside of a larger framework or macro program. For example, if you look at Ernest Hemingway's style versus William Faulkner's style versus Virginia Woolf's style of writing, you will certainly find different strategies used by each author on the micro level that we have been describing thus far. They will each emphasize different representational qualities, points of view, sensory detail, amount of imagination versus memory, etc. But on another level, they are all expressing themselves through creative writing, and there may be similarities which they all share insomuch as they are all expressing inner experiences through the written word.

I think the inability to clearly distinguish between the different levels of information processing has created a lot of confusion in the understanding and implementing of creativity and innovation. For instance, you could say that on one level the process for inventing a new product is the same process that goes into writing a book. On another level, however, there are important and necessary differences between the creative process involved in the two activities.

A common problem of people who have trouble writing, for example, is that they tend to start correcting their grammar and spelling while they are writing. As a result, they forget what they were going to say next or they begin judging their work too early and it never seems good enough. The book or thesis is never done. Rather than write out the whole thing and then refine it, they are editing while they are creating and the two levels of process collide.

This does not mean that micro strategies can't be transposed into other areas. The same micro processes may be applied to making a computer game, making a better

microphone or speaker, writing a book or making a speech—
but they need to be adapted to the higher level framework.
Micro level strategies and programs—sequences of sensory
representations—are 'nested' inside of macro or meta programs, such as 'dreamer,' 'realist' and 'critic.'

Let's begin to bring the R.O.L.E. Model to life by connecting
it to some of your own personal experiences with creativity.
The questionnaire on the next page can help to give you some
insights into the micro and macro structures of your own
creative process.


# Exercise: Exploring the Structure of Your Creative Process

Take a few moments and answer the following questions as
completely as you can.

1. What is a context in which you are able to be creative or
innovative?

2. What are the goals or objectives that you are attempting to
accomplish by being creative or innovative in this context?

3. What do you use as evidence to know you are accomplishing those goals?

4. What do you do to get to the goals? What are some specific steps and activities that you use to creatively achieve your goals in this context?

5. When you experience unexpected problems or difficulties in achieving your goals in this context, what is your response to them? What specific activities or steps do you take to correct them?

Now, look back over your answers to the questionnaire and see which R.O.L.E. Model elements you can identify. Start by exploring the micro level patterns. For instance, what do your answers indicate about how you use your representational systems?

How much does the context in which you are able to be creative involve seeing? How much does it involve hearing? How much does it involve feeling or doing?

How do you represent the goals you are trying to accomplish in that context? Do you visualize them? Do you verbalize them to yourself or others as statements or key words? Are your goals something that you primarily feel?

If you picture your goals, are they images that come more from memory or fantasy? How exactly do you see your goals? Are they bright? Are they in color? Are they moving images?

If you verbalized or heard your goals, did you say them only to yourself, or externally to others as well? What kind of voice tone and tempo do you use to state your goals?

If you represent your goals in terms of feelings, do you feel them as emotions or as actions? Are they familiar feelings or feelings you imagine might be possible? Where in your body do you feel them?

Which representational systems do you use to check your progress toward your goals? Do you know you are getting closer to accomplishing them based on what you see, hear or feel? How much of your evidence comes from the outside world and how much from your own inner experiences? How clear does your evidence have to be? How intense? How precise?

When you are taking steps to reach your goal how much physical action is involved? How much verbal communication? To what extent does it involve looking at or showing something? To what degree does it involve vision, action, logic or emotion? Perhaps you use a combination of imagery, words and feelings or actions. If so, what is the sequence? Do you "Look before you leap?" In your case, do "Actions speak louder than words?" Does a "Picture say a thousand words?" Are there any synesthesias involved in your creative steps? Do all of your steps involve the external world, or do some involve fantasy or memories?

When you had problems or difficulties how did you respond? Did you have any feelings about it? What kind? Did you ask questions? Did it change your image of what was going to happen? Did you say something to yourself or to other people?

How did you adjust what you were doing to address the problem? Did you look at it more closely? Did your feelings get stronger? Did you change the way you talked to people or to yourself? Did you change to a different mode of thinking? Did you use logic? Did you become more emotional? To what extent did you draw on memory? To what degree did you use your imagination? How important was what was happening in the outside world?

These are only some of the questions you might ask yourself. Take a moment and explore your answers for anything else that might be a clue to your micro strategy.

Were you able to learn anything about your most developed, most valued and most conscious representational systems? One way to think about it is that your *goals* would probably be associated with your *most valued* representational system. The representational system you use to find *evidence* for those goals will probably be one of your *most conscious*. The representational systems you use or *change* to attempt to achieve your goals or respond to problems will probably be the most developed ones.

As you consider your answers, think about where there is flexibility and where there is not. For instance, if you changed the representational systems you used to represent your goals, would it significantly change the result of the process? If you substituted words for images, say, as evidence, what impact would that have on the way the process functions? If you watched instead of acted, what difference would it have made?

All of these issues relate to the micro structure of the strategy. Let's shift to the macro level for a moment.

First of all, the questions themselves were asked in such a way to uncover specific types of links and effects. In fact, the questions were formulated to draw out what is called a T.O.T.E.

## The T.O.T.E. Model

*The pursuance of future ends and the choice of means for their attainment are the mark and criterion of the presence of mentality in a phenomenon.*

—*William James* Principles of Psychology

A mental strategy is typically organized into a basic feedback loop called a T.O.T.E. (Miller, et al, 1960). The letters **T.O.T.E.** stand for *Test-Operate-Test-Exit*. The T.O.T.E. concept maintains that all mental and behavioral programs revolve around

having a *fixed goal* and a *variable means to achieve that goal.*
This model indicates that, as we think, we set goals in our
mind (consciously or unconsciously) and develop a TEST for
when that goal has been achieved. If that goal is not achieved
we OPERATE to change something or do something to get
closer to our goal. When our TEST criteria have been satisfied we then EXIT on to the next step. So the function of any
particular part of a behavioral program could be to (**T**)est
information from the senses in order to check progress towards the goal or to (**O**)perate to change some part of the
ongoing experience so that it can satisfy the (**T**)est and (**E**)xit
on to the next part of the program. (*See* Appendix C for more
on the T.O.T.E.)

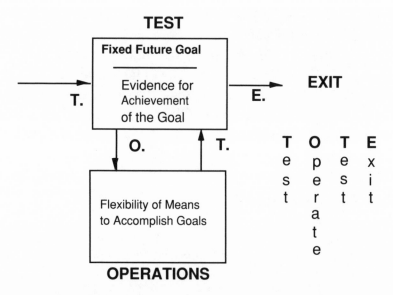

**Figure 1.11. The T.O.T.E.**

For example, one TEST for creativity might be that an idea is
"unique." If the concept you have come up with is not unique
enough you will OPERATE or go through a procedure to
make the idea more unique or to come up with a better
concept.

As with the other R.O.L.E. Model elements, people differ in the way in which they fix future goals (tests) and in their flexibility and choices for varying their means of getting to that goal (operations). Depending on the type of goal and evidence that has been set, for instance, the whole inner program may be oriented toward either:

1. achieving a desired outcome, or

2. avoiding negative outcome.

Individuals will have different ways to TEST for something like "uniqueness" based on personal representational system preferences or proclivities. For instance, something like uniqueness may be determined on the basis of:

1. what someone sees in the outcome.

2. what someone does physically as they are achieving the outcome.

3. what someone feels about the outcome.

4. what someone hears or says in relation to the outcome.

These variations may make a big difference in the kind of result produced by the creative process and in the audience to whom it appeals. Some ideas, for instance, may incorporate features of other products that already exist in the way that they are used but look very different. Other products may look very similar to things that already exist but have a different use.

To summarize, in order to have the minimum information about how someone thinks we must identify:

1. the person's goals.

2. the evidence used by the person to determine progress toward the goal.

3. the sets of choices used by the person to get to the goal and the specific behaviors used to implement these choices.

4. the way the person responds if the goal is not initially achieved.

There is a second set of distinctions which is related to the macro structure of creativity that has to do with the fact that any system of activity is a subsystem embedded inside of another system which is embedded inside of another system, and so on. This kind of relationship between systems produces different levels of creativity or innovation, relative to the system in which you are operating.

## Logical Levels

People often talk about responding to things on different "levels." For instance, someone might say that some experience was negative on one level but positive on another level. In our brain structure, language, and perceptual systems there are natural hierarchies or levels of experience. The effect of each level is to organize and control the information on the level below it. Changing something on an upper level would necessarily change things on the lower levels; changing something on a lower level could but would not necessarily affect the upper levels. Anthropologist Gregory Bateson identified four basic levels of learning and change—each level more abstract than the level below it but each having a greater degree of impact on the individual. These levels roughly correspond to:

- Who I **A**m: *Identity*                      Who?
- My **B**elief system: *Values and Meanings*    Why?
- My **C**apabilities: *Strategies and States*     How?
- What I **D**o or have **D**one:
  *Specific Behaviors*                     What?
- My **E**nvironment:
  *External Constraints*          Where?/When?

The environment level involves the specific external conditions in which our behavior takes place. Behaviors without any inner map, plan or strategy to guide them, however, are like knee jerk reactions, habits or rituals. At the level of capability we are able to select, alter and adapt a class of behaviors to a wider set of external situations. At the level of beliefs and values we may encourage, inhibit or generalize a particular strategy, plan or way of thinking. Identity, of course, consolidates whole systems of beliefs and values into a sense of self. While each level becomes more abstracted from the specifics of behavior and sensory experience, it actually has more and more widespread effect on our behavior and experience.

- *Environmental factors* determine the external opportunities or constraints a person has to react to. Answer to the questions **where**? and **when**?
- *Behavior* is made up of the specific actions or reactions taken within the environment. Answer to the question **what**?
- *Capabilities* guide and give direction to behavioral actions through a mental map, plan or strategy. Answer to the question **how**?
- *Beliefs* and *values* provide the reinforcement (motivation and permission) that supports or denies capabilities. Answer to the question **why**?
- *Identity* factors determine overall purpose (mission) and shape beliefs and values through our sense of self. Answer to the question **who**?

Each of these processes involves a different level of organization and evaluation that will select, access and utilize the information on the level below it. In this way they form a hierarchy of "nested" T.O.T.E.s as shown below.

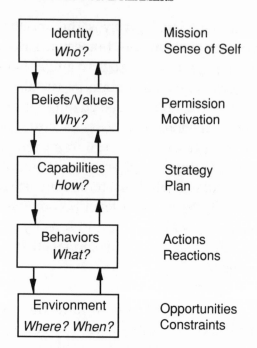

**Figure 1.12. Logical Levels Relating to Creativity.**

Creativity is clearly a multi-level process and requires support from all these levels to be completely effective. Any level that is not aligned with the others can create an interference to the creative process. As an example, someone may have been able to do something new in a particular context (specific behavior) but not have a mental model or map that allows them to know how to continue doing new things or to do innovative things in a different environment (capability). Even when someone is capable of generating creative options, they may not value creativity as an important or necessary function so they rarely use it. Even people who are able to be creative and believe it is an important function do not always perceive themselves as "innovators" or "inventors."

The following statements show how limits to creativity could come from any one of the levels.

**a.** Identity: *"I am not a creative person."*

**b.** Belief: *"Creativity can be difficult and disruptive."*

**c.** Capability: *"I don't know how to think creatively consistently."*

**d.** Behavior: *"I don't know what to do differently in this situation."*

**e.** Environment: *"There wasn't enough time to do something innovative."*

## Discussion: Macro Patterns of Creativity

**RBD**: The way in which you answered the questionnaire earlier in this chapter can give you a lot of insight into the various levels involved in your creative process.

Context has to do with the *where* and *when* of creativity and is linked to our perception of the environment. Goals are indicative of the values that we have and how they relate to our perception of our identity in a particular context. Goals are most often related to the *why* and the *who* of creativity. The evidence we use to determine the successful or unsuccessful achievement of a goal is linked to the internal maps and mental models we use to represent our goals. Evidence relates to *how* we implement a particular value or belief. Specific operations and steps are linked to the behavioral manifestation of creativity—the *what*. How we respond to problems and difficulties also relates to our values and beliefs as well as our map or plan. It involves the link between the *how* and the *why*.

Let's explore some of the potential implications of these questions and your answers.

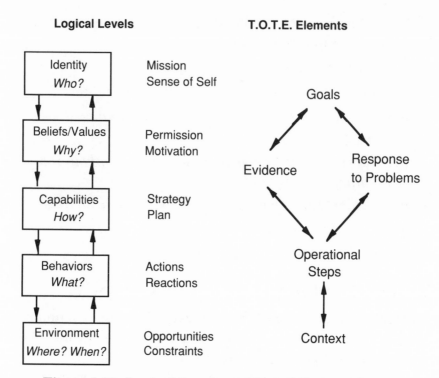

**Figure 1.13. Logical Levels and T.O.T.E. Functions.**

## Contexts

A particular context may be perceived as either a constraint to creativity or an opportunity for creativity. What one person perceives as a limitation another might perceive as a challenge. What is it about the context that you've chosen that allowed or stimulated you to be creative?

Sometimes we restrict ourselves from using a strategy which we developed in one context in other areas of our lives. Often this is because we don't have a way of extracting the content-free elements of its structure. In a later chapter we will demonstrate how to take a strategy for doing well in one context and apply it to another by adapting certain aspects of it to fit the new context.

Of course, a strategy that works well in some contexts might not work well in others. Sometimes people try to apply a creativity strategy that works well in one situation to something that is inappropriate for that strategy if it is not properly adapted to the new context. You've got to adjust the strategy to fit the goal and the context.

I was once helping a woman who was an interior decorator. Her strategy was to walk into a room and get a feeling of what she'd like the room to be like as she walked in. She would start visualizing things changing in the room until she formed a picture that fit with the feeling she wanted. Then she would go out and buy what she needed and decorate the room according to her picture. Her strategy worked well when it came to designing rooms. However, this poor person had a heck of a time in relationships. She'd get the feeling of what the 'perfect man' would be like and she would make a picture of him. Then she'd go out and find the man who looked like her picture. The problem was that she couldn't just change the other pieces that weren't quite right. You just don't decorate the interior of a human being the same way you do with a room. A human being is not as easy to deal with. She would keep going from person to person. It was like love at first sight: this person would fit exactly the picture she wanted. Everything would be great for a while but then she'd begin to have difficulties communicating with him verbally. Words and language may not be so important in decorating a room, but they can be essential in a relationship.

One of the most important motivations and causes for creativity comes from the need to adapt to changing environments and contexts.

When you look at different types of inventions, some of the most creative periods have been when we were at war, and we were inventing ways to kill people. Wouldn't it be great if we could grab the strategy from that context and continue to apply the process with the same vigor but without the unfortunate implications of the context?

The contexts in which you are creative are linked to beliefs and values. Because of their beliefs, people will perceive certain contexts as inappropriate for creativity or not requiring creativity.

The contexts in which you value and implement creativity are even linked to your perception of your identity. For example, people often say they need to learn more about creativity because they are "a designer" or "a manager" or "an engineer." Yet many of these people are also parents with children. They feel the need for creativity in their job but not in being a parent. If you make a mistake as a manager or inventor, you lose time, money or a product. But if you make a mistake as a parent you could lose the whole person. If Adolph Hitler's parents had used more creativity in dealing with their son, maybe the world would be a different place today. Creativity is needed everywhere.

**Goals**

The goal for being creative or inventive makes a tremendous difference in the kind of links you will select. The goal serves as a kind of filter. It is most closely related to the "why" of creativity. Goals have to do with the motivation for creativity.

Are you doing it to make money? Are you doing it because you want to contribute something to the world? Are you doing it because you want to communicate? Why are you doing this?

Some people invent when they are bored. Some people invent when they are angry. Some people invent only when they feel comfortable, when they feel inspired. The "why" can be an important stimulus. It can also become a limitation. Some people can only be creative when they are going toward something in the future. Some people are most creative when they are trying to avoid a problem in the present. What do your goals indicate about your values and beliefs?

On a micro level, different kinds of goals lead to different kinds of results. As an example, in my work with computer programmers I've found some fairly significant differences in how software designers create video games. Some designers aim for a certain feeling while playing the game. Others rely on a specific character for direction. They'll say, "This is the character that I want to have. What can I do with him?" The designer comes up with random ideas for the character and finds out if people like it. That is a very different approach from saying, "The program has to make me feel a certain way and I don't care what the character looks like."

The designers who started with feelings, first created their programs in simple squares and blocks. They would have a square here and a block there, and they would engage in the interaction The other designers would first start with a character. They couldn't figure out what action was going to take place until they had a character. These different kinds of goals and ways of representing goals produce very different results, and they appear in other types of creativity as well.

The sensory system and orientation you choose to represent a goal will also have an influence on how effectively you achieve something. For instance, one common strategy for creativity is to develop an internal picture of an outcome. The creative process organizes around the attempt to make the outer world match that picture. This works great in wood shop, but if you're a father and you think your family should look a certain way, and you're trying to get everyone to act in that way, this could create problems.

The same goal could be represented in terms of images, logical or verbal descriptions or specifications, emotions or kinesthetic actions. Which representational system do you tend to use to represent your goals? How would it change your creative process if you switched to another?

There are a number of key macro level or 'meta program' patterns that appear in relation to commonly stated goals for creativity and innovation (*see* Appendix D for a listing of Common Meta Program Patterns). For example:

1. Getting to something that's "unique" is often a goal in the process of creativity or innovation. "I want to make something that's totally different from anything else around today."

2. Avoiding an irritation. You can have an irritation that you are trying to get around like, "It sure is irritating to have to take five days to get across the Atlantic Ocean to reach Paris or London. Wish we could get across there faster. What do we do?"

3. Identifying and filling a need. "It sure would be easier and safer when you are driving at night if there were little bumps that you could see and feel that let you know where the lanes are."

4. Finding an answer to a new question. "If the world is round, I wonder if you could sail all the way around it?" A question creates a hole or vacuum and you try and fill it in. "Where does all the light in a room go when you turn the switch off?" "Is it absorbed by the walls?" "If the walls were made of mirrors so it wasn't absorbed, would the room still stay light?" "If you were riding on the end of a light beam and looking in a mirror, would you see your reflection or not?" People like Einstein were trying to answer questions like these.

5. Probably the most common meta program for creativity is the desire to fulfill a dream—to accomplish a goal. It's been said that "a goal is just a dream with a deadline." There doesn't have to be a need. They say, "Necessity is the mother of invention," but it is just as true that, "Invention is the mother of necessity."

**RWD**: That's like Marconi's development of the radio, "I want to talk here. I want it to be heard over there. And I don't want any wires." Similarly, in the Little Orphan Annie comic strip, years ago, there was a Daddy Warbucks. He had a television set back in the 1920's. There was the desire to see pictures that have been transmitted from one place to another with no wires.

**RBD**: Even when there's no immediate need, when there is a clearly defined goal, you want to find out how to get there. Sometimes trying to reach the goal becomes an end in itself. A solved problem is like a boat out of water. It's like a finished crossword puzzle. Who's going to hang it on the wall? A lot of inventors seem to have that kind of meta program.

As we said earlier, goals are often highly linked to beliefs, values and identity. One of the most powerful beliefs driving the creative process seems to be that "It is possible;" "I can impact this situation or person;" "I can do something." Sixty years ago, people did not think it was possible to get to the moon. They couldn't see any way to do it. Until someone really believed it was possible, it was considered a waste of time to try to develop the technology.

The film *2001: A Space Odyssey* is an interesting example of creating the belief that something is possible. It installed a picture in people's minds of a Pan Am space ship going to the moon. People said, "Gosh, that's possible. I think that can happen." Even though it wasn't really happening, it built an image, a goal, that inspired tremendous interest in the development of the space shuttle.

**RWD**: Possibility is very important in the area of industrial espionage: knowing what your competition is doing. If you find that your competition has succeeded in generating a megawatt at 50 gigacycles, then you know it can be done. You put your money there and you put your people there.

**RBD**: I've sometimes mused that we should have a political rumor company. You leak rumors such as, the Russians have invented a way of teletransporting people from one place to another. Someone would probably come up with a way to do it.

As an interesting note, the conception of this whole project on creativity and innovation came when the Russians invaded Afghanistan a number of years ago. There was a tremendous concern about their control over the oil. My father (RWD) and I were discussing it, and it occurred to me that if we found an alternative energy source, the perception of the situation would change dramatically. Imagine if you came up with something that made getting energy so easy that you did not have to worry about who had the oil. The Russians would be seen as being in control of just a lot of sand. It seemed to me that the way to stop the Russians is not by building a bigger bomb but by making the need to bomb irrelevant.

In light of the changes that have happened since in the Soviet Union and Eastern Europe, it seems, in a way, that is what happened.

Perhaps the continuing problems in the Middle East are still crying out for the need to invest more creativity into the issue of alternative energy sources.

Or, perhaps, if we came up with a way to get to the moon more easily and if we began colonizing other planets, people would not be so concerned about what happens on the little rock we live on and we would reorganize our values to a larger frame.

### Evidence

What is your evidence for creativity? How do you determine that you've achieved the goals you have set for the creative process?

Do you use your own feelings to decide whether your idea is creative, or do you use somebody else's response to it? That could make a very big difference in what ideas you decide to pursue, whether the idea sells well, or how much protection you get for the idea. If your evidence for uniqueness is something that you can legally protect very tightly, it will make a lot of difference in what you determine to be an acceptable idea.

Goals are related to what are called *criteria* in NLP. Evidence is related to what is called the *criterial equivalence*. Criteria and values are usually very general, abstract and ambiguous. They can take many shapes and forms. Your criterial equivalence is the specific sensory or behavioral demonstration or reference that you use to know if a criterion of value has been satisfied. The *evidence procedure* links the *why* to the *how*.

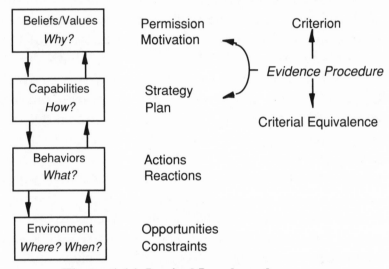

**Figure 1.14. Logical Levels and
Evidence Procedures.**

The form of sensory evidence that you use to evaluate an idea will determine to a large extent whether it is accepted and reinforced, or rejected and ignored.

One key factor in evidence procedures is *frame of reference*. Do you use your own response or someone else's response? In my work with software designers, for instance, I found that some of them designed programs that gave them a certain feeling. Others designed programs that caused a certain response in other people. For example, one designer said he would know if he'd been creative if he had a feeling of success. So I said, "What gives you this feeling of success?" He said he knew he was successful if a game he invented pleased other people. This caused him some problems. He would work on the game until he felt good about it, then he'd show it to other people. Because some people liked it and some didn't, he never had the feeling of being successful. As long as there was even one person who didn't respond to his game, he would feel that he failed.

**TE**: The music business is run that way. If you're promoting a band and you bring a piece of music into a large record company, they say, "That's not what is selling now." That's the way record executives work. They compare it to what's already on the radio and say, "Will this sell in comparison to what's selling now?" What makes new record companies and new producers? People take a chance on something that does not happen to be selling, but which they like. Then that new record becomes the popular standard. How many times have you heard music change over the last twenty-five years? What was esoteric ten years ago, you now hear on the radio everyday. Music you listened to as an adolescent is now musak in the shopping centers. The same thing can be seen in a lot of corporations in this country. They believe that if a product is not like what already exists, it can't be any good.

**RWD**: That is one reason why someone from another industry comes into an established industry and makes inventions. They are bringing other impressions in. They are making associations that were not made before.

**RBD**: Sometimes evidences and criterial equivalences can be too narrow. Sometimes they can be too ambiguous.

In addition to the representational aspect of evidence procedures, the timing of the evidence can also be important. If one of your criteria for creativity is profitability, what kind of time frame do you use to figure out whether a product will make money? When do you evaluate it?

**RWD**: *When* filters are applied is especially important if you are judging whether you are creative by what kind of recognition you receive. In many studies evaluating the inventions, the filter was applied years later to determine which were good inventions and highly creative ideas and which were not. It may have looked very different at the time the invention was first created

**RBD**: The representation and timing of filters and evidence procedures can be very important with regard to how you define creativity. If your evidence for creativity is a certain feeling, then as long as you have that feeling you are being creative-even if you are just remembering the feeling.

Some people only recognize that they have been creative after the fact. They look back at what they've done and say, "Gee, that was creative." Whereas, the other hundred and fifty million ideas they came up with were not creative because they didn't look back on those ideas and notice them.

One of the strategies used by people in the pursuit of artistic creativity, such as musicians and painters, is to organize the creative process around a feeling. Their goal is to represent or convey that feeling through another sensory modality. It doesn't matter how much the picture looks like reality, as long as when you look at it you get the feeling.

There is a story of someone who was riding on a train with Picasso. When he found out it was the famous artist the passenger said, "I understand that you are trying to do something different and unique, but I don't really like your work." Picasso responded, "Oh really, well what *do* you like?" The passenger replied, "I like things that look like reality. You know, that look like things *really* are, like this picture of my wife. That's *exactly* how she looks." Picasso looked at the photo very carefully and replied, "Gee, she's awfully small, isn't she?"

The point is that all maps involve some kind of distortion. We will accept a certain level of distortion and not others depending upon the goal or purpose of the map.

Obviously, evidence procedures and criterial equivalences are also related to values and beliefs.

The most creative software designers, for instance, have a belief that goes something like, "I can always get the machine to do what I want. If I can just define what I want, I can always implement it later." They do not say, "Let's see, what are the memory limitations of my machine? That will determine what I can do."

## Operations

The types of operations used in creativity are another important macro level element. Operations are the most tangible expression of the creative process. They involve the actual steps you go through to produce ideas and actions.

One common meta program pattern relating to operations is what Arthur Koestler calls *Bissociation*: the connecting or combining of several things to make a new synthesis. You put together things on the micro level to make something new on a macro level. In NLP we call this *chunking up*. An example would be Gutenberg's combination of the technologies of block printing, the wine press and the minting of coins to produce the printing press.

Another common operation used in creative thinking is the opposite—*chunking down* or separating. Taking an element and finding ways of separating it out from a conglomeration is another way of being creative—like separating aluminum from aluminum ore. You come up with something new through chunking down things that have always previously come together as a single unit.

Another very common and very powerful operation in creativity is a kind of lateral chunking—through metaphor and analogy. You think of something 'as if' it were something else.

You think of a person as if he were a computer or vice versa. For instance, I may not be able to communicate a certain idea in the form I initially conceived it, but if I gave you a metaphor, even though it isn't exactly the same content I'm talking about, I might be able to get the picture or the feeling or the sounds across that would make it click, fall together, or become clear for you.

For example, until recently our technology modeled muscle as the primary analogy. Now we're modeling mind. The emergence of the information revolution over the industrial revolution comes from the discovery that you don't need strength in order to do things-you need intelligence. Instead of power and strength, technology is interested in creativity, adaptability, flexibility, elegance. Earlier, people interpreted Darwin's principle of "survival of the fittest" to mean "survival of the strongest and most powerful." Now it is interpreted as meaning "survival of that which has the best 'fit'—that which fits in most creatively and ecologically for the whole system."

Shifting ways of thinking about ideas can be important to the creative process-trying to make a picture out of something that isn't pictureable, or trying to make a feeling out of something that doesn't have any feeling with it.

One of the simplest operations for creativity is a noise generator with a filter. That is, you come up with random things and then you filter them and only let certain ones through, like a prism. It filters white light into different colors. It is also a bit like panning for gold. You brainstorm as many wild and crazy ideas as possible and then you filter out a few good ones. This kind of brainstorming is called *divergent* thinking. You try to diverge in as many different directions as possible.

The opposite of this, *convergent* thinking, is also a common operation for creatively accomplishing something. You pick an outcome and just go for it one hundred percent. You only act in accordance with that outcome and you don't do anything

peripheral. You converge on the goal by dropping out everything that isn't directly relevant to achieving it. This is the
strategy of preference in many business-related contexts.

**RWD**: I think generating ideas first and filtering them later
is an essential feature of creative process. I've talked to a
number of inventors who say that they gather all the information they can and then they sleep on it and it comes
together the next morning. Other inventors tell me they sit
down and try to think of all the different ways they could
make the idea work. They do that all at one time, and then the
next day they go back and try to pick out which one will work
and which one won't. They substantially develop the idea one
day and the next day they pare it down.

**RBD**: The point is, not all creativity comes from a single type
of operation. There's an incredible diversity of operations
involved in creativity. Sometimes, the act of creativity requires switching between different modes of thinking. Where
creativity is concerned, it is not so much what is the right
strategy or operation, but what is the range or flexibility of
operations you have available to you, and your ability to shift
strategies. How rich is your model of the world?

   In fact, not all creativity comes at the 'operation' part of the
T.O.T.E. Creativity can come from changing goals and evidences as well as operations. While 'inventiveness' may be
associated with the implementation part of the T.O.T.E.,
processes like 'innovation' and 'discovery' come from changing the other elements of the T.O.T.E.

**RWD**: Shortly after I went to work at RCA, I was talking to
an engineer. We were discussing creativity and inventions
and so forth. He was saying that he was an engineer and he
didn't think that R & D people did anything that was all that
valuable. He didn't see why they got paid a lot of money. He

didn't see what the big deal was about making inventions. He didn't see what was so special about these R & D types. He said, "It's easy. You tell me what to invent and I'll invent it. No problem. Just tell me what to invent and I'll invent it."

**RBD**: He didn't realize that it's the 1% inspiration that makes the 99% perspiration possible and worthwhile. The R & D people were innovating as opposed to inventing. Innovating has to do with changing or enriching goals—with telling someone what to invent. Invention has to do with achieving goals. Coming up with what to invent is as important a creative process as inventing it.

Discovery is not about creating anything new per se. What is discovered may have been around for years or may be a by-product of something else you are doing. Discovery is a result of perceiving something from a different perspective and suddenly becoming aware of something you never noticed before. It comes from changing or enriching your perceptual filters and evidence procedures.

**RWD**: It would be like being the first one to see all seven moons around Saturn. Discovering a new moon may not be an invention but it involves creativity.

**RBD**: Discoveries often come at the feedback phase of the creative process, when you are applying your filters. That is why it is sometimes important to generate ideas first and apply your filters afterwards. You often discover something you weren't expecting, that wasn't even a part of your initial intention or plan.

### Response to Problems
**RWD**: There is a story about a fellow who worked in a saw-mill. One day as he's coming in to work he hears this scream from the other side of the building. He goes running over and

sees one of his co-workers holding his hand and it's bleeding. He's just cut off his finger in a saw blade. "My God. What happened?" the man blurts out. The fellow who's hurt says, "Well, I was just reaching for that board like this and...OUCH! There goes another one!"

**RBD**: One of the most important aspects of the creative process is how we respond when our evidence procedure comes up with negative results. Things don't always work the way we have planned. Even a well-tested operation that has been successful in the past can fail to produce results. One of the most common fallacies in all areas of human activity is that because something has worked in the past it will continue to work. Because our environment changes, something that has been effective in the past can suddenly become a severe limitation.

We often limit our creativity because it's so easy to go back to what we've always done. If fact, past success is often the greatest limitation to creativity. A car company may have successfully sold cars for years and years in a thriving market using a particular strategy. But if the market or the economy changes, that strategy might keep them stuck in a declining market. Eventually the company will have to shift and diversify either its products or its strategy.

Xerox did very well selling Xerox machines for a long time in a world that depended on paper. But with the advent of electronic mail and data storage they realized they were not going to be able to do that much longer. But, of course, nobody in the company wanted to be responsible for the risk of taking a $9 billion corporation and turning it into a $2 billion corporation if they made a mistake. The belief is that if you become successful but then take two steps back, that's failure. Yet, creativity requires the ability to change and to try new things. It is often frightening or risky to try something new. As a result, you rely on the way that you've already done it.

This is another situation where beliefs come in. Sometimes you'll encounter a block in the form of a belief that goes something like, "I've had this strategy a long time. It worked before—it worked great. I don't want to give it up."

You can get around this block by remembering that strategies are not all-or-nothing processes. Being creative does not mean you have give to up the previous strategy or operation. Rather you want to add something else to it. Enrich what already works by adding some more choices. A lot of people believe, "Change means I have to give up what I already have," and, "Being creative means giving up the old." But that is not necessarily true. Creativity and innovation are incremental processes. The people at Xerox thought they had to completely change their strategy as opposed to simply add to what was already working.

The process of incremental creativity and innovation involves a constant feedback loop between goals, evidences and operations. The smoothness of this feedback loop depends on the beliefs we have linked to the process of feedback and evaluation. I've encountered a lot of people involved in creative work who say, "I wish I could have more of a feeling of success. I wish I didn't have such high standards for myself." But at the same time they feel that if they lowered their standards they'd be satisfied with mediocre work. This bind is created by their beliefs.

I once worked with a woman who was constantly getting into these kinds of double binds because of her evidence procedure for success and how she responded to it. She had a strategy in which she would start to learn something, calligraphy for example, with the attitude that if she didn't do it right, it wasn't so bad because she was just a beginner. She initially considered mistakes feedback and as a result learned very rapidly. But as she improved and saw her work more and more closely matching her desired goal, the less tolerant she was of mistakes and felt more and more as if she were failing.

The closer she got to success, the worse she felt if she didn't make it look perfect. In other words, the closer she got to becoming good at something, the more painful it became to stay with it because she would feel terrible if she didn't do it just right. As a result, she would progress very rapidly initially, but as she approached the stage of actually completing something, she would simply drop it because the sense of failure was so intense. She was very creative, but the closer she was to achieving her goal, the more she felt she was not getting there.

Now, her initial response was to say, "Well, I should lower my standards." But that didn't work because if she lowered her standards, she would just feel worse earlier because she came closer to achieving them sooner. The solution came when we explored what the intent or purpose of the bad feeling was-that is, what function it was supposed to serve in the strategy. Her reply was that the purpose of feeling bad about not achieving her standards was to motivate her to continue to try to achieve them. But, of course, that was where the double bind was.

After a certain point the bad feeling actually motivated her in the opposite direction, to give up, because she became so uncomfortable. I asked her what other feelings motivated her to action besides avoiding pain. She said that excitement motivated her as much as pain. So we substituted a feeling of increasing excitement in place of the negative feeling in her strategy, with the stipulation that she could always choose the other feeling if she needed it. This completely changed her ability to accomplish creative goals. In fact, she ended up doing the calligraphy on the brochure for the first *Creativity and Innovation* program we did—very well and very comfortably, I might add.

Dealing with potentially limiting beliefs is an important part of all creativity.

**RWD**: There's an interesting story about Michael Faraday, the discoverer of electromagnetic induction. He discovered that if you had two coils and you passed an electric current through one of the coils, you'd get a current in the adjacent one. He did that in the early 1800's and it was very difficult for him to prove that he was actually getting a current in the second coil. He did an awful lot of work to come to that conclusion. He published a paper and a woman wrote him a letter and said, "Dr. Faraday, that is a wonderful invention. Isn't it possible that you could use this principal to transmit information through space?" And he wrote a letter back saying in no uncertain terms that it was foolish to think that something like this would ever have any use except as a laboratory curiosity. Faraday was a very creative person—and the person who wrote the letter to him was even more creative.

**RBD**: Beliefs determine whether something will be perceived as feedback or as failure. One of my favorite stories is about the two shoe salespeople who get sent to Mexico. Let's say one is Faraday and one is the woman who wrote him the letter. They are both sent to Mexico to sell shoes. After a month Faraday writes back to the home office and says, "Nobody down here wears shoes. They wear sandals. I'm coming home. No market." And she writes back and says, "Hey, send all the shoes you can get down here. No one has any. We can sell them to everybody!" Is the glass half empty or half full? It depends on the meta program and evidence you are using.

**RWD**: That is like the person who invented the automobile. People said, "Well it's a nice curiosity, but it will never replace the horse. First of all, if everyone were really going to have one of these things, you'd have to have tons of this 'gas,' and then you'd have to have these gas stations all over the place because it only goes a limited distance on a tank of gas. And then you'd have to have miles and miles of paved roads, so these things could drive on them. That will never happen. The horse can go on almost any kind of surface and eats grass which you can find everywhere. It's a much more efficient form of transportation. Forget the automobile."

**RBD**: The other story I like to tell is about a kid who's working in a grocery store. He's young and energetic, and the boss has his eye on him. One day an old man comes in to the store and wants to buy a half head of lettuce. The kid politely tries to explain to him that the store only sells lettuce by the head. But the old guy gets very belligerent and says he wants a half of a head and that's all he's going to take. The young fellow wants to do his best for his customers so he finally says, "Well, let me go check with my boss." So he goes to the back of the store, finds his boss, and out of exasperation says, "Some jerk out here wants half of a head of lettuce." Suddenly, he notices out of the corner of his eye that the old guy has followed him back there and heard every word he said. So the kid turns to him and says, "And this fine gentleman would like the other half."

In NLP we believe, "There are no mistakes, there are only opportunities to be creative." Incidentally, the end of the story is that after the old guy leaves—with his half head of lettuce, of course—the boss takes the young fellow aside and says, "That was a really great maneuver. I see you're very creative. I've been thinking about it and I'd like you to be the manager of this store I'm opening up in Toronto." The kid is grateful but a little hesitant. The boss asks him why and he says, "Well, Toronto is in Canada, and I hear that all that's up there are whores and hockey players. I'm afraid there will be nothing there to interest me." "Well," says the boss, becoming angry, "my wife's from Canada I'll have you know!" "Oh," says the kid after a moment's pause, "What team did she play for?"

Sometimes what initially appears to be a big failure gives you the lead-in to a genuine innovation if you can adjust your filters and maintain your strategy and belief. The block turns into a building block.

**RWD**: Part of creativity is maintaining an optimistic outlook. The ability to avoid self consciousness and self criticism is a very important part of the making of inventions. Many inventors simply put aside whatever they come up with that didn't work as relevant to some other problem, just not to the particular problem at hand. I've done that in writing legal documents a lot. I've written something that doesn't fit the particular place, so I put it aside and use it later.

**RBD**: The joke writers for professional comedians like Johnny Carson will always include a backup joke if the initial one fails. In fact, sometimes comedians will like the backup so well that they try to make the first one fail.

The T.O.T.E. Model implies that it is important to explore variations in operations used to accomplish goals, rather than simply repeat the same ones—even if they produced creative results in the past. Because the environments and contexts in which we operate change, the same procedure will not always produce the same result. If you want to consistently achieve your goal, you must vary the operations you are using to get to it. When you always use the same procedure, you will produce a varying result.

In systems theory there is a principle called the *Law of Requisite Variety*, which states that in order to successfully adapt and survive, a member of a system needs a certain minimum amount of flexibility. That amount of flexibility has to be proportional to the variety in the rest of the system. One of the implications of the Law of Requisite Variety is that if you want to get to a particular goal state you have to increase the number of operations which could possibly get you there in proportion with the degree of variability in the system. So, as a system becomes more complex, more flexibility is required. Another implication of the Law of Requisite Variety is that the part of the system with the most flexibility will be the catalytic element within that system—like the queen in a game of chess.

In conclusion, the process of creativity often involves responding to problems in achieving goals. Below are several principles of creativity that are important in effectively responding to difficulties encountered in getting to a desired goal.

1. *Outcome Frame*—Maintain an orientation toward the future goal that you want to achieve rather than away from the problem to be avoided. Even if you are trying to get around a problem, it is important to do it within the broader vision and context of the goal state.

2. *Feedback versus Failure Frame*—If an idea doesn't work, the way in which it failed will give you feedback as to what to do to succeed (learn from your mistakes). Sometimes you even need to do something which you know will not work in order to get the feedback necessary to take the next step.

3. *Flexibility Frame*—a) Always have at least two other choices to fall back on *before* you start implementing a particular operation. b) "If what you are doing isn't working, do something different—do *anything* different." Almost anything is a better choice than what you are doing if you've already demonstrated that it won't work.

## Summary

Creativity is a multi-level, multi-faceted process. We have introduced a number of tools and principles for defining and exploring the creative process centered around the R.O.L.E. and T.O.T.E. models and different logical levels of interaction.

On the micro level, we have discussed how the sensory systems and orientation that we use to map or represent our experience of something is an essential element of the creative process. Creativity is a function of how we think and perceive. The way in which representations are linked together is also a major source of creativity.

Sensory experiences and maps are linked together in the context of macro and meta processes that are happening simultaneously but on different levels. Our perception of our environment is simultaneously linked to our behavioral actions, which are at the same time linked to our inner maps and plans, which are linked to our value systems and beliefs, which are linked to our sense of self. It is this kind of meta level linking that provides the 'logic' behind the sequential and synesthesia links of a micro strategy.

This kind of linking generally assumes the form of the T.O.T.E. and determines:

1. the kind of context in which you are creative or innovative.
2. your goals for the creative process.
3. the type of evidence procedure you use to determine progress toward those goals.
4. the sets of choices you use to get to these goals and the range of behaviors available to implement these choices.
5. the way you respond if you do not initially achieve your goals.

Different types of creativity can be defined in relation to changes made in different elements of the T.O.T.E.

**Innovation**: Coming up with a completely new idea —relates to goal setting.

**Discovery**: Changing your perceptual filters to experience something familiar in a different way-relates to evidence procedures.

**Invention/Implementation**: Operating within a set of parameters to achieve a specified goal—relates to means for accomplishing goals.

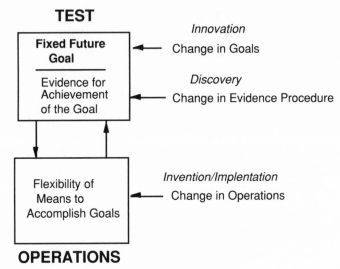

**Figure 1.15. Types of Creativity Related to Changes in the T.O.T.E.**

In addition to micro level structures there are macro level patterns that relate to how we establish and implement the various T.O.T.E. functions. These patterns will influence the scope and style of a particular creative effort. The figure below summarizes some of the key macro level patterns.

An effective creativity strategy will involve a balance of these patterns, typically in the form of a cycle of processes that we have called the *dreamer*, the *realist* and the *critic*. On a general level, the dreamer relates to the establishment of new goals, the realist relates to the process of implementing or accomplishing those goals, and the critic relates to the process

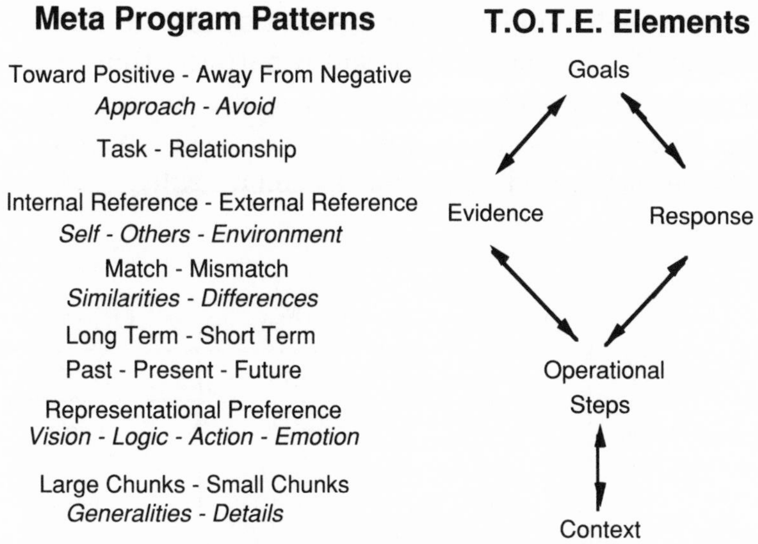

Meta Program Patterns
Toward Positive - Away From Negative
Approach - Avoid
Task - Relationship
Internal Reference - External Reference
Self - Others - Environment
Match - Mismatch
Similarities - Differences
Long Term - Short Term
Past - Present - Future
Representational Preference
Vision - Logic - Action - Emotion
Large Chunks - Small Chunks
Generalities - Details
T.O.T.E. Elements
Goals
Evidence
Response
Operational Steps
Context

**Figure 1.16. Meta Program Patterns Related to T.O.T.E. Functions.**

of establishing evidence procedures and evaluating progress toward the goals.

TEST
Fixed Future Goal
Evidence for Achievement of the Goal
"Dreamer"
"Critic"
Flexibility of Means to Accomplish Goals
"Realist"
OPERATIONS

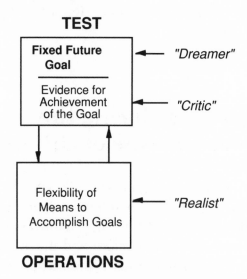

**Figure 1.17. T.O.T.E. Functions Related to Dreamer, Realist and Critic.**

Dreamer, realist and critic processes may also be defined in terms of clusters of meta program patterns that address different aspects of the creative work space. For example, the table below lists some common macro level patterns that could be associated with the dreamer, realist and critic strategies.

| | Dreamer | Realist | Critic |
|---|---|---|---|
| Orientation | *What* | *How* | *Why* |
| *Representational Preference* | Vision | Action | Logic |
| *Approach* | Toward | Toward | Away |
| *Time Frame* | Long Term | Short Term | Long/Short Term |
| *Time Orientation* | Future | Present | Past/Future |
| *Reference* | Internal - Self | External - Environment | External - Others |

**Figure 1.18. Clusters of Meta Program Paterns
Related to Dreamer, Realist and Critic.**

# Exercise: Exploring the Creative Process of Others

As a short exercise, compare the following descriptions made by two well known American fiction writers about their creative writing process. What can you tell about the differences and similarities in their micro and macro strategies? Take note of any patterns in their representational system orientations, goals, evidence procedures, operations and meta programs.

I am always at my most prolific, most genius struck, when I am away from pencil, paper and typewriter. Then countless nebulous ideas take form in the brain like brave new worlds being born. Vivid characters suddenly inhabit those worlds and undertake marvelously complex, though always logical adventures. And all this in passages so fluent, so apt, so powerful that I can only be moved to wonderment by them. And if I had any remaining doubt about it, it is easily put to rest by the glowing reviews which keep appearing-mental reviews, that is—even while my mental work on the dream narrative proceeds. Reviews of one's work, say some authors, can never be too favorable. But watching those imaginary critiques parading before the mind's eye, though I can't really argue with their accuracy and sensitivity, I sometimes do find myself close to blushing at the overwhelming awe and admiration they convey.

So much for the good news. The bad news is there always seems to come a day when I must descend to reality and actually put some of those words on paper. And, in doing so, must recognize yet again that I was born with a faulty connection between mind and hand, something which suggests that I have been thinking those marvelous tales in Venusian, a language notoriously untranslatable into English...

With the deadline date posted large above my desk... eventually, I will write a page. Then I will study it with the horrified realization that, as all good things must, an otherwise promising literary career has just come to an abrupt end... So I rewrite the page, striving to obtain some of that quality I had in mental Venusian, and this time it seems to go a little better. Sometimes, enough for me to risk a second page. And by way of this process, a third and fourth page and so on to The End. Which usually arrives about ten minutes before the expiration of the deadline. Obviously, I am not going to be hanged for something or other if I miss that deadline, but one sound working habit I have conditioned myself to is holding on to the idea that a deadline is sacred. If not for that, I'd be in another business altogether.

There are good days and bad days, frequent wild swings between manic and depressive... at the daily grind one must suffer those qualms, ride those waves of manic-depression, and forever rest uneasy.

**Stanley Ellin**, author of *Dreadful Summit*
and *The Eight Circle*
from *Writer's Digest,* October 1983; pp. 22-23

I don't plot my books out in advance. I have a vague idea of where I want the book to go. I know vaguely what it's going to be about. But the first thing I do is to gather characters in a notebook. I will figure out who the characters are, what they're like, what they sound like. And I give them each a name—if I didn't have a name for each of the characters, then I don't think I would know what to do. So when I get into the writing, I have a pretty good idea of who the main characters will be, but I still don't know exactly how the story will work. And something happens to me in almost every book: A character that, in my mind, may have been fairly minor turns into a major character. I hear him talking, and I realize: This guy is interesting. I wouldn't have known that when I started the book.

I don't have a chapter-by-chapter outline when I start. I don't like having a plot—I think plotting is boring. I don't want the plot to be the main element. I want the characters to be the most interesting thing about the book. I want the readers to be more interested in the characters than the plot. That way, it becomes more like real life. So I don't have a plot outline for the book. But for the individual chapters I will know where each chapter's going. I make myself a few notes so I'll know where each chapter is supposed to head. A lot of times my scenes end with a punch line, and it may take me days to think of the right one. I try to end a chapter in a way that sets things up. I end a chapter with the reader wanting to know certain things. And I try to begin a chapter with something going on. I very rarely start a chapter with description, or with what the weather's doing or something like that. I jump right in.

I want an intelligent reader. I want a reader who's willing to work. When I write something with the hope that the reader gets it, and then I hear from someone that he has, indeed, gotten it—a certain reference or whatever—then that's it for me. That's satisfaction.

> **Elmore Leonard**, author of *Glitz*
> from the *San Jose Mercury News*
> August 24, 1985; p. 9C

The two descriptions provide a fascinating contrast in writing strategies.

On a micro level, Ellin's primary representational system (at least during the dreamer phase of his strategy) is visual while Leonard's is auditory. Ellin writes about "vivid characters" in a "dream narrative" and watching "imaginary critiques parading before the mind's eye." He sees the whole story before he starts writing a word. Leonard, on the other hand, writes about initially establishing what his characters "sound like," giving "each a name," hearing them "talking" and ending chapters with a verbal "punch line." He gets his feedback in what he "hears" from his readers. For him, the book unfolds itself as he is writing.

The fact that Leonard is more auditory in his approach appears to make the translation of his mental process onto paper easier than for Ellin. Ellin claims his visions come when he is away from "pencil, paper and typewriter" and talks about the difficulty of translating his mental "Venusian" into English. This is no doubt because his inner representations are in terms of images as opposed to words. Therefore they do not map over easily into language. Leonard begins by using pencil and paper to gather his characters in a "notebook." Because he actually imagines them speaking, it seems easier for him to transcribe his inner experience onto paper in words. While Ellin describes his process in terms of vision, emotion and logic, Leonard talks of beginning and ending his chapters with actions and words.

The differences in representational systems seems to produce some major differences on the macro level. Ellin's goals center around recording the "complex" but "logical adventures" he has already seen in his mind's eye. In contrast, Leonard's goals center around transcribing the unfolding dialogue of his characters, claiming the characters are more important than the plot. Ellin's more visually oriented strategy involves the movement from generalities to details—he must take his dream narratives and chunk them down adventure by adventure, page by page, word by word. In contrast, Leonard's strategy involves collecting details to make generalities-he builds his story name by name, word by word, character by character, chapter by chapter in a linear progression.

In terms of evidence, Ellin clearly uses an external reference while Leonard applies an internal reference. Ellin must post an external deadline and hold it "sacred" in order to complete his work, and values the reviews and critiques of others. Leonard, on the other hand, describes the kind of reader that *he* wants to have, what he wants them to be interested in and "hopes" that they get what he wants to convey. Ellin judges himself; Leonard judges the reader. As an author, Ellin seems to perceive himself more as a *channel* between his visions and his readers, while Leonard perceives himself as the *source* of his ideas.

As a result, Ellin seems to bounce back and forth between the dreamer and the critic—*towards* the positive and then *away* from the negative; *self* and then *other*; *matching* and then *mismatching*. Because of his external reference he has to contend with "frequent wild swings between manic and depressive." Leonard's process, on the other hand, involves more of a relation between the dreamer and the realist. He produces in present oriented, short term small chunks-his stories unfold like "real life." He is slowly but surely going toward something.

| Ellin | Leonard |
|---|---|
| visual — logical — emotional | auditory — action |
| external reference | internal reference |
| toward — away | toward |
| long term | short term |
| future | present |
| chunk from large to small | chunk from small to large |
| Dreamer/Critic | Dreamer/Realist |

What both Ellin and Leonard share, however, is application of a continuous incremental feedback loop that constantly refines the material with which they are working.

## The Creative Cycle

One way of defining the creative process would be that a well-formed creativity strategy is made up of a sequence of programs that follow a cycle made up of the following stages:

1. Generating and Selecting new ideas—*Dreamer*

2. Implementation of selected ideas—*Realist*

3. Feedback—Incorporation/Rejection of other peoples' ideas and reactions-*Critic*

4. Completion of the project—Exiting the T.O.T.E.

5. Re-Entry—getting ready to start a new project

Each of these stages of the creative cycle can be viewed individually as a separate T.O.T.E. with its own unique set of tests and operations.

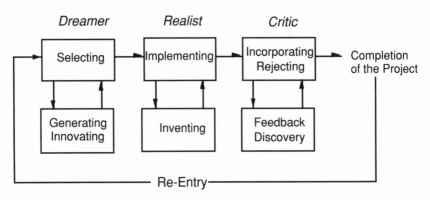

**Figure 1.19. Sequence of T.O.T.E.s Related to the Complete Creative Cycle.**

The criteria used for the test phase of each of these stages roughly correspond to what are called "Well-Formedness Conditions" in NLP. These conditions are used to identify the minimum set of requirements an idea or outcome has to satisfy in order to be "well-formed." The standard set of NLP well-formedness conditions is listed below.

## Dreamer

1. Outcome is stated in positive terms. That is, it states what you do want as opposed to what you don't want.

   **Questions**: *What do you want? What is possible? What is the payoff?*

## Realist

2. Can be initiated and maintained by the person or group desiring it.

   **Question**: *What specifically will **you** do to achieve this goal?*

3. Testable in sensory experience.

   **Question**: *How, specifically, will you know when you achieve the goal?*

## Critic

4. Preserves the positive by-products of the current behavior or activity.

   **Questions**: *What positive things, in any way, do you get out of your present way of doing things? How will you maintain those things in your new goal?*

5. Is appropriately contextualized and ecologically sound.

   **Questions**: *Under what conditions would you not want to implement this new goal? Who and what else could it effect?*

As you will notice, I have organized them into the various phases of creativity to which they are relevant. What makes something well-formed is different at different stages. The criteria of the dreamer T.O.T.E. are primarily organized around possibility and desirability. The criteria of the realist T.O.T.E. are organized around feasibility and workability. The criteria of the critic T.O.T.E. are organized around acceptability and 'fit' in relation to the larger system in which the idea will be expressed.

Clearly, the typical expression of these NLP well-formedness conditions are formed from the point of view of a single individual. Yet, a great deal of creativity, and the creative cycle, involves the work of groups and teams of people—especially in an organizational setting. While the general goals of each T.O.T.E. remain the same for a team, it may be helpful to widen the statements and questions associated with these well-formedness conditions to include the team perspective.

## Well-Formedness Conditions for Evaluating New Ideas in a Team

### Dreamer Stage

1. State It In Positive Terms.

   *What is possible? What is the goal? What will we be doing?* (As opposed to what will we stop doing, avoid or quit.) *What is the payoff?* (Get a consensus.)

### Realist Stage

2. Make Sure It Can Be Initiated and Maintained by the Appropriate Person or Group.

   *Who will do it?* (Assign responsibility and secure commitment from the people who will be carrying it out.)

3. Its Progress Must Be Testable Through Sensory Experience.

   *What are the performance criteria? How will they be tested? How will we know if the goal is achieved?*

## Critic Stage

4. Make Sure It Preserves Any Positive By-Products of the Current Way(s) of Achieving the Goal.

*What positive things do we get out of our current way(s) of doing things? How can we keep those things when we implement the new idea?*

5. Make Sure It Is Ecological For Everyone Effected By It and It Is Appropriately Contextualized.

*Who will this new idea effect? Who will make or break the effectiveness of the idea and what are their needs and payoffs? Under what conditions would you* **not** *want to implement this new idea?*

Thus far we have focused on identifying and defining the key elements and principles involved in the creative process. In the coming chapters we will demonstrate and explore how these principles and tools can be applied to specific contexts and situations involving creativity.

# 2

---

# Micro Tools for Creativity: Strategy Elicitation Using the R.O.L.E. Model

**RBD**: We pointed out in the previous chapter that, according to the Law of Requisite Variety, the process of creativity involves the constant updating, expansion and revision of your creativity strategies and maps. This in and of itself is an ongoing challenge. But sometimes when you want to update one of your maps, you run into another kind of challenge-what and where is the map I need to update? Our mental strategies are so much a part of our perception of reality that we are often unaware of what they are and how they operate, like a fish being unaware of the water in which it is swimming.

Likewise as we seek to identify and benefit from the creativity strategies of other people, we often immediately run into the limitations of conscious awareness. It is a well-known phenomenon that the more you learn something, the less aware you are of what you're doing while you're doing it. For instance, I was satisfied that I had learned to play the guitar to a certain extent when I could talk to someone while playing it, and not pay attention to what I was doing with the guitar. I didn't have to be totally conscious of each step. I had developed some degree of unconscious competence. While this is very efficient with respect to performance, the problem comes when it's been twenty years since you did something consciously, and someone says, "Gee, you're really good at that. How do you do it?" It becomes very difficult to consciously reconstruct for somebody what specific steps you went through.

One of the real contributions of NLP is that it provides some tools with which you can read peoples' minds in a way. Actually, you are reading certain minimal cues that give you information about the form of someone's thinking process (as opposed to the content).

If thoughts are a function of the connection between pictures, sounds, and feelings related together in some sort of ordered sequence like a telephone number or a computer program, we need some way to get access to that process even if the person who is doing it isn't conscious of it. Through the research that we've conducted in NLP, we've found that there are specific behavioral cues that go along with specific kinds of thought processes. Our belief is that the mind and the body are interconnected through our neurological systems. In fact, you can't think without having your body do something on the outside that reflects something about that inner thought. And the more completely you think about something—the greater the commitment of neurology you invest in the thought—the more your body changes.

If you asked someone to think of a time when he was confident and he kind of glanced away for a moment and in a flat tone of voice said, "Sure, I just thought of one," I would not be very convinced that he was really thinking of that experience. But if he looked off into space, and his pupils dilated a little, and his skin began to become flushed, and his breathing deepened and he said, "Yeaah!" in a loud voice, I would believe that he indeed had fully accessed that experience. In other words, the more response you see, the more convinced you would be that a person actually thought of the experience.

The question is, "What is the physiology that goes along with creativity?" One phenomenon that seems to characterize people who are very creative is a highly focused mental and physical state that John Grinder calls a "demon state." (You may prefer to think of it as an "angel state.") Probably all of you have had that experience where you're working on something so intensely that you get into this state where you can't do anything but think about what you are working on. It consumes you. You can't not do it. We've found that people who are highly successful by being creative often talk about being driven as though there's a little demon in them that makes them do it. And there's certain patterns of physiology that go along with that kind of state.

**TE**: Not that there's just one correct physiology. You are not going to be able to identify the creative and inventive people because they all walk with a limp, or have a slightly shorter right arm. But there's going to be a physiology that corresponds to the mental activity of being creative, it's like a hologram and that's going to be part of your creative process.

A hologram is a three-dimensional image. What makes that so important is that the process of creating a hologram involves the storage of information in a specific type of formation. All the information about creating the image is stored in all parts of the image. If you take a hologram produced on a glass photographic plate and break the plate into pieces, the pieces themselves contain all the information about how to create the whole three-dimensional image. If you view one of these pieces with the correct light source at the proper angle, you can still see the entire image although you only have a piece of the original plate that the image was produced on. When applied to the process of creativity, the hologram analogy allows us to understand how all the parts that make up creativity, whether they be representational systems or physiology, contain information about the whole creative process. That means that any aspect of the creative process can be used to access the information contained in the entire process.

Let's say normally you have a certain physiology when you're being very creative, and you sit with your shoulders back, posture erect and breathing in a certain way. Well, if you sit slumped over it may inhibit your mental process, because during the mental process of being creative your physiology is part of it. It is a critical part of accessing that creativity. You cannot separate mind and body.

**RBD**: There's an interesting illustration of this in the movie *Butch Cassidy and the Sundance Kid*. If the Sundance Kid took his time and actually aimed his gun he couldn't hit anything. He had to be moving. If he was falling through the air backwards, and shooting under his shoulder, he could hit anything.

# Identifying R.O.L.E. Model Patterns

As we pointed out earlier, one of the biggest difficulties in identifying mental maps and strategies comes from the fact that *the more one develops the ability to actually do something, the less one is aware of **how specifically** one is doing it.* Most people focus on what they are doing and not the subtle mental processes by which they are doing it. Most effective behavior is characterized by 'unconscious competence.' While this reduces the amount of conscious effort one has to put into achieving a goal, it makes it difficult to describe to others how to develop the same degree of competence. Furthermore, people often downplay critical steps in their own thinking process as being 'trivial' or obvious without realizing that those seemingly unimportant images, words or feelings that they are taking for granted are exactly what someone else might need to know to complete the mental strategy.

Neuro-Linguistic Programming has identified a number of verbal and non-verbal indicators that may be used as clues to uncover pieces of someone's mental processes with or without their conscious awareness.

## Physiological Clues:
## Making the R.O.L.E. into a B.A.G.E.L.

The R.O.L.E. model elements deal primarily with cognitive processes. In order to function, however, these mental programs need the help of certain bodily and physiological processes for consolidation and expression. These physical reactions are important for the teaching or development of certain mental processes as well as for the external observation and confirmation of them. The primary behavioral elements involved in R.O.L.E. modeling are:

**B**ody Posture

**A**ccessing Cues

**G**estures

**E**ye Movements

**L**anguage Patterns

## Body Posture
People often assume systematic, habitual postures when deep in thought. These postures can indicate a great deal about the representational system the person is using. The following are some typical examples:

Visual: *Leaning back with head and shoulders up or rounded, shallow breathing.*

Auditory: *Body leaning forward, head cocked, shoulders back, arms folded.*

Kinesthetic: *Head and shoulders down, deep breathing.*

## Accessing Cues
When people are thinking, they cue or trigger certain types of representations in a number of different ways including: breathing rate, non-verbal "grunts and groans," facial expressions, snapping their fingers, scratching their heads, and so on. Some of these are idiosyncratic to the individual and need to be 'calibrated' to the particular person. Many of these cues, however, are associated with particular sensory processes.

Visual: *High shallow breathing, squinting eyes, voice of higher pitch and faster tempo.*

Auditory: *Diaphragmatic breathing, knitted brow, fluctuating voice tone and tempo.*

Kinesthetic: *Deep abdominal breathing, deep breathy voice in a slower tempo.*

## Gestures

People will often touch, point to, or use gestures indicating the sense organ which they are using. Some typical examples include:

Visual: *Touching or pointing to the eyes; gestures made above eye level.*

Auditory: *Pointing toward or gesturing near the ears; touching the mouth or jaw.*

Kinesthetic: *Touching the chest and stomach area; gestures made below the neck.*

## Eye Movements

Automatic, unconscious eye movements often accompany particular thought processes indicating the accessing of one of the representational systems. NLP has categorized these cues into the following pattern:

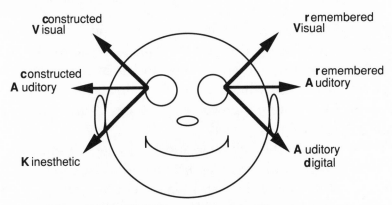

**Figure 2.1. NLP Eye Accessing Chart**

## Language Patterns

A primary method of Neuro-Linguistic analysis is to search for particular linguistic patterns, such as 'predicates,' which indicate a particular neurological representational system or sub-modality, and how that system or quality is being used in the overall program of thought. Predicates are words, such as verbs, adverbs and adjectives, which indicate actions or qualities as opposed to things. This type of language is typically selected at an unconscious level and thus reflects the underlying unconscious structure which produced them. Below is a list of common sensory-based predicates:

| **Visual** | **Auditory** | **Kinesthetic** |
|---|---|---|
| see | hear | grasp |
| look | listen | touch |
| sight | sound | feeling |
| clear | resonant | solid |
| bright | loud | heavy |
| picture | word | handle |
| hazy | noisy | rough |
| brings to light | rings a bell | connects |
| show | tell | move |

By identifying the way in which people use and combine their senses while thinking through the tools listed above, we can come not only to understand the process of creativity and innovation more fully, but also to help train and develop these aspects of the thinking processes of others to improve their thinking capabilities as well.

By examining the behavior and language of people who have done something creative or innovative, we can begin to get a general idea of the cognitive structure of the thought process behind creativity and innovation. What is important for R.O.L.E. modeling is not the content of a creative product or behavior but rather the concrete sensory elements of the thought process that produced them. It is this underlying structure that can allow us to transfer the productive elements of thinking to other topics or subjects.

# Strategy Elicitation
# Procedures and Principles

**RBD**: I usually elicit a strategy the way that I draw: I make a general sketch **first**, then I add the details (*see* Appendix E for an overview of Strategy Elicitation procedures). I might start by simply asking, "What do you consider to be the specific steps in your own creative process? What, specifically, do you see, hear or feel internally and in what order?"

Another way to get a general sketch is to do is what is called a **contrastive analysis.** It is often much more difficult for someone to answer a question like, *"How are you creative?,"* than a question like, *"Think of a time that you were really creative and then think of a time that you couldn't be but wanted to be. What's the* **difference** *between those two situations? What went on differently in your mind when you were able to be creative versus when you weren't?"*

By giving someone something to compare, you get a much higher-quality answer. The *major differences* will pop out, i.e., what is different about them, and that's really what you're after. What you want to know is: *What was the difference that made the difference?*

Another general principle of effective elicitation is that of *similarities* and *differences of content.* On the one hand, you want to try to get examples of very similar content areas that match each other in all aspects but the outcome of the strategy. This way you can be sure the difference was due to the **strategy** alone and not the content. For example, asking somebody to contrast a time when they were able to be extremely creative in answering an essay question with a time when they got stuck answering an essay question, may give you more information about the *essence* of that person's creativity strategy than if you contrasted getting stuck on an essay question with a time they got stuck cooking or selling something. This is because a good deal of *"noise"* and other variations are introduced by the differences in the content of the strategy if the contexts are very different.

Similarly, you may get higher quality information about the essence of a person's creativity strategy if you can find a contrast between essay questions on the same test (same day, same teacher, same subject, etc.) where the only difference was the person's ability to be creative. The fewer influences that are brought to bear by the differences in the content of the strategy, the more you can be sure your focus is on the difference in the actual strategy alone.

On the other hand, contrasting examples of creativity that involve very different content areas and noticing what is the **same** about the strategies can also give you a great deal of information about the essence of creativity for that person. That is, if the person uses the **same** strategy to be creative when they are cooking as they use when they are coming up with a creative solution to a business problem then we know that it is a significant strategy.

Another important principle of elicitation is that a *behavioral example* of the strategy you are after will give you higher quality information than *talking about* an example. What I mean by *quality* of information is this: It's much easier for me to give a person a test and ask, *"Which questions were easy for you and which ones were hard?"*, than it is to say, *"Think of a test you took three years ago. What, specifically, did you do in your mind as you were answering those questions?"* That's more like 'Neuro-Linguistic Archaeology!' The information is going to be too coded in with all kinds of other "noise," introduced by the memories of the past three years. You want to get the highest signal and the least noise.

You will get higher quality information by **watching the person engaging in the activity** of writing an essay question than by asking them about one they have already written. If you want to find out about somebody's strategy for a certain academic subject, give them some test questions, sit down and watch them. You will be able to **see their strategy as it happens**. Then right afterwards say, *"Contrast for me now: Which one was the easiest for you and which one was the most difficult? What's the difference between those?"* Then ask, *"As you were answering the one that was easiest for you, what did you go through in your mind? What were you aware of?"* What they might do at that point is to **look up and left** and say something like, *"Gee, I don't know."* In other words, what they've done is to say, "I don't know." But they've in fact just **behaviorally demonstrated** it for you. If you say to somebody, *"Think of a test you took three years ago,"* and they look up and left and say, *"I can't remember,"* then you can't be sure you are not just getting a part of their memory strategy. But if you said, *"Now you just went through this. What did you do in your mind?"*, it's going to be a lot less memory strategy and more recapitulation of what they just went through.

So, optimally, you want to set up something that they can do right there—high quality. Then you contrast: *"Which of these was most difficult?"* That makes the differences start to pop out. Then I might just ask, *What **specifically** did you go through in your mind?"*, and watch what they do again to make sure I see a repetition of the general pattern I think I have been observing.

Of course, it is not always possible to get ongoing behavioral examples. You should also keep in mind, however, that very often *people do what they are talking about.* That is, people will often reiterate what they did in a situation while they are telling you about it because they begin to reaccess the strategy as well as the memory. For instance, it is common for people to become angry again as they tell you about a person with whom they got into a fight. So be sure to keep your eye out for patterns at all times.

If I have to rely on the memory of the person I am interviewing then I ask them to think of at least three different instances of creativity. This allows me to find the pattern that emerges. In this case I will be less concerned with the immediate details of the person's thinking strategy than the elements that are the same in all three examples.

Once I get done with these initial steps, I usually have a basic idea, or sketch, of what their strategy is. With just a couple of simple questions, you can get a good idea of what the physiological and representational differences are between a successful and unsuccessful strategy. For instance, I might quickly discover that when the person is creative they *lean back, move both of their hands, look up and right, and are aware of making internal images.* In contrast, when they are stuck, they *tighten their shoulders, stop breathing, shift their eyes between down left and down right, and are aware of vague critical internal voices.*

In order to get the details of the strategy I would explore the structure of the process a little bit more. To find the evidence procedure I might say, *"When you've **got** the answer, when you are done, when you know you have the answer to that question, how, **specifically**, do you know it?"* It should be a lot easier for them to answer that question after I've done the general sketch than if I started out with it. Now that they've thought about it, now that I've had them go through a few times already I ask, *"How do you **know** when you have the answer?"* That is probably one of the most important parts of the strategy since it will identify their criteria for success.

And it is critical to remember that what the person **says** and what actually happened may be very different. A person may *look up, take a deep breath* and say, *"I saw that it was right."* What they saw may have let them know it was right **or** it may have been a *feeling* that is so habitual that it seems more like "reality" than a feeling.

In general it is always a better idea to *give more credence to the non-verbal response.* If someone takes a deep breath, and leans back, it indicates they probably made some sort of shift in their internal state. They may have felt or got some other physiological indication that let them know the answer.

Perhaps they felt a shift from tension to relaxation. And that's how they **knew,** *"OK, that fits in there."* Whenever you ask an elicitation question the primary issue for success is to know when to watch for the answer.

If you read an elicitation question off of a piece of paper and then look up at your subject, there's a good chance you may have already missed all of the important information. *It's the unconscious, immediate reaction that is going to carry more information.* All the subject can do at a verbal level is to *interpret* their reactions *consciously.* That is, the person you ask the question of is going to go through the answer, and then they're going to try to put it in some words that they think **you** want to hear. For successful elicitation, however, you don't really care what they have to **say about** it. You just want to know what they actually **did.** So the timing of your observations are very important. As soon as you ask the question, for about *three or four seconds*—that's what you want to watch. You don't want to sit there and, as they go through twenty thousand eye movements, keep track of them all. You want to get the ones that happen right at the critical time.

In so many studies that I've heard of, the researchers are getting someone's conscious opinion about their thought processes and not their accessing cues.

Once again, the closer that you can get to an actual behavioral example, the better. That will save you from a lot of guess work. If you absolutely can't find a way to engage the person in the activity then pick the most recent experiences that you can, because those are going to be the ones that will elicit the information that you want with the least amount of noise from memory and interpretation.

So, to review, get a **behavioral demonstration** of the strategy or pick your example as near to the present as possible. **Contrast** this example with as **similar** an example you can find but where the **outcome was the opposite.** After you do the contrast and have the subject oriented, ask,

*"What did you do with the one that was successful? What, specifically, did you just go through in your mind?"* You may also want to **contrast** the strategy with as **different** an example as you can find but where the **strategy was the same**.

These are all basic orientation questions and will give you a chance to watch the strategy go by a number of times. Remember, if it happens fast and you miss it the first time, don't panic. If it is really their strategy it will happen over and over and over again. It is the patterns that repeat that you are the most interested in anyway. By the time you've oriented your subject you are probably going to have seen the strategy go by two or three times, and will have had a chance to get a general opinion. **Then**, right after you set up the contrast say, *"Well, what did you just do in your mind?"*, and watch them. You're not going to be particularly interested in what they say about it at this point. Typically, they're not going to give you the information you're seeking. For instance, you can probably bet they're not going to say, *"Well, I **pictured** this, and then I **said** this to myself, and I got this **feeling** with the **picture**, but it didn't **look** right yet, so I **asked** another question..."*

In fact, the purpose of a lot of the elicitation procedures is just to focus the subject on this actual *fraction-of-a-second experience* that's really the key to the whole thing.

So first you ask, *"How did you know when you got the right answer?"* **Then** you are going to want to ask: *Was it **picture, sound, feeling**?*

To start **detailing** the strategy, I've found that it's usually easier to peg the **end** of a strategy than the beginning. If I ask, *"When did you start being creative?"*, it is typically more difficult to answer than: *"Now that you have done something creative, at what point did you **know** that you were successful?"*

Most people don't know where, when and how they started being creative for a given problem. Almost everyone, however, can identify when it was **finished**. You might be able to trace back influences on the start of the process to years ago. But the *end is usually a definite point*. It's a little easier to pinpoint. When you're done, you know that you're done.

I use this "rule of thumb"—to start at the end—unless there's some reason to start somewhere else. If you are taking a written test then the point at which you looked at the question is usually a good beginning point. But many strategies don't have such a definite beginning point.

Once you are at the end of the strategy you ask, *"What specifically did you see, hear or feel?"* Then you can simply ask, *"And what happened just **before** that?,"* to get the details of the strategy **sequence** and **links**.

To elicit the **effect** of each of the strategy steps, I ask basic T.O.T.E. questions and watch for which of the cues I've observed thus far recur as they are answering or thinking of the answer. In addition to the T.O.T.E. questions posed in the questionnaire in the last chapter, I have listed some other examples below.

1. What are your *goals* when you are being creative?
   a. What steps do you go through to select an idea?
      1) How, specifically, do you know when you have a good concept that you want to continue with?
      2) How do you sort good ideas from bad ideas?

2. What steps do you go through to *implement* your idea?
   a. When and what kinds of constraints do you introduce as you are forming and implementing your idea?
   b. Where are your go/no go points?
   c. What parts of your experience or environment do you utilize in order to get to your goal?

3. What, specifically, do you use as *evidence* to know if you are making progress toward your goals?

4. When do you want *feedback*?
   a. What kind?
   b. From whom?

5. What *stops* you from being creative/productive?
   a. How do you tell the difference between "procrastination" and "gestation"?

6. How do you respond if you run into *problems*?
   a. Think of a time you were stuck and were able to break out of it. What did you do?

7. How do you protect yourself from *interruptions*? From *distractions*? From *criticism*?

8. What would the ideal creativity manager make you do?

# Exercise:
# Basic R.O.L.E. Model Elicitation

**RBD**: We'd like to present a short exercise on some basics of strategy elicitation.

As I said before, one of the fastest ways to elicit information about peoples' thinking processes is to do contrasts. If I want to find out where a person is having difficulty, I make a contrast between a time where there was no problem and a time where there was a problem. This is going to focus me on the nature of the difficulty a lot faster than if I just used a trial-and-error method of search like a checklist.

If I want to find out what the critical event is in spelling, for example, I get two kids of the same age, same height, same cultural background, same amount of education, who attend the same school. The optimal situation is to have two identical twins where one is a good speller and one is a poor speller.

I ask them each to spell a word. I have the optimal contrast because whatever is the same about them is obviously not relevant to what produces their difference in spelling performance. It's only what is different about what they do that focuses me on what could be significant to their spelling.

It is the same for creativity. Contrast tends to focus you very quickly on the significant events. For instance, in the following exercise you will be asked to review in your mind times when you were creative and times when you wanted to be creative but couldn't. After finding out any processes that were at all effective in both of the contrasting instances, you can screen out everything else that is the same. Then you can look only to what is different in the instance in which you were able to be creative and that will give you some very important clues to your creativity strategy.

In this exercise we want to start exploring the process of elicitation with a procedure that allows you to observe and record different R.O.L.E. Model elements. On the following page is a questionnaire with some spaces provided for you to keep track of key R.O.L.E. model information.

This exercise is best done with one or two partners to help with observations of details that may be outside of your own conscious awareness. You can try it alone of course, but it's hard to watch your own eye movements in the mirror!

The observers should be facing the person who is exploring his creativity process. After you ask each question on the sheet, check off the boxes which correspond to positions the explorer's eyes move to as he is thinking and answering the question. The boxes give you a way to record the sequence of eye movements.

For the time being, don't worry about trying to interpret or transpose the eye movements-just record them as you see them. In other words, if I'm sitting opposite you and I look down and to my left, you will see my eyes moving to your right. Don't worry about whether it's my left or your right,

| Question | Eye Movements | Representational System | Body Posture And Gestures |
|---|---|---|---|
| *Re-experience a time when you were best able to be Creative* | 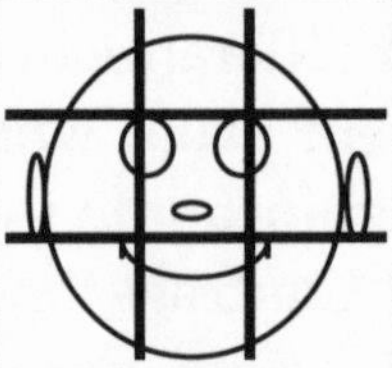 | O Picture(s)<br>O Words<br>O Sounds/Tones<br>O Feelings | |
| *Relive another time you were really able to fully be Creative* | 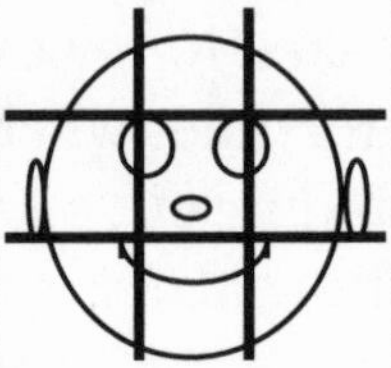 | O Picture(s)<br>O Words<br>O Sounds/Tones<br>O Feelings | |
| *Re-experience a time when you wanted to be Creative but got stuck.* | 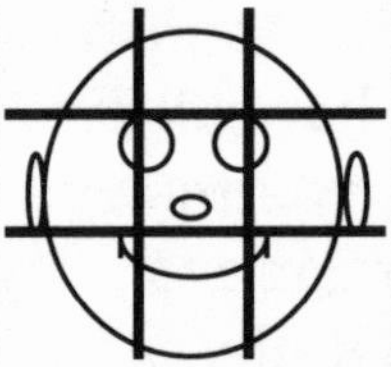 | O Picture(s)<br>O Words<br>O Sounds/Tones<br>O Feelings | |
| *Re-experience another time you were unable to be Creative* | 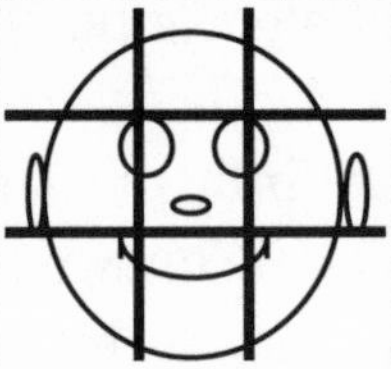 | O Picture(s)<br>O Words<br>O Sounds/Tones<br>O Feelings | |
| *Pick something easy and try to be Creative right now.* | 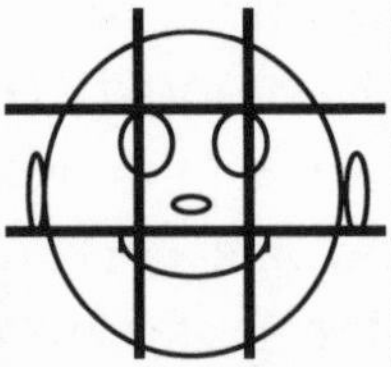 | O Picture(s)<br>O Words<br>O Sounds/Tones<br>O Feelings | |
| *Choose a difficult subject and try to be Creative right now.* | 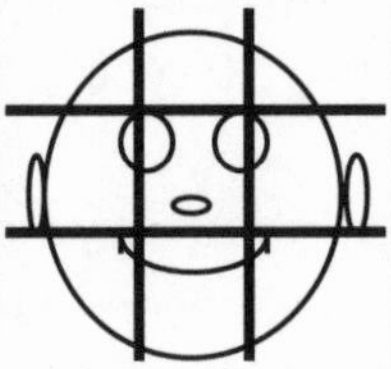 | O Picture(s)<br>O Words<br>O Sounds/Tones<br>O Feelings | |

**Figure 2.2. Creativity Strategy Elicitation Chart**

just mark it as you the observer see it-as if the grid was on a piece of glass that you are looking through and you are just tracing what you see.

**RBD**: It is probably a good idea to work out a signal system between the observers and explorer so that the observers wait until the explorer has the idea or the experience in mind before they start noting details. Otherwise you may get arti-facts from his "memory strategy," If you say, "Think of a time when you were creative," that person is first going to have to go through the process of recalling that experience and you will be observing the cues associated with that process more than with creativity.

**TE**: For example, a person might first go inside and repeat the question, "When was a time when I was really creative?" The person may not be thinking of that specific time yet. He may be using some other process, something in order to access that particular time and place. You can be getting information about the recall process as well as the motivation process.

**RBD**: So have your partner signal you when he's identified the specific instance. Then say, "Now relive it again in your mind." As he relives the experience, watch the eye positions he goes through. Keep a record of the sequence of the eye positions he goes through on the chart. The simplest way to do this is with numbers and arrows as shown in the figure below.

As we mentioned earlier, it is often useful to do this exercise in a group of three. Then you can have one person observing and writing the eye movements down, and the other person validating the observations-you get a 'double description' to check your observations. You both watch and agree on what you see, but only the one person needs to write them down.

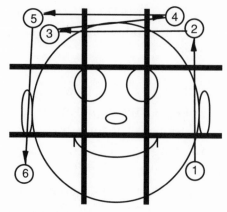

**Figure 2.3. Sample Record of Eye Movements**

What is interesting about this exercise is that you're literally watching the person's thoughts. You're watching what's going on in that person's mind. You'll know a lot about that person by observing them this closely.

Use the same process for the instance in which the person wanted to be creative, but couldn't. Ask the person to think of a very similar instance when he wanted to be creative, but couldn't. Have him identify it and signal you. Then say, "Relive it again in your mind," and keep track of his eye movements. You may notice that his eyes start in the same place, but in this second scenario, his eyes might then end up, say, down and to the left instead of up and to the right. Try to find out what the difference is.

It is useful to use a couple of different examples in order to find a pattern in the eye movements. If it's really a thought pattern, that person's eye movement sequence will happen again even if the specific content of the example has changed.

Also, be creative and curious. If you notice that the person does shift their pattern, ask them, "Were you thinking about it in the exact same way? Did you suddenly add something in there?" Because what you're going to find is that you'll be able to tell, if someone shifts their pattern, that they uncovered something else. You'll be able to see the difference. If you do notice something that isn't consistent, find out whether the person is really thinking of it consistently.

In addition to recording these eye movements and making these comparisons, ask about the link between what you see and what's going on inside them. That is what the 'Representational System' column is for. Make a note of which of the senses was being used in what ways during the different experiences. You can start by having the explorer check his own subjective experience by asking something like, "Are you more aware of pictures, sounds, feelings or words when you are in this experience?" Check off which representational systems were involved in each experience.

As we mentioned before, however, there may be parts of the R.O.L.E. Model that are outside of the explorer's awareness. So, as an observer, if you notice something interesting, ask the explorer about it. If you notice he looks up right and stays there for a long time, you might say, "What are you doing up there? Were you picturing anything?" Begin to connect what you see with what's going on inside that person. My rule of thumb is: "When in doubt, check it out."

Another guide you might want to use to help uncover unconscious processes is the NLP Eye Movement chart, shown below, that we presented in the R.O.L.E. Model section. You can use this chart as a guide to give you an indication about what might be going on inside of the explorer when his eyes are in certain positions.

**Note**: While we have found that the senses indicated by the position of the eyes tends to be consistent for right-handed people across different nationalities and cultures, there will be many left-handed people, and a few right-handed people, for whom these functions may be reversed. That is, they imagine while looking to their left side and remember while looking to their right. It is important to remember that the

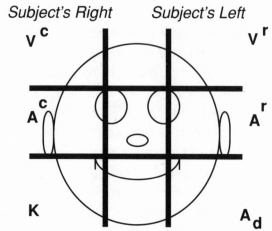

**Figure 2.4. Representational Systems
Indicated by Eye Position.**

model should be made to fit the person, not the person to fit the model!

Also remember that the senses do not function in an all-or-nothing fashion. When you're talking to yourself, it doesn't mean that the visual part of your brain turns off. It is still working and it is indeed possible to have a multi-sensory experience at any point in time. In NLP we call the ongoing process of multi-sensory experience a *4-tuple*. Eye positions merely indicate which of the senses is the focal point at a particular time.

As the subject, you may find it difficult to be conscious of what you did when you are asked these questions. And when you finally became aware of part of what you did, it won't be any one thing, but kind of a mishmash of things. In creativity, a person rarely just goes from a single picture to a single feeling. It's often an integration of two things: pictures and words, or sounds and feelings, or feelings and pictures, and so on. The creative process is often a combination of both-a *synesthesia*. This kind of combining makes identifying any particular eye movement associated with creativity inappropriate.

In fact, when a person's eyes are in the middle of the chart, and not to the right or left, it is a pretty good indication that there is probably some kind of synesthesia or overlapping of different sensory information going on.

Really explore the sensory orientations and links that happen in the two experiences. In general, the up-down position of the eyes tells you which representational system is being used; the left-right positioning of the eyes tells you some basics about the orientation of the representational system; and the sequence of movements tells you about the links between the representational systems.

There are a number of different kinds of patterns that you might find as a result of an exercise like this. The goal is to work with your partners to find your own particular pattern for creativity. For example, you might find that when you are thinking creatively your eyes tend to sweep around from up and to the right to up and to the left. Whereas when you get stuck, your eyes shift to one place and stick there.

The question of which representational system is being used is not as important as *how* that representational system is being used. Maybe for creativity, you have a lot of mental activity accompanying multiple inputs, whereas in getting stuck, there is input from only one channel and a person cannot shift out of it.

This kind of pattern for creativity can be contrasted with a strategy for effective memory, such as spelling. When a good speller is remembering a spelling word, her eyes will typically go up and to the left and stay fixed as she reads off the letters in her memory. When someone has difficulty spelling, her eyes will move all over the place, searching for the information.

The quality of the eye movement is an analog to what's going on in the person's head. As the observer in this exercise, you want to pay attention to the pattern of how the eyes move

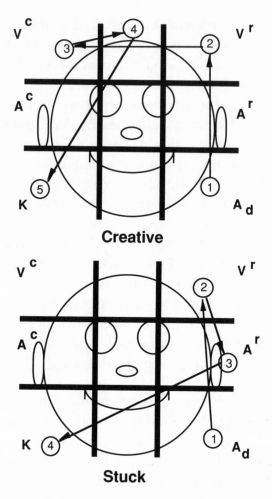

**Creative**

**Stuck**

**Figure 2.5. Example of Difference
Between Creative and Stuck
Eye Movement Patterns.**

as well as where they move. Mark down the number of times your partner's eyes move and how they moved: Did they move slow or fast?

Be careful of bringing in any preconceptions that might effect your observations. In contrast to the example I gave above, you might find that when your partner is being creative, his eyes move very little and when he's stuck, his eyes move all around. For one person, creativity might be sticking to something and following it through instead of changing his mind, whereas, for someone else, it might be coming unstuck and moving the eyes at random.

**TE**: The pattern of eye movements can also change depending on what you are being creative about. In certain contexts, you may be creative by accessing all quadrants. In other contexts, the way to be creative may be to stick just to that representational system. There are differences between being creative about cooking or writing a song or painting a picture. They involve a focus on different representational abilities: taste, sound and vision.

**RBD**: At this point in the elicitation process it really helps to put your full attention on the explorer. For instance, you will find that people often answer your questions with their eyes much earlier than they do with a verbalization. If you only start watching someone after he begins speaking, you miss a lot of the accessing cues that lead to that response. The person may not know what to talk about until that person gets the picture first. Usually, by the time the words come out, it's too late. The critical information comes right after you ask the question and before they actually start to verbalize their thoughts. This is also the time they will be the least conscious of what and how they are thinking.

  If you asked Albert Einstein, "How exactly did you come up with the theory of relativity?", he might say, "I don't know," but look up and right and then down and right with his eyes. He has answered you with his eye movements even though he can't answer it consciously.

  While it is important to reduce your reliance on the words that a person uses, there are certain language patterns that should be noted as we mentioned in the B.A.G.E.L. section. For instance, phrases like, "I see what you're saying," or, "It sounds right to me," or, "I can't get in touch with this," indicate different types of mental processing. Other examples might include:

**Visual**

SHOWED the options. Which choice LOOKS best. FOCUS on a particular option. I wasn't CLEAR about what to do. LOOKED at it from a different PERSPECTIVE.

**Auditory**

ASKED myself if I needed any more information. It SOUNDS good. There was nothing else to TALK about, so I SAID, "Let's TUNE in to what to do next." Something just CLICKED.

**Feeling**

In order to get a FEEL for the process I tried to get a HANDLE on the first step. There was a lot of PRESSURE so I just JUMPED right into it. There was something I FELT we needed to TOUCH on next so I tried to get a SOLID GRASP on it.

Keep in mind, however, that most of the quick thinking happens in front of your eyes before people even start talking.

You should also be aware that the wording *you* use when you ask a question is going to have an influence. There's a difference between "remembering an experience" and "reliving it." What you really want from asking this question is to take this person back through the experience. It's best if the person responds from first person, present tense, such as "I am doing this, I am thinking that" etc. If the person goes back into the experience and speaks in past tense saying, "Well, first I did this, then I did that," he is probably not actually inside himself and his experience as it occurred but is disassociated from it and thinking about it rather than reliving it. He is probably remembering back and analyzing what he did as opposed to re-experiencing it. These two types of experiences are very different. Your goal in modeling creativity is to determine the explorers's creativity strategy, not his analyzing strategy. You want to get the person inside that experience. You don't want the person to think about what they did, but rather to actually go back into the experience.

**TE**: If the person is analyzing what possibly could have occurred, try to create a situation where that person has to engage in being creative right now. If all he can do is analyze or vaguely remember where he was, but he can't remember what happened when he was being creative, then say: "Well, suppose you had to be creative about that in a different way right this minute, what would you do?" This allows you to get away from the interference of his memory strategy. You can have him engage in that activity in the present. This way you're going to get the purest form of information from the explorer if he's not capable of doing it by remembering.

**RBD**: So if you can't get a memory, then go to an ongoing example. You will attain a higher quality of information.

Another strategy is to ask the person to think of the last time she created. Sometimes a person is trying to remember back too far. Ask her to think of something that happened last week. Oftentimes, you might get information that's too clouded by other experiences.

Eye movements, of course, are just one form of what we call *accessing cues* in NLP. The last column on the elicitation questionnaire is for notes about significant patterns in body posture or gestures. For instance, a person who talks to herself a lot may assume an 'auditory' body posture. It is the same posture as that of Rodin's "Thinker." The body is leaning forward, the head is pointing down and to the left, and one of the hands is touching the face or jaw. People tend to touch the sense organ that they are using to process with at a particular moment. This kind of posture tends to go along with talking to one's self. We sometimes call it the "telephone posture" because it is as if you're on the telephone-talking to yourself long distance.

Postural changes can make a big difference in your internal processing. If you lean forward, it's going to change your breathing. It's not just the fact that your point of view changes. If you lean forward, it is very difficult to take a deep breath. Whereas if you lean back, you can easily take a deep breath in your chest. Your internal processing is affected by the way that you sit, the way that you hold your head, the way that you position your eyes and your breathing. For example, sit forward, droop your head and shoulders and try not to feel depressed. As long as a person stays in that posture, that is going to influence the type of thinking that person experiences. It is important to understand the interplay of physiology in creativity.

Other accessing cues include breathing, gesturing, and voice tone and tempo. Breathing is one of the most powerful accessing cues. I've done some drawing and drafting. I would spend all day not breathing. When I am drawing, my breathing is either shallow and in my chest, or there's hardly any breath at all. As a result, my shoulders are usually all hunched up. And it's not that I'm uncomfortable about what I'm doing. I find that in order to really project visually, I go into that sort of physical state.

When people are into feelings, they tend to breathe more abdominally. They take much deeper breaths. If you're breathing deeply your voice is much slower and lower and you go into a physically more relaxed state.

For instance, if I say, "Everybody sit back and go deeper into a relaxed state," and my voice is slow and deep, it makes it easier for people to access that condition. The voice tone cue works very differently when I say the same words quickly and with a choppy, nasal voice as opposed to when I say the same words slowly and deeply with pauses between the words.

That would be the case if I am asking you to do something feeling-oriented. On the other hand, if I say, "I'm going to ask this person some questions and I want you to watch and record the sophisticated pattern of eye movements," a slow, low-pitched voice with a lot of pauses may not help to access a state congruent to that mode of processing. To cue that state I might need to use a high-pitched, quick-tempoed voice. So, tone and tempo of voice tend to cue responses as well.

So, if someone speaks low, slow and breathy, it may be a clue that he is thinking in terms of feelings. If someone speaks in a rapid high-pitched voice it may indicate visual processing. In any event, you may want to note what kind of vocal qualities accompany the creative and stuck experiences.

**TE**: One of the most important things that you might learn from this exercise is that other people think differently than you do. I don't know how many times I've heard people say things like, "Doesn't *everybody* make pictures when they are creative?" "Doesn't *everybody* talk to themselves?" "Doesn't *everybody* have strong feelings?" The important thing to remember here is that there is no "right way" to be creative, and to celebrate the difference.

**RBD**: Another important thing to learn from this exercise is how to observe and interact with people on another level.

People typically tend to focus on the content of what is said rather than the thinking process used by the person saying it. For example, if an inventor talks to someone about his invention, the listener will probably concentrate on the technical concepts rather than observing how the inventor is thinking about his invention. The listener becomes too caught up in what the inventor is saying rather than how he is saying it.

Our first goal here is to find out what's going on in terms of the strategy for thinking. A thinking strategy is not determined by the objects or contents upon which it is operating. The form of a strategy is independent of what you put through it. It is important to recognize the distinction between the form a response takes versus the content associated with that response.

I heard of a sales-training course instructor who says something like, "If they touch their face it means they are ready to buy." That's silly from an NLP standpoint. Our interpretation is, "If someone touches his face, it is a signal about *how* he is thinking—with internal words—not *what* he is thinking." To me it signals that the person is talking to himself. He could be talking to himself about buying or not. The idea is to learn how to relate what you are observing to the other person's subjective experience without interpreting or judging.

When you see someone processing thoughts internally, the first step is to learn how to see what you see and how to hear what you hear rather than simply making a judgment or an interpretation based solely on content.

Not everybody thinks or responds in the same way and not everybody is creative in the same way. Our creativity allow us to do very well in certain activities. By knowing about the structure of our creative process we can generalize our creativity to other activities.

There are different types of strategies for being creative, and they have different degrees of effectiveness in different situations.

The following transcript provides a demonstration of how this type of process can be used to help draw out and define the creative process of an exceptional musician. Michael Colgrass is an award-winning composer who illustrates a number of the creative processes and principles we have outlined in this book. As you read over the interview, pay special attention to the language patterns and what they tell you about how Michael links together his representational systems.

# Interview with Michael Colgrass: Pulitzer Prize Winner for Music (1978)

**Michael**: You say I'm a successful composer and what is that? As a profession, many people don't know what a composer is. This has been my experience. You say, "I'm a composer." And they say, "Oh, does that mean you write pop tunes? You have any hits on Broadway?" I say, "No, I write music for symphony orchestras and string quartets. I'm a so-called classical composer in the lineage of Beethoven, and Bartok, and all that. Then they say, "Yeah, I've got the idea... You make much money at that sort of thing?" *(Laughter)*.

Anyway, there are many ways of defining success. There's the artistic way, and then there's the business way. In music or any of the arts, success is almost a dirty word. Artists say, "He doesn't really write, he's not really good, but he's known to the public." But I would say I'm successful. I make my living at it and was awarded a Pulitzer Prize. But there's only one basis in which this success is important to me; and that is, that I can write the best piece of music possible at the moment. The next piece must be the best piece I can write. And, it must be in a lineage of pieces that are always getting better and always changing.

One of the characteristics about my works that my publisher mentioned is that each one is different. He said, "I see the thread of your personality through all of them." And I like that.

**RBD**: That helps me to get a sense for your macro level goals and evidence for composing. Can you tell me what it is like when you are actually in the process of composing?

**Michael**: Some are like long hard extended work moments *(eyes shift from down right to down left)*. Others are moments where things go very fast *(looks up and right and snaps fingers)*. When you're writing well *(leans back and looks up and right)*, it goes by itself.

My idea has always been that if I have a pencil in my hand, I can do whatever I want *(leans forward and gestures as if holding a pencil)*. If I want to write a b flat, I say, "b flat," and I write b flat. I mean, the pencil has no choice. But that's not composing, for me.

Once you set up your idea of the material *(leans back and raises both hands)*, you kind of sit back. You look at it *(eyes up and right)*. You think about it *(eyes down right)*, and you feel it. And then, if you're sensitive to it, it starts to tell you what it wants to do. It's like it starts to move in a certain direction. If you're sensitive *(leans forward and gestures as if holding a pen)*, you'll—I'm not calling it automatic writing at all—but you'll just kind of say, "um humh," and then you'll just start writing it down.

**RBD**: It certainly seems like you use all of your senses during the composing process. But I would like to get a little better idea of how the different pieces relate to one another. What is it like to be stuck? How do you know if you are stuck? And how do you respond to it? How do you break out of it?

**Michael**: Let's say you're stuck. It's a terrible thing to have happen, not because you're not going to get unstuck *(looks down right)*—I will get unstuck, there's no question about that—but *(eyes down left)* when I'm stuck *(eyes up left)*, I feel that I've either done something wrong or I'm about to do something wrong.

So I look back *(eyes up left to level left)* at what I've done and I sing it through repeatedly. I will sing phrases over and over *(looks level left)* and over again. This is why I can't compose

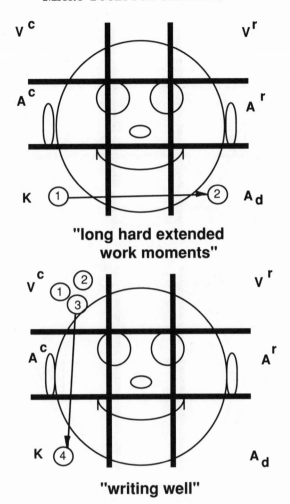

"long hard extended
work moments"

"writing well"

**Figure 2.6. Contrast of Eye Movement Patterns for
Difficult Versus Effective Composition.**

while anybody in the house is sleeping, because I can get
pretty noisy *(leans farther forward and looks up left and
right).*

I have to use my feet. I have to use my hands. I've got to feel
the music *(moves body and hands up and down).* I've got to be
inside the music literally. I might have to go, *(eyes up left and
raises right hand)* "Da da da ta ka ka ka kuk;" That's not right

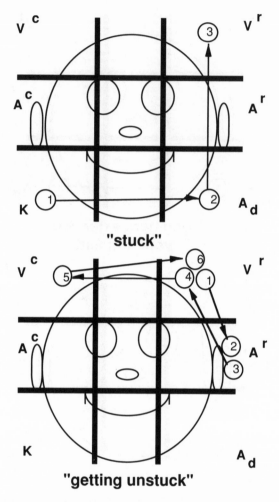

**Figure 2.7. Comparison of Eye Movement Patterns for "Stuck" Versus Getting "Unstuck".**

yet *(eyes remain up left, pause in breathing)* "Da da da ta ka ka ka ka ka kuk;" Needs a slight change, *(moves head up, shakes head rhythmically and increases tempo)*, "Da da da ki ka ka ka ka kyak;" *(leans back, eyes up left, raises left hand, pause in breathing and then leans forward)* "Da da da ki ka ka ki kyak;" *(leans farther forward and moves backwards as he sings)* "Di di ta ka ki ka ka ka ka ki kyak." *(leans back and holds up index finger of both hands)* I like it.

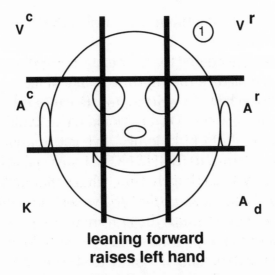

**leaning forward
raises left hand**

**Figure 2.8. Posture, Eye Movement and Gestures
For Ongoing Process of Composition.**

**RBD**: What let's you know that that's the one you like?

**Michael**: I don't know, but the momentum of it satisfies me.

**RBD**: The momentum of it satisfies you. So you have a certain feeling that this thing's got to have and it isn't until you find the auditory tones that carry that feeling along with their progression that you'd go, "That one makes a match with my desired state. That sound gives me a feeling that matches the feeling that I want to have."

**Michael**: Yeah, right.

**RBD**: You indicated earlier that you begin with a feeling. Does the feeling stay with you the whole time you're working on a piece?

**Michael:** Unless I stop for some technical kind of stuff; what I call 'idiot work' *(hand gesture down and left)*. Like when I have to write out something. But most of the time my senses are working together.

When I was just doing that, for example *(eyes up and left)*, I have to also picture the rhythm. It has to feel right, but I have to also see how it's written, too. Because if I'm going to make a choice between "Da da ta ka ki ka ka kyuk" and "Boh boh boh da da da ki ki ki kyuk," I've got to know how it's written *(leans forward)* RIGHT NOW. I can't spend two hours figuring out, "What's that rhythm, what's that meter, what's the tempo we're in?" *(eyes up far left)* I've got to know it's *(moves body side to side and snaps fingers)* snap...snap...snap *(leans back)*. That's the tempo it has and I've got to know where it starts, what instruments it's going to start in, and I have to know what the rhythm is immediately *(repeats phrase silently to self and moves hands)*. That's what the conductor would be doing to represent that.

So, my conscious mind *(eyes up left and touches index finger to temple)* has got to be involved in this. It's got to be saying, "4/16, 1/16th rest and four notes of a quintuplet with the first fifth missing." And then "ta ta da da da;" I might have to run it several times to see what it is, but it's a sextuplet finishing on a 1/16 which *(leans forward)* will complete the third beat, and a *(leans far forward and snaps finger)* ... snap... silence on the fourth beat. If I don't know that technically then I'm going to be going nuts because I sang something that I like and I don't know how to write it down-see. So, I've got to know how to write it down, and I've got to have the musical linguistic *(eyes down left)* exactly for it.

**RBD**: So if you know how to write it down, then it can be preserved. If you have feelings and they produce certain sequences of sound, then if you don't have some way of representing them permanently they could be lost when your feelings change.

**Michael**: *(Eyes level left and points to the left)* But I'll always remember what I just sang. Years later, I'll be able to remember *(eyes level left)* what I just sang here in front of you.

**RBD**: How do you do that?

**Michael**: Well, that's a new one. How would I do this? *(Eyes up left)* I picture it, I guess. *(Laughs)* My eyeballs are screaming at me. I'm conscious of watching my own eyeballs.

**RBD**:Your eyeballs are screaming, there's a lot of sensory overlap in your descriptions. Words being represented as pictures, sounds as feelings, feelings as sounds. They're all very much overlapped with one another.

**Michael**: *(Leans back, eyes up left, raises both hands)* When I'm like this, in an important moment, writing it down, I'm feeling it *(eyes remain up left, gestures down right),* I'm hearing it *(cocks head to right),* and I'm seeing the mathematical subdivisions of the rhythms that have to be written down. And I want to get that, see *(leans forward and takes pen from pocket).*

Say my son comes in, and he wants me to go and pitch for the boys playing baseball, because it's five o'clock. And I'll say, "Not now, Neil. Not now!" He might go, "Come on, Mike. I'm going to bang my hands down on the keyboard, I'm going to bang both hands now. You get till the count of five." And I just... *(eyes up left and body poised forward holding pen as if to write).* So he'll go over here and write a note. It'll say, "Are you going to come in two minutes, in one minute, or are you going to kill yourself?" One time he did this, and I saw the note and I marked, "kill myself," and I handed him the note back. And I went on like this because it was very clear to me and I was going to write it down now.

I wouldn't care if there were an earthquake. In this hypo-thetical moment—but it's not hypothetical it's a real hypo-thetical moment—I would tell the earthquake or whoever *(eyes remain up left, body poised forward holding pen)*, "In a minute." Because this is like an encapsulation of everything that's important to me as a person to do. And not doing this, or abrogating this, or leaving it hanging like that forever and forgetting it would be a self-abdication *(looks down right and gestures down with both hands)*.

**RBD**: Is it the feeling that keeps the continuity of the piece and adds your personality to it?

**Michael**: Yes, but also there is something else that comes through. The way you start something will have an effect on the way you finish it. There's something suggested by the beginning *(eyes level left)*. If it's a stormy opening it might be a stormy close. Or stormy openings might seem to call for quiet closes or vice versa. Those things generally seem to suggest themselves to you *(eyes level left)*.

**RBD**: So, do you lay out for yourself the way that you want the piece to progress right from the start?

**Michael**: *(Leans back, touches hands together, eyes up left for a long time)* I've got to be satisfied that something has hap-pened and it's completed itself. If that's happened, I can finish quietly. Maybe something has partially happened *(separates hands and lifts index finger of left hand)* but not completely yet and it's going to be part of the finish. It's going to have to finish bigger *(moves both hands to the right)* and bigger and bigger to satisfy me. That's one way of thinking about it.

Another thing that I often do is *(lifts and separates hands, eyes straight down)* to write music in chunks. I used to make the mistake of saying *(claps hands, leans forward)*, "Well, I'm in bar 126, what's bar 127 going to be?" It's natural, but I've learned since, "Don't write that way." If you wake up and you're thinking of something that seems to be irrelevant *(gestures left)* to bar 126, just go and write it! *(Leans forward, gestures right, eyes down left)* So I'll write, and I'll just forget what I have so far. And later I'll discover this *(gestures down right)* might just fit right there *(gestures up left)*. Maybe it had not seemed logical at all, but this is really what bar 127 would be *(eyes level left)* if it continued on. Or, I might say, "Right, *(gesture up left to right)* push this forward, this goes in right at the beginning *(gesture down right to up left)* and now it's coming clear, and this goes here *(eyes down, gestures from down to up as eyes move up)*."

Now you start constructing *(eyes up left and right)* to a certain extent and building. You can actually sit back *(leans back and raises both hands)* and start to see blocks coming together. Sometimes people say, "How do you write pieces?" And I'll say *(still leaning back with eyes up left)*, "You build them." You do write with a pencil *(gesture with hand)*, that's the mark you make. But you do build, you construct. And as these pieces start to go in, then they suggest other pieces.

And a certain detachment begins to take place too *(leans farther back, eyes farther up left)*. Because as you detach yourself, you are getting a Gestalt view of what's going on here, see. Because this piece is going to last twenty minutes but you've got to be able to see it, *(eyes up left to right)* "Swooch," as finished. You've got to be able to see from here to here *(points up left to right, eyes move up left to right)*. You can't sing through twenty minutes *(points up left to right)* every time you want to check something here at the seventeenth minute *(points towards right side)*. So you've got to be able to go *(eyes move left to right)*, "Zzzuh," like that and take in the emotional runnings *(eyes closed and head down)*, things, feelings and events *(eyes up left)*. Events and feelings that have to take place fast. So that you can get to this point and not have to waste a lot of time.

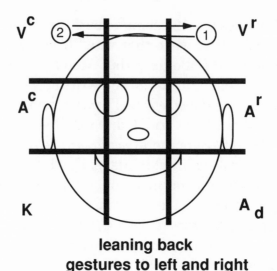

**leaning back**
**gestures to left and right**

**Figure 2.9. Posture, Eye Movement and Gestures**
**For "Constructing" Whole Composition.**

**RBD**: You store the piece visually so you can see it all at once. If you stored it kinesthetically or auditorily you'd have to go through it sequentially. But if it's processed visual to kinesthetic you can rapidly go through the whole complex of feelings. Do you automatically see the notes for each sound?

**Michael**: Well, actually these are amorphous images that I am speaking of now, not the eighth notes or sixteenth notes or b-flats. *(Looks up left to right and gestures with hand up left to right)* It's kind of like a painting, but not exactly. It's an abstract image.

**RBD**: So this kind of abstract visualization comes more at the beginning and during the composing process, whereas seeing the specific notes comes more towards the end.

What I'd like to do now is to see if we can organize this information into a simple and explicit set of steps. For example, one of the ways I'd know if I had a well-designed strategy is to answer the question, "If I had a second grader here and I wanted him to do what you do, could I tell him exactly what to do in a way he could follow it and be successful at it?" What would I tell him to do first? Would I tell him to start by getting into a feeling?

**Michael**: I have worked with children as well as adults, teaching them to write music. And we usually write a piece of music in 35 to 40 minutes.

**RBD**: Perfect. What do you have them do?

**Michael**: I may start warming them up by telling them to move around, change their posture and position and start making any old sounds. (I myself will often stand on my head when I'm preparing to compose.) And the room becomes cacophonous with noise from people howling and screeching and grunting, and clicking their mouths. And I ask them to think of a mark they could put on the blackboard that would represent that sound.

They don't know how to write pitches and all that. If you were going to teach them that it would take months. So you don't do that, you just say, "Make a mark that represents a sound." Anybody can make a mark on a blackboard. So when somebody has a sound in their mind I instruct them to hear the sound, and go to the blackboard. Then I tell them to think of the left side of the blackboard as the beginning and the right side of the blackboard as the end; the top of the blackboard as high and the bottom of the blackboard as low. And make a mark that represents your sound.

So the person goes up to the blackboard and makes a mark. Of course, you could talk about that mark for a long time. You could say, "Well, exactly how high or low is it?" But you'd go nuts because there is no way of measuring it. So I say, "Well, we'll let that go for a moment and approach it differently."

If the person has made a mark that looks like a little curly-cue, I'll ask, "Can you sing that?" And he might go, "Buuwhuit,"because the mark kind of went like that.

Then I'll say, "Will somebody else come up here and make a mark?" You could also have the same kid working, but it's fun to have different people doing it. It's a good idea to do a collective piece. So I'll ask somebody else to come up and make a mark, but now there's one big difference. I'll point out, "You already have one sound there and the second sound you're going to make has got to be in relation to that sound, but independent of it. It's got to come before it or over it or below it or after it. It may be quite different from it, or extremely similar to it."

So a person says, "Yeah, I've got a sound." And they go up there, and they might make something like, "Whup whup whup whup whup," like little inverted apostrophes or something like that.

So the first person made this "buuwhuitt." The second person made "whup whup whup whup whup" underneath that, or just after it. Now we have two things there. Now the third person comes up and I ask him, "What do you want to hear? What do you think belongs there?" He might say, "Well, right after that I want to hear 'click click click click click click click click.'" By now they are seeing, too. I think this is impor-tant because people often have a lot of trouble hearing. As you have pointed out, we're more visual than auditory in North America. So, when they can see the sound, as it were, then they can hear the sound better. That's why I go to the black-board with it.

And so, the child hears, "Click click click click click click." So I'll ask, "What mark would represent that well on the black-board?" Maybe he makes a big mistake, given what's already there. Maybe he'll draw a bunch of little circles. So I'll ask, "Does everybody understand that to be 'click click click click

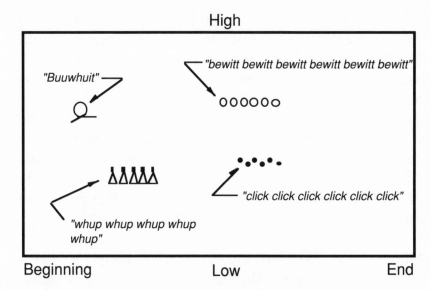

**Figure 2.10. Drawings of Sounds on a Blackboard.**

click click?'" And the rest of the group will say, "No, that's 'bewitt bewitt bewitt bewitt bewitt bewitt.'" It's great, the sounds you'll get. And so I'll say, "What will make 'click click click click click click?'" And somebody will say, "Well, the sounds all have to be all like little dots." And I'll go, "O.K., did you hear what your colleague said? Go make dots instead of circles."

In this process, incidentally, I like them to do it. I don't ever go to the blackboard and make the marks for them. I don't tell them what to do. Instead I'll ask the group, "Are you satisfied with what he's done?" Because in this way the whole group's learning at the same time.

**RBD**: It makes sense that a notational system has to be one that's developed by all the people, otherwise they're not going to have a reference experience for what all the marks stand for. In fact I would think that's what language or written music is all about.

I know that when I was a kid learning about music you studied pre-existing music theory. Instead of beginning with feelings and sounds, you started by looking at the notes and went from the notes to trying to figures out what the sounds were. It was a preset perceptual frame. We never could have gone, "Click click click click click." That wasn't within the scope of the visual representations that you could make. By starting with the auditory, you are creating a completely different purpose for learning notation. It seems like it would be a lot less tedious because one would be developing a way to represent something that he himself has created.

**Michael**: To help them complete the piece, I might act like a little bit of a rudder. I'll ask, "Does anybody want any more on the piece? Is it finished?" When they're finished, I might have them discuss what they hear and see what lets them know that.

Then I ask them, "Now, how are we going to perform this?" This is very important because they have created a work now, but it hasn't come to life yet. And to understand the whole process, they've got to perform it. Now, if I tell them how to perform it, then they will not have divined for themselves how a performance can take place. They will not have fully understood what the composing process is. So I say, "Anybody got any ideas? Come on, we're gonna all make these noises together now."

So someone might say, "I've got an idea," and they go up to the board and they'll try it their way. One person might say, "All of you on the left side of the room do the first song, and all of you on the right side of the room do the second song." Somebody else might say, "I'm going to run my finger across the board. Wherever my finger touches, everybody just sing what you see." One kid, one time, said, "Everybody do anything they want, whenever they want to. Look at the sounds that are there and finish when you are finished." I thought that was a wonderful one. The piece sounded terrific when they did that. It had all kinds of parameters that the written one didn't have.

This is one way of teaching conducting. Another way is saying, "You do this and you do that." You basically teach it. You elicit the performance by leading them in a certain direction.

So now what they've done then is: They've heard sounds, put those sounds together in a composition by creating their own notation for it, conducted it, and performed it. In that one period of forty or fifty minutes, the past thousand years of music history has been re-created for them.

I like to point out to them, "Now, what you have done here is exactly what a composer does, no different. Except, you have not specified exactly how high or how low the sounds are. How long, how short, how dark, how thin, how loud, how soft. A composer has notations for those and those notations can be easily learned." I might take the mark for the "buuwhuit" mark and write some quick musical notes, and put the beams on the tie and add a little crescendo mark or something and it looks like 'real' music then. And they see how that abstract mark can be transferred into the notation which is usually a foreign language to them. I'll go through the whole piece that way, kind of like just quickly. Then they see a whole score right in front of them, and they understand the essence of the score.

People say, "How do you compose music, what do you think of first, aren't you a genius to do that?" and all that sort of thing. And I like to point out to them that the process we've gone through is exactly the process a composer goes through.

As a composer you've got to think of how to start, what to do next, and how to finish. That's what really is involved. If you can do that, you can compose. Someone might say, "Well, I don't know anything about music." That doesn't make any difference. If you can do the process I was just describing with blocks of sound, you can compose. The learning of the musical linguistics, as it were, is just a question of time and sophistication. And it does take time and all that.

But I've seen professional composers try and do this exercise and they don't do it very well. I've seen some non-composers that have never written a line of music go up to the blackboard and they'll be fearfully imaginative. And I'll say to them, "I sure wish you would learn notation and start studying some of this, and sit in orchestras and play an instrument and so forth because you sound like a composer to me."

# Exercises for the "Mind's Eyes"

**RBD**: Since creativity involves thinking in new and different ways, another approach to developing creative ability is to find habitual ways of thinking and then change or add to them. One obvious way to find and break habitual ways of thinking using NLP is through eye movement patterns. Since our eyes reflect patterns of our internal processes they may be used as a tool for both diagnosing and changing habitual thought patterns.

We mentioned earlier that people tend to have most highly developed, highly valued and most conscious representational systems. These proclivities are often reflected in eye movements and patterns.

## Exercise: Exploring Representational Systems Through Eye Position

As an exercise, try the following experiment. Keeping your head oriented straight in front of you, put your eyes into each of the basic eye positions indicated on the eye movement chart. Hold each eye position for 30 seconds. Have a partner keep track of the time for you so you are not distracted.

# 3

---

# The Dreamer

## Tools and Strategies for Generating and Selecting Ideas

**RBD**: As you can see from the interview with Michael, once you have identified the elements of an effective creative process you can begin to develop those skills in other people.

We would like to have you do a couple of exercises that will give you some "brains-on" experience with some of the operational aspects of creativity that we've been discussing —particularly in relationship to the dreamer. We want to get you involved in exercising your own brain. At the most fundamental level creativity comes from "thinking about something differently." Whether you're trying to put value to it, get around it, get rid of it, whatever you're trying to do with it, creativity involves thinking of it differently.

As we said earlier, the simplest creative operation is in the form of a noise generator inductor. That is, you generate random things and filter them. The creative product or out-come is whatever comes out the other side of the filter. If you change the filter you're going to output different things.

In this next exercise we'd like to give you control of some mental 'knobs' that you can use to change your perceptual filters. You could even get into groups and turn each other's 'knobs' up and down and backwards and forwards. The basic idea is to just sort of 'randomly' think of things differently and discover what happens. Change the perceptual filters you use to make sense out of things.

**TE**: Find out how you would habitually approach something and then change it—just for the heck of it. For example, close your eyes for a minute, and think back to this morning as you prepared for the day. What do you do habitually? Maybe it's the way you brush your teeth. Maybe it's which hand you wash with or which side of your face you wash first. Do you put your socks or your pants on first? Do you usually put on your left sock first or your right sock?

What would happen if you went back and just randomly thought about doing it in some other sequence?

**RBD**: When you open a door, do you do it with your left hand or your right hand?

**TE**: What would happen if you randomly in your own mind right now started doing things differently than you normally do them? What do you have to do in your own mind to get things to be different?

**RBD**: What if you walked backward down the escalator?

**TE**: What if when you turned on the light in your room it became darker rather than lighter? What if when you turned on the coffeepot in the morning it cooled down rather than heated up?

**RBD**: What if, this morning, every thought that came into your mind was a surprise to you?

**TE**: What would happen if you were fascinated with the fact that as you put a pen down on a paper it left a mark? When was the last time you were fascinated by the fact that a pen leaves marks on paper?

**RBD**: How long has it been since you doodled?

**TE**: How long has it been since you acted as if you were seven? When was the last time you got to act like a child without somebody scolding you for it?

**RBD**: This is the kind of attitude we'd like to have you take into this exercise.

In addition to mentally thinking of things differently, we'd like to have you play with your physiology in some new ways to enhance the process.

Michael Colgrass, talked about how he prepares to write music standing on his head. He stands on his head in order to shift the way he would think about things.

There is another guy I know who is a real estate investor. And one of the things he would do when he needed to be particularly creative was to do everything he normally did right-handed with his left hand—he was right-handed. If he was really trying to solve a problem, he would try to do this for about a week, in order to stimulate the other side of his brain.

There are ways you can use your physiology to help you access different states of awareness that most of us just don't utilize. Think about it for a moment. How many of you, if you get stuck with something, would roll around on the floor? I mean, if you crawled around for a bit, it might change the ways that you think about something. Imagine yourself trying to think about a domestic problem in the same old way if you found a nice grassy knoll, jumped on it and rolled all the way down to the bottom of the hill. When you got to the bottom of the hill, would you still be thinking about it in the same way?

**TE**: There's someone I heard about recently who would lay down if he got into a stressful situation. He would just lay down. He'd be at work talking to somebody in the office, and if things got stressful he'd go down right out there in the middle of the floor. He'd lay down, and continue talking to them. He'd do it in the hallway too. I don't recommend it for everybody, but think about how that change things a little bit.

If you can't solve a problem by "thinking on your feet" then try laying down. Think of a problem you're working on right now and imagine for a minute that you're standing up walking around. Now, what happens if when you're thinking about solving that problem you imagine yourself laying down? Does it change your response to it?

**RBD**: I don't think I can take it standing up.

**TE**: Just knocked you off your feet, huh?

**RBD**: The point is, changing physiology will help to change thinking-which is the essence of creativity.

**TE**: The worst that will happen is that you will become stuck in a new and different way.

**RBD**: Eventually even new approaches become "old hat." So, what you want to do is put on your thinking cap instead of your old hat, and do something different.

This brings us to a couple of other operations you might use to help stimulate creativity that we've discussed—the use of metaphor and anchoring. Some people may actually put on a "thinking cap" as an anchor for creative thinking. Some people have a special location or chair, that they go to when they really need to think about something creatively.

Another important aspect to thinking differently is being able to wipe the old slate clear. A lot of times you get started doing something a certain way and you build up a kind of inertia in it. Because you've invested so much time in that first approach, you keep trying to figure out how to modify what you've already got rather than just crumple it up, throw it away, and start from scratch so you can look at it through completely new eyes.

**TE**: Of course, for some, it's "wiping the slate clean," for others it might be "stopping the chatter." For certain people, it's a different way of thinking if they look at the pictures and stop listening to the voices. Turn the volume off and just look at the pictures. For other people it works the other way. They want to blank the screen out and just listen to the words for a while. For example, try repeating a mantra without having an internal voice—I dare you.

**RBD**: Or try to talk over it.

The bottom line is, in these exercises be a dreamer. Let the dreamer in you run wild and give him or her the tools of physiology, anchoring, metaphor and representational systems. Start by noticing how you habitually start thinking about something and then begin to change it. Whatever you are doing, do something different—do **anything** different.

## Exercise: Changing Perceptual Filters

Let's say you were given a pencil, a piece of paper and a stone and told to make something out of it. How would you start? Do you make a visual image in your mind's eye? Do start talking to yourself in your head or ask yourself questions? Do you try to get a feeling for what would be interesting?

If you made an image in your mind's eye, was it in color? Was it moving? Did you see yourself in the image (as if you were watching yourself on television), or were you imagining how something would look from a "first person" point of view? Did you see everything at its normal size and its normal speed or did you distort time in any way? The answers to these questions can determine a lot about how you are creative and how easily you may succeed, or not, in different types of situations.

Would you use the pencil and paper to draw or write out your ideas or would you try to incorporate them into your result? Depending on how big you visualized the stone, you might have begun to design a sculpture; or you may have imagined breaking the stone into chunks and building a house, pyramid or chimney. You may have thought about using the stone for self-defense or as a way to send a message through someone's window. One person thought up the idea of pretending that the rock was a pet, wrote instructions for its care on the paper and made a lot of money.

Now, pick a situation from your own life that you would like to be creative with; whether it is with your children, writing music, solving a business problem, being nice to the bank teller, etc. How do you think of that situation in your mind? Are you seeing yourself in the picture? Do you have more feelings associated with this situation than with the rock? Do you hear any sounds?

Try changing some things around and find out if it affects your experience. If you have a picture that is in color, make it black and white. Imagine people singing instead of saying their words. If you have a feeling in your stomach or chest, move it into your fingers. If you have an image that is static like a snapshot, make it move; if it is moving, try running it backwards or running it faster. What happens?

This exercise is the kind of "thought experiment" that lead Albert Einstein to revolutionize the field of physics. Remember, it was Einstein's ability to direct his mind's eye to visualize the world in a different way, not his mathematical ability, that inspired his creative genius.

Being able to be aware of and direct your internal thoughts is an important skill for everybody. Not only in terms of problem solving but in terms of innovation and generativity.

## Exercise: Turning Something Valueless into Something Valuable

Let's do a second exercise. Take a moment and find something that is the most useless thing that you can think of. Identify an object that you think has absolutely no value to it at all. Be creative about finding it.

Now try to give that useless object some kind of value by changing your perception of it—by thinking of it in a different way.

Let's say you have a popsicle stick—your valueless thing is a used popsicle stick. How could you turn it into something of value by thinking of it differently?

One specific strategy to use is to change the qualities of what you see, hear and feel.

For example, if I say, "popsicle stick," how do you first think of it? Do you visualize it in your mind? If you have a picture of something, like a popsicle stick, what would you have to change about it so that you would perceive it as something different—so it wouldn't just be a "used popsicle stick" anymore? Size would be one of the qualities, shape, texture. What would you need to change about an object so it would become something else? Alter the brightness, shape, depth, focus, quantity or perspective.

**TE**: What would happen if you painted it a different color?

**RBD**: When I was a kid we used to change the shape of the popsicle stick by scraping the sides on the pavement and making a point on the end of it.

**TE**: Put an edge on it. Soak it in water and bend it into a new shape.

**RBD**: Get the competitive edge. Whenever you felt licked you could take your popsicle stick out as a creative link.

**TE**: Defend yourself in the parking lot.

**RBD**: How big is the popsicle stick in your mind? Imagine you could put a knob to it: As you turn it, the popsicle stick becomes bigger. Then you could have a popsicle stick that was ten times normal size. You could make a surfboard out of it.

You could make it smaller, like a toothpick. Then you could take a whole bunch of them with you, or a half of one. Chunk it differently. Make it bigger, smaller, more, less.

**TE**: You could take a whole bunch of them and glue them together and make those phony wood logs. Get enough of them and you could make screens for your windows.

**RBD**: Now we're bringing in something else, which is what we've called chunking. You could chunk the popsicle stick smaller or larger. If you chunked it up, a popsicle stick is just another example of a handle. What could you think of doing with handles? Would a popsicle stick be a better handle for something than something else?

Instead of changing the object itself, try changing the background in which you are visualizing it.

**TE**: Changing the environment or the context in which it exists.

**RBD**: Seeing a popsicle stick in a food store or a toy store. Taking it into a government building.

**TE**: How could you send a popsicle stick with your tax forms and have it be interesting? You might write a little note on it, and tell them what they could do with it. Right? (Laughter.)

**RBD**: Another way to think of it differently would be to put a different representational systems to it. If you gave that popsicle stick a voice, what would it say to you?

**TE**: Get gestalt with it: Who is that popsicle stick?

**RBD**: You never know what that popsicle stick might have heard.

What if you sent secret messages with it? That might give it value. You could put a joke on it. What if after you got done with that popsicle stick, there was a joke printed on it, like with a fortune cookie—a fortune stick?

**TE**: It goes, "You've been stuck."

**RBD**: One important distinction in sound, that is associated with the two different hemispheres of your brain, is whether you represent something as words or tones. There's a difference between saying, "yesss," and "YES!" or "Nooo?" and "NO!" In other words, the word stays the same in both cases but the sound changes around it. Some people respond primarily to the words and others just to the intonation.

What tone of voice would your popsicle stick have, if it had a voice? A lot of comedy is based on giving inanimate objects voices.

As you consider how you might associate sounds with that popsicle stick, shift the non-verbal qualities as well, like volume, pitch, tempo, rhythm, location and timbre.

**TE**: For those of you not yet familiar with these auditory distinctions, timbre is kind of the auditory equivalent of shape. It is the quality that makes a particular instrument sound different from the others. If you play a middle C on a violin and a flute they sound different. If you take a synthesizer and play A = 440, it would sound completely different from a guitar or a piano or some other instrument.

**RBD**: If you were going to use words and describe the popsicle stick, what kind of language would you use?

**TE**: Our culture tends to emphasize the overlap between pictures and words. As youngsters we are taught to describe things with visual language. We have lots of words to describe the way things are visually. We are used to describing what we see in terms of shapes, colors, brightness, etc., but we're not taught to describe a sound in terms of its frequency, its duration, it sustained quality, its amplitude. We aren't taught to describe things auditorily with the same precision as we do visually. Instead, we sort of imitate the sound with our mouth. We go, "It went 'bruuuuuuph,'" instead of going, "It was an increasing pitch with a brief duration, and volume dropped significantly towards the end."

**RBD**: In general people tend to interpret more than observe. In NLP training programs, we spend a lot of time teaching people the difference between seeing and hearing and feeling, and interpreting. There is a difference between saying, "That person's voice had a high pitch, and it tended to come sporadically," and saying, "That person's voice was angry."

There's a difference in saying, "The dress was red, with checks on it," and saying, "It was pretty." Pretty is a judgment as opposed to a description. People tend when they hear sounds to interpret them, to make a judgment about them. These judgments can limit our experience of something.

Like sounds and images, people tend to interpret or judge feelings. There are "good" feelings and "bad" feelings.

**TE**: The electrical theory of human behavior—you have positive and negative feelings, and you get all charged up.

**RBD**: We don't necessarily subscribe to that model in NLP. We don't believe that if you have a "bad" feeling the best way to get rid of it is to blow it out, or that if you don't get rid of it, it's going to stay there.

Freud believed that creativity was the sublimation or "discharge" of stored up sexual feelings through the brain instead of the genitals. He believed you had to trade off sexual frustration for creativity. If you had a good sex life, tough luck, you couldn't be creative.

In NLP we don't perceive your guts as big libido-storing capacitors that have to be periodically discharged. We believe that feelings are a response to some ongoing state of your mind-body system—they are a *communication* to you about something that's going on in your system. The key is not in the content of the feeling but in how you respond to it—and that depends on how you perceive it.

**RWD**: Many people believe fear is bad, but many actors say, "It's that fear right before, the butterflies in my stomach, before I go on stage that gets my adrenalin going and then I know I'm really going to give a good performance. If I don't have the butterflies, if I don't have the fear, then nine times out of ten, my performance isn't as good."

**RBD**: Likewise, most people think of frustration as a bad thing and a limitation to creativity. But for some people, when they're frustrated, it's the only time they can be creative. And if they weren't frustrated, they'd never be creative.

When I was in high school, I couldn't write papers until it was the night before, when I was going, "Oh no! Now what am I going to do? I'll never get this done in time!" Then I would get creative. But if I sat down three weeks before, with all the time in the world, I'd be blank.

There's that old saying that "when the going gets tough, the tough get going"—but only when the going's tough. That's probably why there are so many heart problems at the executive level. They are people who are in that position because they operate well under stress. They are creative under stress. And so, in order to keep them busy, you have to keep them under stress. I have a postcard in my office that says, "Don't tell me to relax. My tension's the only thing that's holding me together." One person's pain is another person's pleasure.

What do you do when you are successful and there are no more problems, no more stress?

**TE**: Get creative! Attach the process of innovation to something other than stress. Maybe starts with fun or curiosity.

**RBD**: Change your perceptual filters. Changing your perceptual filters and evidence procedures in relationship to feelings can really help to generate new choices. In fact, I think that is the key to what Freud was calling "sublimation"—redirecting the flow of activity in your mind-body system by adjusting your perceptual filters.

I remember talking to a person who had lost about twenty pounds by changing his response to a certain feeling. He tended to overeat to avoid feeling "hungry." He took the feeling of being "hungry"—being "hollow," "empty"—which is a bad thing that you want to go away from, and shifted his perception of it. He had done some weight training, and in weight lifting there's a term called "burning." Burning is desirable. When you are "burning" you are using calories to build muscle mass. He realized that "hungry" and "burning" were similar feelings and that if he shifted his awareness of certain feeling qualities he could change "hungry" into "burning" which was something that he wanted. So all of a sudden it wasn't a bad feeling any more to not be stuffed. So, instead of laying in bed at night going, "Oh God, I'm hungry, I'm torturing myself," that feeling then indicated, "Oh boy, I'm burning, keep it coming."

The way we feel about something is probably one of the most common ways we determine its meaning and value. The point we've making is that any particular feeling is neither inherently good nor bad. You change the way you feel about something by shifting how you perceive it. Rather than interpret and judge feelings, creativity comes by changing some quality in them.

The qualities of feeling include intensity, location, position, texture, temperature, shape, pressure.

For example, if we return to our popsicle stick, how could we give it value through changing some quality of feeling? How could you get that popsicle stick to give you a different quality of feeling

If you were trying to lose weight and you liked ice cream, you'd have this magic wand that would have the flavor in the popsicle stick. So, if you wanted to feel like you'd just treated yourself and ate something, you'd lick the popsicle stick and...

**TE**: Lick-a-stick. You'd use it to put honey in your tea. Add in some taste.

You could use it to butter your toast. You could use it to paint with. Play doctor—Freud would go for that one.

**RBD**: This is what we call chunking laterally. Chunking laterally would be like shifting from a popsicle stick to an ice cream stick or a swizzle stick: They're not bigger or smaller. They're on the same level. You could take this and start to generate other possibilities with it. You could make a cake stick, where you put a piece of cake on it instead of ice cream. Why not? A cookie stick.

**TE**: A fish stick.

**RBD**: Which is another thing: You don't have to keep it wood.

**RWD**: Plastic, dry ice.

**TE**: Ice sticks.

**RWD**: I saw a man hammer a nail in a board with mercury once. He took a popsicle stick and stuck it in mercury, then put the mercury in liquid nitrogen. He froze it and pounded nails with it.

**RBD**: So you could take the temperature of the popsicle stick and make it hotter or colder.

How else could you give a popsicle stick value? Could you understand something about physics from it? Could you do something with mathematics? With art? Like taking a plate and spinning it on the popsicle stick?

**RWD**: Remember Michael Colgrass: You've got the color and the thickness of the sound. You know, a piccolo makes a little skinny squeaky sound that's very silver. The bassoon makes a great big wide noise that's orange and green. What sound does a cold popsicle stick make? What color is it?

**RBD**: Another whole strategy is to use synesthesias between the senses-to connect the qualities of the senses together.

How does a sound look? How does it feel? There's the overlap between representational systems. If you take the intensity of a feeling, what would its analog be visually? Would it be brightness, would it be size? Would its auditory analog be volume? Pitch?

If I change the brightness do I change the feeling? If you make too sharp an image you might get hurt. (laughter) You got the point.

A third strategy for changing the way you think about something is through analogy and metaphor. In fact, one of the most powerful forms of creativity is that of metaphor.

The broken stem of a flower may seem pretty useless. If you look at that stem, it might in itself be nothing, but if you said, "This stem is like my life," it will start shifting your perception of it.

If it stays grounded it'll grow on its own.

Analogy is a very powerful form of creative thinking.

How is an empty matchbook like something else? Is it like somebody that you know? A business you know?

The fire has gone out, but it flares up every once in a while. That's a striking analogy.

If you're a minister, metaphor can be one of THE most powerful parts of your presentation because you can take something like a concept that is not easily understood and say what it means. Parables are one of the most often-used forms of metaphor to communicate things on a spiritual or identity level.

Jesus Christ, Milton Erickson and some of the world's best communicators use metaphor, use analogy as a way of communicating.

## Exercise: Stimulating Group Creativity

**RBD**: Try this exercise with a group of people. Get together with three other people. One person shows his 'valueless' object. Each of the other group members is to be in charge of one of the senses.

*Person #1* is in charge of the visual system. Person #1's job is to help you to shift your visual filters regarding your object. What can they help you change in terms of shape, brightness, depth, size, location, movement, etc. Make it bigger, smaller. Imagine more of them, fewer of them.

*Person #2* is responsible for auditory qualities. Person #2's job is to ask things like, "Does it make a sound?" "Can you put a sound to it?" "Can you make a sound with it?" "If it's not something that has a voice, can you put a voice to it?" "If you talked about it, what would you say?" "If you gave it a voice, what would it say?" Change the sounds, make them higher, lower, faster, slower, louder, softer, etc.

*Person #3* will help to shift feelings. Person #3 might ask things like, "What kind of feeling could it give you?" "How would it feel if you changed the feeling in some way?" Could you shift the location in some way-say, to the tongue or to the hands. What happens if you changed the temperature, the weight, the texture?

Below is a listing of the possible submodality distinctions you could change.

| **Visual** | **Auditory** | **Kinesthetic** |
|---|---|---|
| BRIGHTNESS (dim-bright) | VOLUME (loud-soft) | INTENSITY (strong-weak) |
| SIZE (large-small) | TONE (bass-treble) | AREA (large-small) |
| COLOR (black & white-color) | PITCH (high-low) | TEXTURE (rough-smooth) |
| MOVEMENT (fast-slow-still) | TEMPO (fast-slow) | DURATION (constant-intermittent) |
| DISTANCE (near-far) | DISTANCE (close-far) | TEMPERATURE (hot-cold) |
| FOCUS (clear-fuzzy ) | RHYTHM | WEIGHT (heavy-light) |
| LOCATION | LOCATION | LOCATION |
| ASSOCIATED/DISSOCIATED | | |

Just shift them and find out how your thinking varies. You're not supposed to do anything with it yet. This is just to take it and find out what happens if you vary these things randomly.

One way to enhance the whole process is to find out from the other people in your group what they do to get creative— like the person who stands on his head, the person who lays down, the person who gets into a meditative space. Then you can try out each other's creative physiology. Try the physiology someone else uses to be creative.

If someone does ballet steps in order to get into a creative space, give it a try. It'll definitely get you into a different way of thinking.

**TE**: There is not any particular outcome or goal for the exercise other than discovering something new about thinking creatively. This is the land of the dreamer—creativity for its own sake.

**RBD**: Feel free to talk to each other about whatever comes to mind. Of course, the other members of the group are going to be looking at your object and changing their thinking about it too. A lot of creativity doesn't come from one person but from the synergy between people. You know, "Two heads are better than one." If you put two people together the end result is greater than the sum of their combined capabilities. It's more like a logarithmic function.

When you come up with an idea, feel free to blurt it out. What we're trying to get you to do is experience something in as many different ways as possible. There should be no goal yet. We're going to add these steps later. The three group members' function is to adjust your three sensory knobs: feeling, auditory and visual.

And as you do this keep in mind that the brain of the person next to you...

**TE**: ...could be your own.

## Discussion: Examples of Changing Perceptual Filters

**RBD**: Part of creativity is thinking of things as something else-like Picasso looking at a bicycle and seeing the bicycle seat and handlebars as being the head of a goat. How do you take that broken head of a pin or that flower stem and make it into something useful? Is it possible to use that to stimulate creativity for something more "serious"? I think that a certain amount of random thinking is very useful. "A little nonsense now and then is valued by the wisest men." A lot of creativity comes from thinking of nothing in particular or taking things and just varying them.

As a result of this exercise you'll probably realize that you can come up with an idea a minute, and some of them might be good. The next step is to engage the realist. What's the difference between what you are engaging in here and what's useful and realistic? You might legitimately ask, "This is great fun, but so what?" The "so-what" brings in two other things, criteria, that is, restraints that focus you toward something; and filters, that is, things that screen out certain possibilities. Criteria relate to "what am I going for" and filters relate to "what can I or can't I do." That's going to be our next step.

In fact, people actually do this kind of thinking and put it to use.


**RWD**: For instance, if you drive from San Francisco down Highway 5 toward Los Angeles, you'll see barren mountains off on the right. If you drive back in those mountains, there's a pile of tires in there. There's a mountain of tires in there. And that's not the only place where these piles exist. There are several places in the United States. Usually they are concealed. They are dumps. The tires are piling up. There are mountains of used tires and it's getting worse.

Modern tires have steel fibers and all kinds of reinforcing in them. You can't bury them. When I first saw tires sticking out of the mud in the San Francisco bay I thought that people had thrown them there. That isn't the case. If you bury a tire it'll eventually work its way out of the ground. It'll move. It'll get carried along. They won't stay where you put them.

When the U.S. Army left Vietnam, one of the things they did was pile up all the used tires, and the Viet Cong set fire to them. They burned about three months. The tires were piled something like 600 feet high: a pyramid of rubber tires.

The point is: "What to do with a mountain of old useless tires?"

Well, if you can grind them up, if you can reduce their size, you can turn them into something of value. This mountain of tires in California is worthless. A particular client of mine made a device that will cut the tires into smaller parts.

As soon as they have been cut, they immediately have value and you can insure them. Why? Because the big chunks have value as fuel. You can sell them to a power generating plant: They use them like coal. The small chunks are used in highways. Most of our highways today are made of oil with ground-up rubber in them. If you fall on the street now you bounce. If the chunks are very tiny they turn into carbon filings and those have a high value in a laboratory as a chemical. It's carbon. Very fine grindings of the tire have the highest value.

A mound of tires is like ore, it's like iron ore in the ground. As soon as you dig up this dirt and run it through the processes that take the iron out of it, you have something of value. As soon as you take these tires and cut them up into pieces, even large pieces, you can insure them.

The mountain of tires was built because a man was charging people 50 cents each to dispose of their old tires. In other words if they'd give him their tire and fifty cents he'd cart it away and they didn't have to worry about it. The trouble is, if that mound catches fire, it'll burn for months and there's nothing he can do to stop it. He could lose his whole livelihood. On the other hand, if he grinds it up in pieces, it'll immediately have a sale value and he can get insurance to cover that value.

**RBD**: Once you've changed it, once you've chunked it differently, even before you've sold it, you could borrow against it or insure it. By grinding it up—changing its size—not only did you get your fifty cents, but now you have something you can insure and you can borrow against it. It makes a molehill out of a mountain.

**TE**: I've seen sandals that were made from tires. They were a very popular use of old tires in Vietnam.

**RBD**: There are many ways to give something value. What makes something useless or valuable? Is it the product itself? Is it the process? Is it the result of the process? Where does value come in?

Many times, in order to change one representational aspect you have to change others as well. That is the source of a lot of creativity. Sometimes it's the innovation that you make in order to accomplish another innovation that becomes even more valuable.

**RWD**: A good example of that was one of my clients, Oscar Heil, who developed the Heil speaker. It's a fascinating device. One of the interesting things about it is you can't localize it. If you're going to make a piano sound come out of an amplifier and speaker, one of the problems is that you can localize it, whereas with a real piano the sound comes from all over. The sound of a piano doesn't just emanate from a single source the size of a speaker. In a concert hall, for example, the sound comes from all over. You often can't localize it to a specific place unless you can see the piano. Even if you're in a room with it, you may not be able to tell exactly where the sound is coming from.

The Heil speaker is made so you can't localize the sound. You can hear it, but you can't really point your finger at where its coming from.

An ordinary speaker is a big cone that has a magnetic coil on the bottom which moves the cone back and forth and this pushes the air back and forth and sets up the sound wave that you hear.

The Heil speaker is like an accordion made out of plastic. It 'squeezes' the air rather than pushes it. It's very light and very quick.

With a standard speaker, if you're trying to imitate a piccolo playing a very high note, you have to move that big diaphragm back and forth as fast as that note moves—and you can't do it. With a little very lightweight piece of plastic you can do it at immense speeds.

Furthermore, what you're trying to do with this big speaker is *couple* into the air. And the air doesn't weigh anything. It's like trying to throw a cherry pit. You take a cherry pit and throw it as hard as you can and no matter how hard you try, it'll go a little way and then drop. But if you take the same pit and put it between your fingers and pinch, you can probably squirt it just as far as you can throw it with your whole hand, maybe farther. You have better coupling. So this speaker has very close coupling with the air. It's very lightweight and very quick.

I've heard that with most speakers, no matter how good the system, a good piano player will always recognize it as a recording. You can't fool them. The reason you can't is that they hear the hammer hit, they hear the arms move. They hear all the little squeaks of all the mechanisms that are in the piano that the average speaker can't reproduce—like the impact of the hammer on the string that makes the string vibrate. The Heil speaker is so light and so small, it could pick up things like the fingernail hitting the ivory on the keys.

**TE**: The thing about it that's interesting to me as a musician is that it never became as popular as it could have for people who wanted good sound reproduction. People were so trained in directionalization from their stereos that somehow it didn't sound as good when it was coming from all over. It was a case of perceptional bias and belief. They paid a lot of money to get localization. They wanted to know when they sat in the living room that it was coming from the speakers over there, not that they couldn't locate where the sound was coming from.

**RWD**: Oscar Heil's argument was that most people seem to think their most delicate sense is the sense of sight. He firmly believed that the sense of hearing is a lot more delicate. He gave a number of examples. He said, if I had one of these bathroom windows that's corrugated and clouded, and you could see just a faint image, you could see my face through it but you probably wouldn't recognize who I am. But if I call on the telephone, which produces an extremely distorted version of your voice, you can recognize people's voices even though it's a highly distorted input.

**TE**: You can phone somebody and recognize them even if it's a bad connection. Even though it's crackling, you still know, "It's Mom!" It's a function of a feature detection process that your brain uses to reconstruct the hologram of the whole voice.

**RWD**: Speaking of chunking, the telephone company takes your conversation and they split it up. They cut it up into little bitty short segments and they mix it in with ten other people's voices and they send it across the country and when it gets to the other end, they take all these little bitty pieces that they chopped your conversation up into and put them back together.

**TE**: So, the next time you're talking to somebody on the phone and you're not communicating with them properly, it could because you are getting the wrong part of the conversation. Next time you don't make that big sale, blame it on phone company chunking.

# Exercises for the "Mind's Eyes"

**RBD**: Since creativity involves thinking in new and different ways, another approach to developing creative ability is to find habitual ways of thinking and then change or add to them. One obvious way to find and break habitual ways of thinking using NLP is through eye movement patterns. Since our eyes reflect patterns of our internal processes they may be used as a tool for both diagnosing and changing habitual thought patterns.

We mentioned earlier that people tend to have most highly developed, highly valued and most conscious representational systems. These proclivities are often reflected in eye movements and patterns.

## Exercise: Exploring Representational Systems Through Eye Position

As an exercise, try the following experiment. Keeping your head oriented straight in front of you, put your eyes into each of the basic eye positions indicated on the eye movement chart. Hold each eye position for 30 seconds. Have a partner keep track of the time for you so you are not distracted.

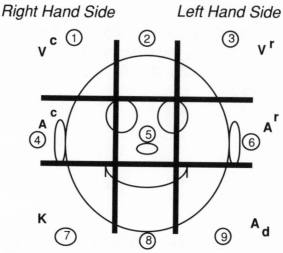

**Figure 3.1. Eye Positions for Exercise**

Notice the differences you experience between each position. Are some of them more comfortable, natural or familiar feeling than some of the others? Does it feel to you as if you are actually holding your eyes for a longer time in some of the positions than others? In some of the positions you might find yourself thinking or making certain types of associations. In others, you may just draw a complete blank. Which eye positions do you associate more with creativity? stuckness? being a dreamer? a realist? a critic?

## Exercise: Exploring the Effects of Eye Position on Problem Solving

As a further experiment, take some problem or idea you are working on and simply hold your eyes in these different positions for a few minutes while you are thinking of it. Notice how it effects your thought process in relation to the problem or idea. Be especially aware of how you are affected by the unfamiliar eye positions. How has the way in which you are thinking about the idea or problem changed as a result of each eye position? Do any of the eye positions bring out certain kinds of feelings, sounds or imagery? Does moving your eyes to any of these locations change any of the qualities of the images, sounds or feelings you already have associated to the problem or idea?

## Exercise: Exploring Patterns of Eye Movement and Synesthesias

Our physiology, and in particular our eye movements, form the underlying circuitry through which our strategies are manifested. Thus, our strategies are only as effective as the neuro-physiological circuitry which supports them. As we have already explored, much creative thinking comes from our ability to link our sensory representational systems together-as in a synesthesia. Patterns of eye movements also reflect which senses we tend to habitually link together and how strong those links are.

As another exercise, try moving your eyes between various combinations of the different eye positions; say, from up left to down right and back again, or from up right to up left and back again (if you use all 9 positions, there are about 45 possible combinations). Some of the most common and significant patterns are shown in Figure 2.12.

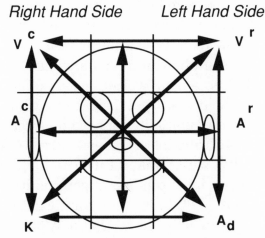

Right Hand Side    Left Hand Side

**Figure 3.2. Some Basic Eye Movement Paths**

Move your eyes back and forth between the two eye positions you have chosen about 6 times. Start by moving your eyes very slowly at first and then speed up the movement. Try to move your eyes between the two positions in a straight smooth line. Then switch to another pair of eye positions and repeat the process again. Keep choosing new pairs until you have covered all of the basic pairs of eye positions.

Find a partner to act as an observer. Have your observer notice exactly how your eyes move between the two positions. You will probably soon realize that movement is seldom perfectly linear. Often the eyes will move in little jerks, pausing briefly in certain places along the path of trajectory. Often the eyes will arc rather than move in a straight line from one location to the other. Sometimes the eyes will move farther in one direction than the other.

Patterns of eye movements are a way of linking various parts of your neurology together by laying down a physiological track or path between the various parts of your brain that you use to represent information about the world around you. The ease or difficulty you have in moving your eyes to these different positions can help you to assess which neurological pathways are most open and smooth. In fact, we sometimes use this particular procedure to make what we call an "eye print" of an individual. Like a finger print, a person's "eye print" is a representation about an individual's unique characteristics—but on a neurological instead of physical level. Eye prints can help you to get insight into which parts of a person's brain are habitually connected or separated, and thus what kinds of thinking processes a person might excel at or have difficulty with. This in turn can help assess what kinds of aptitudes, inner conflicts or personality traits a person might be most likely to experience and express. It can also be used as a way to define areas that may be improved and enhanced.

As in the previous exercise on eye position, take note of which patterns of movement seem most comfortable, familiar and natural. Do some patterns seem more related or conducive to certain types of thinking? Once again notice which patterns of movement seem more connected with creativity? stuckness? being a dreamer? being a realist? being a critic?

## Exercise: Creating and Strengthening New Neurological Pathways

Take the patterns of movement which seemed the most difficult, awkward or uncomfortable and "beat a path" between the to eye positions by moving your eyes back and forth between the positions. Your partner can help you by using his or her finger as a guide for your eyes. Have your partner hold a finger about a foot to a foot and a half in front of you and move the finger back and forth between the two eye positions you want to link together more strongly. Your partner should begin by moving the finger very slowly at first in a smooth, even, linear path. As your eyes accommodate to the movement, ask your partner to increase the speed of the finger motion, tracing the same path. You may do this without a partner by drawing a line on a piece of paper and use it as a guide by holding it in front of you at the proper angle.

To assess the impact of creating these new links, once again take some problem or idea you are working on and notice how using each new circuit effects it. First take note of how you are thinking about the problem or idea. Is it primarily feelings, words, sound, or images? What qualities or submodalities seem to be emphasized in your current representation of the problem or idea? Then, without consciously focusing on the idea or problem, have your partner (or the paper guide line) lead you through the new eye pattern. Notice how it effects your thought process in relation to the problem or idea. How does the way in which you are thinking about the idea or problem change as a result of the new pattern? What changes in terms of the qualities of the images, sounds or feelings you had initially associated to the problem or idea?

## Exercise: Exploring and Creating New Circuits Through Eye Movement Patterns

Clearly, more sophisticated thinking patterns tend to require more sophisticated patterns of eye movements. During the elicitation exercises you probably noticed that a person's eye movement patterns can assume some fairly involved sequences. Some patterns appear to be almost circular; others may be triangular, rectangular or some other type or combination of shapes (some examples are shown in Figure 2.13).

As an experiment, try tracing some of these basic kinds of shapes with your eyes. Make a circle, a square, a triangle or some other shape. Make sure you repeat the pattern a few times to get a sense for how it effects you. How easy or comfortable is it to move your eyes in that pattern?

Now try changing some aspect of the eye movement pattern. If you traced the circle in one direction, reverse it. If the base of the triangle was on the bottom, turn it upside down. What effect does that have on you or your state of consciousness?

As with the previous eye exercises, take some problem or idea you are working on and notice how using a new pattern of circuitry effects it. Once again, note the cognitive structure of how you initially think about the problem or idea. What aspects of imagery, sound and/or feeling seem to be emphasized in your starting representation of the problem or idea? Again, go through the new eye pattern without consciously focusing on the idea or problem, and notice how it effects your thought process in relation to the problem or idea. How does the way in which you are thinking about the idea or problem change as a result of the new pattern? What changes in terms of the qualities of the images, sounds or feelings you had initially associated to the problem or idea?

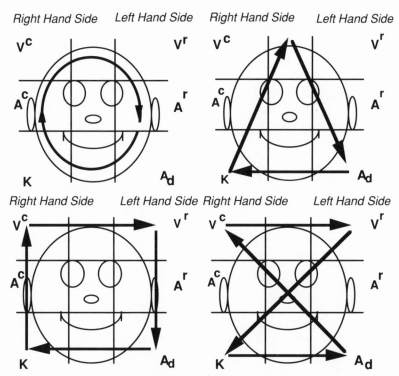

**Figure 3.3. Some Basic Eye Movement Patterns**

In NLP, these types of eye movement combinations are used in a more precise way to develop new thinking strategies. In a later chapter we will demonstrate how they may be used to do this with the New Behavior Generator strategy.

Sometimes habitual synesthesia patterns can cause problems as well, and may need to be interrupted. The process of breaking and reestablishing synesthesia patterns is described in detail in *Changing Belief Systems with NLP* (pp. 25–53).

# 4

---

# The Realist

## Tools and Strategies for Implementation

**RBD**: Once you have generated and selected an idea, the next challenge comes in implementing it. At the dreamer stage of the creative process you are merely thinking of what is *possible*. At the realist stage you are concerned with what is *workable*. This involves considering the constraints of technology, time, environment, etc.

The implementation process can be broken into two phases—the *conceptual phase* and the *operational phase*.

At the conceptual phase of implementation, the primary criterion or test is one of *feasibility*. The function of the test part of the conceptual T.O.T.E. is to filter out unfeasible ideas—this is the go/no-go stage for an idea. A main concern at this point is that one might judge too quickly.

The operational part of the T.O.T.E. is directed toward getting the *initial expression* of the idea as a 'mock-up' or design example. The primary feedback loop is organized around making mock-ups and bouncing ideas off others. This involves initially looking at alternative representations.

At the point where there is an idea it is important to seek conceptual feedback, primarily broad feedback on major concept ideas. That is, "Is it a good concept?" Since there is nothing tangible yet, it is important to look for constructive feedback at this point. If the feedback is too critical it will squelch the dream as opposed to improving the expression of the dream. In fact, many creative people choose to wait for feedback until after they have completed a prototype expression of the idea.

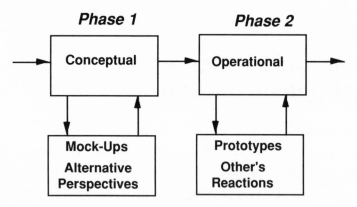

**Figure 4.1. T.O.T.E.s Involved in the 'Realist'
Stage of the Creative Process.**

At the operational or 'mechanical' phase of implementation, feedback goes on all the time-primarily through other people's responses. Since the goal of this phase is to refine the tangible expression of the idea, specific comments are important as well as comments about other concepts that fit in with your basic idea. Many creative people feel that they should get as much feedback as possible, as early as possible, in the final implementation stage. At this stage, "anything goes"—that is, almost all feedback is welcomed, "because it's important," not because you like it or want it. For this reason it is important to seek feedback ONLY when you are ready.

There is often less variation between individual strategies for the operational aspects of implementation than there is for generating and selecting ideas. In other words, there is less variation in the 99% perspiration than there is in the 1% inspiration. Mozart and his father most likely were more similar in the way that they implemented a symphony than they were in the ways they generated and selected which material to orchestrate. This is true of electronic engineers, video game designers, mechanics, seminar leaders, patent attorneys, etc. As you bring something from the map to the territory there are more constraints and restrictions, and fewer variations allowed in the creative process.

While all stages of the creative cycle require feedback, the realist stage requires the shortest and tightest feedback loop. The timing cycle for feedback in the dreamer and critic stages can come in relatively longer intervals than at the realist stage. To implement an idea, the more immediate and direct the feedback, the better.

Dreamer   Realist   Critic

**Figure 4.2. Frequency of Feedback for
Different Stages of Creativity.**

Because the feedback loop is so immediate and the focus intense in the implementation phase, probably one of the most important skills to develop is that of handling interruptions, distractions and blocks to creativity.

It is not an uncommon experience for a creative person to be interrupted in the middle of a project. After an interruption, it can be difficult to get back into the same state or 'creative space' that you were in before it occurred. This can slow down your productivity or even severely inhibit it.

Distractions have to do with the diffusion of attention at a time that you are trying to focus. Often distractions come in the form of other goals or projects that compete for your attention so that you are not "all there."

While interruptions and distractions primarily come from external sources, blocks come from the inside. Blocks are most often recognized as the places you get stuck or the impasses reached in your progress. Often many little blocks or stuck spots are encountered and shaken loose in the course of the creative process.

Obviously the timing of feedback or input makes a big difference in each of these interferences to creativity. Sometimes an interruption can actually be conducive to the creative process, because it gives time for an idea to gestate. Can you recognize the differences between procrastination and gestation in yourself? Certainly, one of the first steps in developing the skills to address these issues is the ability to recognize creative versus stuck states in yourself and others. During times of external non-productivity a person is not necessarily being uncreative internally.

# Exercise: Calibrating the Physiology and Body Language of Creativity

The purpose of this exercise is to sharpen your abilities to observe and "calibrate" the non-verbal cues that accompany creativity strategies. The information gathered during this exercise can help define what physical states or actions can help to intentionally break stuck states and become creative.

1. Find a friend or associate to work with. Facing your partner, ask the following questions and observe everything you can about the non-verbal response.
   a. *Think of a time you were really in a creative state and not available to interruptions or feedback.*
   b. *Think of a time you were procrastinating or stuck and needed to be interrupted or to receive some feedback.*
2. Now have your partner randomly pick one or the other of the two experiences and see if you can guess which one he or she is thinking of by observing the changes that you see in body language.

We find this to be an especially useful exercise to do with people who work together on projects in organizations or in teams. (It can also be great help to the spouses and mates of creative people!) A common problem that happens in creative work, especially between people who work closely together, is that someone unintentionally disrupts the creative process of a team member or partner because he or she thinks the person is "not busy" when, in fact, the person is deep in the kind of inner process necessary for productive thinking. Another type of problem can occur when a partner or team member doesn't recognize a person as being deep, or 'lost', in a creative state and interprets their lack of responsiveness to their communications or feedback as a lack of interest or lack of caring. A first step in improving the creative process is by recognizing, acknowledging and respecting it when it is happening.

This exercise can also give you some further insight into the Representational Systems, Orientation, Links and Effects associated with your creative process.

Another way to help avoid interruptions is to set up signals to let other people know what state you are in. It could be something like putting a red light on your door when you are unavailable for interruption, and a green light when you are. Or it could be something as simple as having your door opened or closed.

# Tools for Dealing with Interruptions: Leaving and Re-Entering a Creative State

Of course, there will be times when interruptions are necessary, and having the skill to be able to leave something and then pick up again where you left off can be very important. There are several simple strategies that you can use to help with the process of disassociating from and re-entering a creative state. The following steps (which typically take 30 seconds to 1 minute to accomplish) will help to facilitate the exit from and re-entry into a state of creativity from an external interruption.

1. Take a mental snapshot of your progress. Focus especially on your last point of success.
2. Memorize your body position. Note your posture, breathing rate, head and eye position.
3. Make quick notes (key words) or sketches on your work and body position.
4. Find a creative cue or metaphor. See if there is something in your environment that you can associate with the creative state as a trigger or as a metaphor to the kind of state or thought process you are in.

Take a moment and try them out, even as you read this book. Follow each step, and then put the book down and go do something else briefly. When you return, see how quickly you can get back into the same state of focus and attention you had before you put down the book.

These steps help you to set *anchors* to get back into the creative state you were in prior to an interruption. In NLP the term *anchoring* refers to the establishment of links between other R.O.L.E. Model elements. Anchoring is a process that on the surface is similar to the "conditioning" technique used by Pavlov to create a link between the hearing of a bell and salivation in dogs. By associating the sound of a bell with the act of giving food to his dogs, Pavlov found he could eventually just ring the bell and the dogs would start salivating, even though no food was given. In the behaviorist's stimulus-response conditioning formula, however, the stimulus is always an environmental cue and the response is always a specific behavioral action. The association is considered reflexive and not a matter of choice.

In NLP the process has been expanded to include other logical levels than environment and behavior. A remembered picture may become an anchor for a particular internal feeling, for instance. A touch on the leg may become an anchor for a visual fantasy or even a belief. A voice tone may become an anchor for a state of excitement or confidence. A person may consciously choose to establish and retrigger these associations for himself. Rather than being a mindless knee-jerk reflex, an anchor becomes a tool for self-empowerment. Obviously, anchoring can be a very useful tool for helping to establish and reactivate the mental processes associated with creativity.

Most often anchors may be established through simply associating two experiences together in time. In behavioral conditioning models, associations become more strongly established through repetition. Repetition may also be used to strengthen anchors as well. For example, you could ask someone to vividly re-experience a time she was very creative and pat her shoulder while she is thinking of the experience. If you repeat this once or twice the pat on shoulder will begin to become linked to the creative state. Eventually a pat on the shoulder will automatically remind the person of the creative state.

If your goal is to quickly leave and then re-enter a state of creativity to handle an interruption, however, repetition is not always a viable strategy—unless you have set up your anchor ahead of time. In the case of an interruption, repetition must be replaced by redundancy. That is, establishing more than one anchor for a particular state or experience. Having multiple anchors increases the chance that you will be able to reaccess the state you want. That is the purpose of making several types of associations. It is often useful to make associations in each representational system: physical, visual and verbal, as this technique suggests.

Some creative people like to make or establish general creativity anchors. Listening to certain types of music may help to anchor you into a naturally creative state. Gathering certain books around you or putting up certain kinds of pictures can remind you of creative experiences. Having special objects near you that you can hold, touch or 'fidget with' can enhance the entry into a focused creative state.

Naturally, it can be of great value to develop specific cues to signal others that you are engaged in the disassociation or re-entry process so that other people don't misinterpret your actions and think you are actually being unresponsive. It can also help to set some procedures for how they can respond appropriately and respectfully to those cues.

# Tools for Dealing with Distractions

Distractions tend to originate externally, but usually in a more general way than interruptions. Distractions often come from a confusion or competition between priorities-such as family, other projects and responsibilities, etc. The best way to help deal with distractions and stay focused is through time management and project management strategies. The purpose of these strategies would be to sort out and allocate the time blocks to be devoted to the various elements of the project, other projects occurring simultaneously and other parts of your life.

In my work with creative people and organizations, I have found that the most effective strategy is to create *multiple representations* of the project elements and sequencing, so you have many ways of seeing how all the pieces fit together. While the whole area of time and project management could take up an entire book in itself, and is beyond the scope of this work, the most effective strategies involve the visual organization of different chunks of time—i.e., calendar for day, week month, year—in which elements and events are related together. In a way, these structures are ways of setting up anchors, on a macro level, for leaving and re-entering the creative process. A little organization ahead of time also prevents congruency problems that arise from conflicts of priorities.

The figures below shows a number of different ways you can represent how the various elements of a project fit together and fit with other parts of your life.

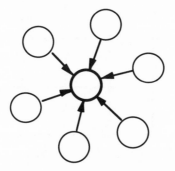

**Figure 4.3. Overall Project Elements.**

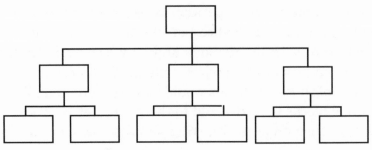

**Figure 4.4. Breakdown or 'Chunking'
of Project Elements.**

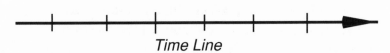

*Time Line*

**Figure 4.5. Time Sequence of Overall Project.**

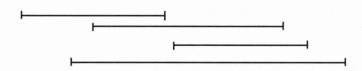

**Figure 4.6. Coordination of Sequencing
of Project Elements.**

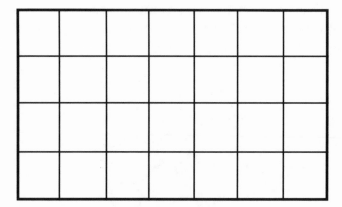

*Project Calendar*

**Figure 4.7. Timing in Relation to Other Projects.**

**Figure 4.8. Priority Line**

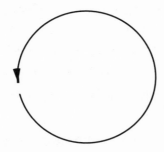

**Figure 4.9. Project Cycle**

As an exercise, take some creative project that you are working on and think of it in the context of the different frameworks implied by these figures. Notice how it clarifies and enriches your concept and awareness of how different pieces fit together.

Keep these representations around as anchors. Later on, if you find yourself distracted from your project, look at the different representations. You will probably find that different ones help to refocus you or give you ideas about how to proceed or what to do next at different stages in your implementation.

In an organization you will often find that different organizational functions and team members will tend to arrange their perception of the project more within one or the other of these frameworks. It is often important for them to share all of the ways of perceiving the timing and structure of the project.

# Tools for Dealing with Creative Blocks

One of the most challenging aspects of the implementation stage of creativity is dealing with internal blocks and impasses related to the manifestation of your ideas. In previous sections we have already presented and explored some tools that can be used to help move from a stuck state to a creative state at any stage in the creative process, including:

1. Putting yourself into a creative body posture and physiology.
2. Multi-sensory check-make sure you are using all your senses when you are thinking about the particular problem or goal you are dealing with.
3. Try alternative representations-change various aspects of the images, sounds or feelings you have and find out if it changes the way you experience the problem/goal.
4. Bounce ideas off someone else.
5. Choose alternative approaches BEFORE beginning a particular part of the project.

Some other approaches to breaking out of stuck states and creative blocks include:

1. Consider the problem in all parts and then go to sleep, meditate, exercise or simply distract yourself—ideas will often come spontaneously later on.
2. Transfer a creativity process from some other area in your life.
3. Try other peoples' strategies.

One question that often arises with respect to developing more creativity is, "If a person who wants to improve his creativity is having trouble, do you try to enhance his strengths or do you try to improve his weaknesses?"

One approach is to appeal to the strength, "What representational system has this person developed most fully? How can I build more on that existing strength?" The other approach is to try to build up the system that the person has developed the least. That could produce some of the most generative results.

If you apply the principle of pacing and leading, of course, you end up doing both. You use an individual's strengths in order to enhance their weakness. You can borrow a creativity strategy from one area of their life and creatively apply it to another area. This process is called 'utilization' in NLP. An effective process from one context is utilized to enrich, widen or expand an ineffective process in another context.

# T.O.T.E. Utilization Process

One of the most basic utilization procedures is to elicit the four elements of the T.O.T.E. loop for both the effective and ineffective strategies and contrast them for the key differences. The effective strategy may be utilized to enrich the ineffective strategy in two ways:

1. by replacing the elements of the ineffective T.O.T.E. with the corresponding elements of the effective T.O.T.E., or

2. by adding the elements of the effective T.O.T.E. to those of the ineffective T.O.T.E.

The figure below shows an example of two contrasting T.O.T.E.s for contexts involving communication. The chart has been filled out by a creative teacher who gets stuck and inflexible when she has to delegate a specific task to someone. As you can see, the two strategies differ in some important and significant ways.

| | eg. Teaching<br>Effective Context | eg. Delegating<br>Ineffective Context |
|---|---|---|
| *What are your goals?* | Sharing knowledge with others and having fun. | Getting task done the right way. |
| *How do you know you are achieving your goals?* | The look on people's faces and my inner feelings. | The end result of the task. |
| *What do you do in order to reach your goals?* | Use many examples and pictures. | Explain instructions clearly. |
| *What do you do if you are not satisfactorily reaching your goals?* | Say the same thing in different words.<br><br>Try to get the audience into a more open state. | Become angry. |

**Figure 4.10. Example of Contrasting T.O.T.E.s for Communication Situations.**

Rather than judge the limiting strategy as 'bad' or 'wrong' and something that she shouldn't do, we asked this teacher to simply add the elements of her teaching T.O.T.E. to her delegation process. That is, we asked:

- When you are delegating, can you make your goals to get the task done quickly *and* share knowledge in a fun way with others?

- Can you use the end result of the task *and* the looks on peoples' faces and your own feelings while the task is being carried as evidence that you are achieving your goals for the delegation?

- Can you explain instructions clearly *and* use examples and pictures as you are explaining them?

- If the delegation goals are not being satisfactorily achieved, can you *add the choices* of saying the same instructions in different words and trying to get the person you are delegating to into a more open state of mind as other alternatives to getting angry?

Notice that there are a few adjustments that need to be made to adapt the effective strategy to the new context. Sometimes this requires a little creativity. But often it can be done fairly simply.

## Exercise: Transferring an Effective T.O.T.E.

As an exercise in utilization, fill in the form below for a context where you have been able to be effectively creative, and a context in which you often find yourself stuck or inflexible.

| | Effective Context | Ineffective Context |
|---|---|---|
| *What are your goals?* | | |
| *How do you know you are achieving your goals?* | | |
| *What do you do in order to reach your goals?*<br><br>*What do you do if you are not satisfactorily reaching your goals?* | | |

**Figure 4.11. T.O.T.E. Utilization Chart.**

Contrast the different answers you've given for each of the two strategies. How could you enrich the ineffective context by adding in elements from your creative T.O.T.E.?

## Demonstration of T.O.T.E. Utilization Process

**RBD**: So, C., what is a context in which you are able to be effectively creative?

**C**: Making a presentation—in a training program for instance.

**RBD**: What is the context in which you would like to improve your creative abilities?

**C**: Selling my presentations.

**RBD**: OK. Selling your presentations. This sounds like it ought to be interesting!

What I want you to do first is step into what it is like when you are presenting and imagine you are there doing it. What are your goals?

**C**: To improve people's know-how. That is basically it.

**RBD**: All right, step out of that.

Come over here and step into the "trying to sell" process. What are your goals?

**C**: To sell and make them pay!

**RBD**: OK. Here we have an interesting difference in goals! One of the interventions you might already begin to think about is to imagine approaching selling as just being about increasing people's knowledge of your product.

Who says that selling has to be about making people pay? Selling could be just giving them the know-how to make the decision.

Let's return to effective presentations for a moment. How do you know that you are increasing people's knowledge in a presentation? Do you see things in their faces, do you hear things in their voices?

**C**: Yes, there are all these things you have said, and perhaps some more concrete tests like doing exercises.

**RBD**: So, you have an activity; then what do you do? During the activity, how do you tell?

**C**: Afterwards, by the looks on their faces as I'm talking. And they make richer propositions and have better questions.

**RBD**: So one is the look on their faces and the other is somehow in the content of what they are saying. You do an exercise and that you listen for enriched questions and propositions.

Let's go back to the ineffective selling process. How do you know that you are going to successfully make people pay?

**C**: That may be where I have a problem. When they pay, I guess.

**RBD**: Here the only evidence is from the result after it is all over; whereas with the effectively creative process the evidence is going on during the process.

Now let's explore some of your operations. What do you do in order to increase people's knowledge, and get the kind of looks on their faces, and the kind of enriched propositions and questions?

**C**: I pay a lot of attention to their language, to their representational systems. I start by gathering as much information as possible about who they are, then I try to make my actions fit with their image of the world.

**RBD**: What do you do if you are running into trouble during a presentation when it doesn't seem that it is going well?

**C**: I think then that I made a wrong analysis and I try to recycle the analysis of their image of the world.

**RBD**: We have some basic simple things.

- I pay attention to their language
- Find out about who they are and what their world view is
- Try to make actions that fit with their world models
- If I am having trouble I recycle to gather more information, to recheck my understanding of their models

What do you do when you try to sell a presentation to somebody?

**C**: The same thing, but maybe I have the belief that I can't spend so much time.

**RBD**: So you do listen to their language?

**C**: Yes.

**RBD**: And you do find out who they are and try to make your actions fit with their models of the world, and if you have trouble you just recycle and say, "Oh, I probably misunderstood their model of the world?" Or do you go, "Oh, no!"?

**C**: That's it. Maybe I don't think that I have enough time and I shouldn't be using up their time

**RBD**: So you don't recycle?

**C**: Not as well as I should.

**RBD**: So when you don't reach the goal you just quit. Your basic operational steps are the same but your response to resistance is different. You mentioned that there is a kind of belief that popped up here which is probably one of the reasons why you are not as effective as in the presentation context.

| | Effective Context | Ineffective Context |
|---|---|---|
| *What are your goals?* | Improve people's know-how. | Sell people and make them pay. |
| *How do you know you are achieving your goals?* | Looks on their faces. Enriched propositions and questions. | When they pay. |
| *What do you do in order to reach your goals?*<br><br>*What do you do if you are not satisfactorily reaching your goals?* | Pay attention to language. Find out about their world view. Make actions that fit their model of the world.<br><br>Recycle to gather more information about their world view. | Pay attention to language. Find out about their world view. Make actions that fit their model of the world.<br><br>Feel that I shouldn't be using up their time. |

**Figure 4.12. Comparison of C's Effective and Ineffective T.O.T.E.s.**

But there are also other differences between the two T.O.T.E.s. In the ineffective T.O.T.E. you use essentially the same operation, but have no ongoing evidence and a different goal. It's sort of like saying, "Hey, this process works so well for presentations that I will just use it for this other situation where I have no evidence and a completely different goal. Why isn't it working?"

My point is that the fact that you do the same thing is irrelevant if you don't have the appropriate guidance at the upper level of the T.O.T.E. Doing the same behavior for a different set of values will make a completely different result.

There is a difference between listening to someone's language with the intention of showing friendship and to create rapport versus listening to their language for the purpose of manipulating him to do something. An effective strategy is not only a function of the *what* and *how* but also of the *why*.

One of the other things that seems significant to me is that while you say that you believe you don't have enough time, you do your whole sales presentation before you check whether you are being effective or not. That seems like a terrible waste of the little time you have. When you are improving people's know-how you are checking constantly. If you only check once every hour it might take three hours to get better. Whereas, if you checked once a minute you might be able to pack a lot more into the time you have. When you delay your feedback as long as you do in your sales presentations you can only be a dreamer or a critic, not a realist.

Let's now explore how we can utilize the elements of your effective T.O.T.E. to enrich your own know-how in selling your presentations.

If you took the goal you have when you make presentations and brought it into the selling context, what would happen? You are not going to get rid of the other goal, by the way. You are just going to add the goal of increasing their know-how to the process of selling. It is not a matter of either having to increase these people's knowledge or make money. Some people think that ethical selling is a contradiction in terms. It doesn't have to be.

If you step into the selling context and think about increasing their knowledge, increasing their know-how about what you are selling, what changes?

**C**: First of all I just realized that, in my therapy practice, every person that has been referred to me was sent by other therapists, who saw me working. I did what you have just said.

**RBD**: How would you do that same thing in selling your trainings? Maybe you don't have to make the sale right away anyhow. So you don't have to worry about time. You don't want to manipulate people. You want them to make an advised, appropriate decision. And if they make that decision without the knowledge, it could be a lot worse for you because they will be disappointed.

**C**: I know. I've had cases like that.

**RBD**: I think it is to your benefit to add in that goal. Put yourself back into one of those selling situations, and just imagine that you are not only trying to sell something, you are giving them important know-how.

OK. Let's also take the evidence procedure that you use when you make a presentation into this selling situation. How would you act and engage them in activities in which you could stimulate enriching propositions and questions? They might be a lot more apt to come to a program if they know they will be enriched by it.

Take the same group of people that you are having trouble selling to, and imagine looking at their faces *while* you are in the process of selling them.

**C**: Their questions are about the content of what we are exploring. It's completely different. It's even fun!

**RBD**: And now you have an opportunity to recycle instead of quitting. In other words, you can tell a lot sooner if you are fitting their model of the world.

So that is how you are going to double sales in the next five years!

**C**: Thank you!

**RBD**: All communication is just communication. This is one belief that I found in creative managers. They say there is no difference between delegating or negotiating or persuading or teaching. It is all communication. The difference between persuasion and teaching is only in your inner map, not in how you interact. The principles that make you effective in both are the same. The same goals, evidences, and operations are effective for both.

## Exercise: Cooperative Learning

**RBD**: Effective strategies may be transferred between two people. For example two teachers, or two musicians, or two inventors may have different strategies for accomplishing the same kind of task in the same context. Eliciting and sharing goals, evidence procedures and operations can help to widen and enrich the range and scope of your creative abilities.

Find a partner and choose a common task or a situation that requires creativity. Each fill in the T.O.T.E. information on the chart below and compare your answers for the similarities and differences. Imagine what it would be like to add your partner's operations, evidence procedures, goals or responses to problems to your own strategy. How might it change or enrich the way you approach the situation?

Who knows how many potential Einsteins there are reading this book? Certainly all of your brains are capable of it. I don't think there's a relativity gene or a physics gene that Einstein had that you don't have. By sharing these strategies, we can multiply their number by at least the number of people reading this book.

**TE**: In one of our modeling workshops, we spend about five days on that subject. We call it "stealing behaviors." You steal other people's mental processes, not just for creating, but for doing just about anything they do. The mental process you used to go through your life and to do all the different things you do can be used by other people for things you never even imagined you could use it for. And likewise, you can use theirs as well. This is not limited to creativity.

**Context:** _____

| | Person #1 | Person #2 |
|---|---|---|
| *What are your goals?* | | |
| *How do you know you are achieving your goals?* | | |
| *What do you do in order to reach your goals?* | | |
| *What do you do if you are not satisfactorily reaching your goals?* | | |

**Figure 4.13. Cooperative Learning T.O.T.E. Chart.**

# Exercise: R.O.L.E. Model Utilization

**RBD**: You can expand the depth and precision of the T.O.T.E. utilization process by adding to your elicitation the other elements of the R.O.L.E. model we've been exploring. For instance, you can include the specification of physiology, representational systems, and submodalities. Because of the need for physiological observations, this exercise is best done with a partner.

We often find that in contrasting the two contexts and strategies it is helpful to spatially sort the two states by literally locating them in different physical locations. So that you would actually move to a different place in the room as you are thinking of the two situations. This physical sorting process also keeps the two states from overlapping or mixing together before you are ready.

Another helpful procedure is to establish what we call a *meta position* in NLP. A meta position is a physical location that is separate from either of the two states you are examining—where you can think about them without being overly involved or associated into either one. When you are comparing the two experiences for differences and similarities, it is best to do it from a meta position.

The steps to the R.O.L.E. Model utilization process are similar to those of the T.O.T.E. utilization but incorporate filling in a bit more detail.

1. Select a **specific physical location** somewhere in front of you to your right. Step into this location and associate into the experience where you have been able to be effectively creative, and silently **relive** it.

   The observer should note any significant physical clues associated with the experience (i.e., **p**osture, **e**ye movements, **g**estures).

2. Sometimes it helps to identify and relive one or two other examples of the effective strategy. Continue to use the **SAME** physical location to relive each resource experience.

   The observer should note any similarities or patterns between the physical clues associated with all of the creative examples.

3. Identify a past or ongoing situation where you want to be more creative or flexible, but experience difficulty. Select a **DIFFERENT physical location** from your creativity examples, associate into that experience and silently relive it.

   Observer notes the **most significant differences** between the physiology associated with the problem situation and effectively creative situations.

4. From a **Meta Position** compare the problem and creative situations and notice what is different in regard to

the internal R.O.L.E. model distinctions (representational systems, submodalities, synesthesias, etc.). Especially notice differences in the basic T.O.T.E. functions—how the goal is represented and evaluated, and what choices and operations are used if the goal is not met.

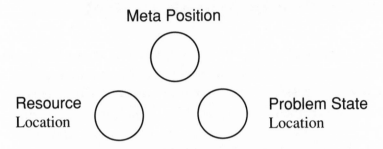

Figure 4.14. Locations for R.O.L.E. Model
Utilization Process.

5.    **Transfer** the key elements of your creativity strategy by stepping into the creativity location and focusing on the physical and mental patterns that you have discovered from your meta position analysis. That is, think about the body posture, accessing pattern, submodalities, T.O.T.E. elements, etc., of the creative resource. Then step back into the problem state location and add these elements to your experience of the problem experience.

Find out how you can adapt your effective creativity strategy to the problem context. Again, sometimes this requires a fair amount of creativity in itself. If you have difficulty you can always return to meta position to get a more distant or general perspective.

The following transcript demonstrates how a creativity strategy may be elicited and transferred to a problematic situation. While the process followed in the transcript does not exactly follow the steps to the exercise, it illustrates some of the ways in which the elements of one strategy may be transferred from one context to another, as well as give more fascinating insights into the nature of creativity.

# Interview with Inventor Lowell Noble, March 18, 1983

**RBD**: I'm going to ask you some questions about times that you're creative and find out if we can observe any patterns. You are a successful inventor, with a number of patents in the field of electronics. When you think of being creative, do you think of it as being a specific state that you go into? Do you think of it as being something that happens periodically for a short time, or is it something that you work into?

**Lowell**: It's usually a process that occurs when I've tried to organize and to think about something as much as possible. It usually is oriented towards solving some kind of a specific problem or reaching some kind of a specific goal. I think it can be a very slow procedure. My actual creative thinking often occurs in bed between 7:00 and 9:00 in the morning when I'm lying flat on my back. But I usually do a lot of preparation, and get a lot of information into my mind ahead of time so I'm letting it digest over night and most of my thoughts come to me in the morning. I wake up and I am well organized.

**RBD**: When you say you are well organized, does it mean that you can say to yourself specifically what to do, does it mean you have a visual image of how it is going to fit together; do you have a list, an outline, a picture? What specifically do you have in your mind?

**Lowell**: Oh, I usually consider any problem in a sense like a mathematical equation, in order to solve an equation, with $n$

roots you have to have $n$ variables, too. So in order to conduct any experiment, there are four or five things you want to vary—you like to visually have a knob that you can twist. I know when something is well organized when I think I know what is going to make something happen, and I have control over a sufficient number of variables, preferably over those variables that will make the most effect.

**RBD**: I noticed that your eyes went up and left when you said that you have to see this chain of causes and effects between these variables. When you think of that organization, are you making a visual image in your mind of them?

**Lowell**: Frequently it will be visual, yes. I prefer to visualize things. For instance, I prefer to visualize an experimental set up, before I know whether I can even do it or not. You can control everything visually.

**RBD**: So when you visualize a certain set of controls, you don't first think about whether you can actually do it yet. You just picture what the experiment would be. My understanding is that there is no filtering yet, all you want to do is to create that as a mental structure.

**Lowell**: Sometimes, you cannot have controls over everything you'd like to. But sometimes, one knob controls two or more variables.

**RBD**: Now you talk about knobs, do you see knobs? And do you label them, like this is such and such control, and that is such and such a control?

**Lowell**: Well, I usually have a list of variable knobs. When you have ten knobs, you try to reduce them to two knobs or three knobs. The other thing is you like to simplify everything conceptually as much as possible. To reduce the number of knobs is very crucial.

**RBD**: I'd like to go to a specific example. Is there something specific that you could talk about that you organized in this way?

**Lowell**: I recently invented a three-dimensional display device that hooks up to an Apple computer and that is not holographic nor stereoscopic. Instead of having a flat screen, you can have an image basically floating out in space. It's been a common misconception that in order to see things you have to have a screen. But by using certain principles of optics you don't have to have a screen and can make three-dimensional images.

**RBD**: Sounds fascinating! Now, when you first came up with that as a conception, was it to solve a specific problem?

**Lowell**: Oh, I saw an ad where somebody had done it and they were charging 220,000 dollars for it. And I said, "Gee, I'd like to have one, but there must be a simpler, easier way. So somebody had made a device that made images floating out in space. But in my estimation it is a very crude method of doing it. So I said there had to be an easier way of doing it that I can do with my Apple.

**RBD**: So when you started to visualize this, how did you do it? Did you start by seeing an image, did you see a device in your mind's eye?

**Lowell**: No, actually, I went to optics books and started reading different things about optics, and what you can do. I had a background in optics, so I was familiar with the very fundamentals. So I started reviewing, because I hadn't really been active in the field for about ten or fifteen years.

**RBD**: I want to review the steps up to this point. It seems almost as though someone put an image in your mind, by saying, "I've made this great device." And you had sort of a basic idea of an image floating out in space in front of a screen. So, that was your goal, no screen, just an image floating out in space. You'd know you were successful when you had something that could do that.

**Lowell**: For less than 220,000 dollars.

**RBD**: It seems that an essential part of creativity is coming up with that image to begin with. I would identify that as "innovation," which is coming up with something completely new. For example, coming up with an idea that no one else has seen or the picture that you are going to start with. This is different from what I would call "invention," which is the process of making something do what you see in that picture. They're both just as creative. Getting the idea to start with is what I call innovation, and invention is: "Now how do I implement that."

**Lowell**: Frequently in order to innovate you need a device that approximates what you want to accomplish.

**RBD**: So after you've got that, you start gathering information. Now, did you screen out information? Did you only look for a certain kind?

**Lowell**: I knew it had to be some kind of a projection system. I had to project light out into space. So I looked at different kinds of optical projection systems.

**RBD**: So you weren't just studying anything about optics. In other words, there was probably a lot about optics that you didn't need to know. In fact, there might have been some things that you needed not to know. There's a lot of useless information. There is erroneous information. Somebody might have even said it was impossible to do this.

**Lowell**: Yes, everybody always said, "You need a screen." And that's an erroneous piece of information I think, but it's widely believed.

**RBD**: So there was one thing you went in there with, the belief that you were going to find a way around the need for a screen. And even though you might have read that it was not possible, that became filtered out as part of the process.

**Lowell**: Yes, I'd say I'd honestly believed that was not true. The thing that spurred me on was that somebody said that they could make images in space. That upsets the general concept that you need a screen. So I said, "Do you really need a screen to think about it? You really don't. You see things all the time and there's no screen there." So then if you don't need the screen, what other mechanisms do you use to have a light image focused in space?

Conceptually then, the next thought is, "How do you see things?" And you really see things by the rays of light coming into your eyes. So all you're going to need then is just to control the angle at which the rays come into the eyes. That's my approach. The big change was in the ways you look at and visualize things. When you are seeing something you look at ray orientation more than at screen orientation or reflection orientation. The information I was looking for is how you actually physically control the angles of rays of light. And that's what you do. You're looking at refraction and lenses and mirrors.

**RBD**: So after you had the picture in mind, you began to build an image of, "How is that image going to appear there, how am I going to be able to perceive it?" And all it comes down to is a matter of how the rays of light go into your eyes.

**Lowell**: That's right. You can forget about the optical specialities, because all that you're concerned about is the angle that the rays come into your eye lenses.

**RBD**: So it seems that your first dial was to adjust the angle of rays of light. What was the next step?

**Lowell**: Well, I looked at basically how lenses worked and how lenses are used in projection systems. I looked primarily at systems that are used to project television images onto big screens in bars, which are basically a simple set of lenses that are already available.

**RBD**: You needed to get something that controls angles of light. So you explored simple systems that already existed to do that. You didn't want to reinvent the wheel, and yet you didn't want to look at everything. So it seems you have a filter that says, "I don't have to look for anything beyond this now, I don't have to be searching all over the world. Here is something that seems to be a simple way of doing what I want."
  What other dials did you put into it?

**Lowell**: In order to control the dials for the same things the T.V. does, you've got the T.V. set and all the knobs over here, and you have a projection system, which usually has two lenses on it. So then you have to have knobs to control the distance between the T.V. set and the first lens, and the distance between the first lens and the second lens, and the distance between the second lens and the resulting image. If you can control all those, then you can control the distance after the image.

**RBD**: So you've got knobs that control the distance between the lenses. You've got light projected through these lenses in a certain way, and you are going to control the different angles of light coming through the lenses.

**Lowell**: You can physically control those by moving the lenses back and forth varying all those physical spacings. You have three physical spacings that you can control.

**RBD**: So you mentally move the lenses back and forth to find out how it will come out. You were doing that in your own mind, moving the lens and so forth.

**Lowell**: Sure, with no screen.

**RBD**: One of the things I saw you doing with your gestures was actually spatially placing the T.V. knob and the other knobs in a particular location. Was the image in your mind three-dimensional? Did you see the lenses from the side?

**Lowell**: Normally, when you think about optics, you think about an optic bench. It's long so you can slide things back and forth. You have a light source and the lens and the screen. In this case the set up would be that the projection screen would be in front of the T.V. monitor, then there would be two lenses in front of the projector, and then the image would be floating out in front of them someplace. You'd think about how you can pull all the lenses back and forth. Conceptually you're looking down on the optic system.

**RBD**: So you viewed it from the top as opposed to from the side as it is normally envisioned. You literally rotated the perspective in your mind's eye. A different perspective could actually lead to different conclusions.

**Lowell**: I think that there are basically three perspectives that people visualize things from: (1) what I would call the God's eye view, it's like looking down at the earth, a long ways away; (2) then there is the driver view, where you are seeing what you would be seeing if you were actually there, like actually driving a car, or actually sitting in front of the optics bench; (3) then there is the right shoulder view, where you've visualized yourself from a short distance away, usually slightly up and behind. Those are three basic ways of visualizing systems. In visualizing a whole system, the God's eye view is the best, then the driver view, and then the right shoulder view.

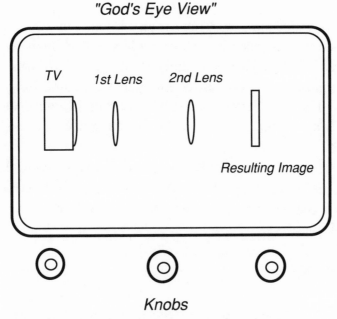

Figure 4.15. Visualization of Optic Bench.

**RBD**: Well, it seems that each would give you a different type of information.

**Lowell**: You get different information, and you get a different feeling, too.

**RBD**: Once you've got the image set up in your mind, how do you make it real? How do you know when to stop just conceptualizing it in your mind and start working on it? My guess is that you didn't start working on the equipment until you had a certain set of things in your mind that you needed.

**Lowell**: Well, there's no sharp demarcation; whenever you think you understand it well enough.

**RBD**: How do you know if you understand it well enough?

**Lowell**: I figured I had how many knobs I needed, and it shows three, in order to control the lenses and the distances. And I said, "O.K., I know roughly what's going to happen, how it's going to work. So, let's get going, let's get something to try it out." The first thing I did was try and find two lenses. The only thing I could find was my wife's magnifying glasses.

**RBD**: I've seen a couple of different eye movements and what I'd like to do is just find out what those were indicating. My guess is that the whole process that you went through wasn't just all pictures.

**Lowell**: No, there were a lot of mathematical terms.

**RBD**: So, at the time you were doing this, were you talking to yourself, or were you getting feelings about what you were doing?

**Lowell**: I guess I tried to organize what I was doing, to make sure it was all there.

**RBD**: So how did you do that?

**Lowell**: Basically, when I accumulated all the information I went to bed. That's my standard procedure: to get as much information as I can, go to sleep, and get up in the morning.

**RBD**: Do you say anything to yourself before going to sleep, like "I'm going to work on this particular problem?"

**Lowell**: I usually think about it. You think about it a lot and try to organize it.

**RBD**: "Thinking about it a lot," what does that mean? How do you think about something? If I were thinking about something like you do, would I be asking myself about it, or making lots of pictures, or something else?

**Lowell**: No, probably half of it is language, and half of it is pictures.

**RBD**: Which half is language? What do you do with language?

**Lowell**: Language would be concepts, I think; "focal lengths," or "virtual images," or "real images;" words that generalize concepts.

**RBD**: When you talk about concepts, do you mean words that stand for a certain type of action in your image?

**Lowell**: It can be, but I usually think of words as something you cannot easily visualize. I try to organize things as much in pictures as possible. But if you can't picture it then you have some concepts that you have to organize verbally, and with mathematical relationships.

**RBD**: So something you can't visualize you give a label?

**Lowell**: You give a label to it, right.

**RBD**: So, you have your picture and then the things you can't picture you give a word. Now are there any feelings involved in the process?

**Lowell**: Yeah, I try to feel or visualize or think up what it would be like to be in the situation; to see a three-dimensional exploded view of the final result.

**RBD**: As you're looking for that final feeling, is there a point where you get a certain feelings that goes, "Ah, that's it, that's what I need?"

**Lowell**: At which stage are you talking about? The whole process is composed of a series of little steps.

**RBD**: In each one of those little steps as you go along, are there feelings associated with how far along you are?

**Lowell**: I think so, if there's an improvement as you go along each step, you can see things are looking better. I don't mean just visualizing things looking better. It has more to do with the quality of the images that you are looking at. Are these real, are they moving, in color, appear to be fully formed or less than that?

**RBD**: And that feels different from when they are not?

**Lowell**: Sure, sure. Basically, when you're trying to accomplish something like this, you try to make sure you're making progress all the time and moving along toward the goal. You never know how long it's going to take you to get there, but as long as you're moving, making progress, it'll be satisfactory to you.

**RBD**: Was there a certain point that you felt you had successfully completed what you set out to do?

**Lowell**: In reality or visualization? I did it first in visualization. I thought I could do it and I knew what kind of image I really wanted to have. But I set up the equipment and for about two weeks nothing happened. And what finally happened really was amazing. My wife came down one day and said, "What's that image floating out there in space?" I couldn't see it. And that was really fantastic. I had accomplished it but I couldn't see it.

Now you get into the psychological aspect of it, not the mechanical detail. People vary tremendously in their ability to see things in three dimensions. About 20% of the population cannot see things in three dimensions. If I show the same things to different people, some of them, my brother for instance, can't see them at all. He's my best critic. When I can finally get this rigged up so he can see it, it proves it's great. My wife can come down and see things floating easily. It's just a difference in the connection between the eye and the brain.

**RBD**: It would be interesting to explore whether the ability to see three dimensions in objects externally correlates with the ability to visualize internally in three dimensions. Do you know if your brother can visualize in three dimensions?

**Lowell**: I don't believe he does.

**RBD**: I saw your eyes moving a couple of different places as you answered some of these questions. What I'd like to explore a little further for a moment is the way you use your different senses.

For example, I find that many people might use words to criticize themselves instead of labeling things that they can't see, which is a very different way to use your internal voice. For instance, if you tried something that didn't work, did you say, "Oh that was stupid," or, "You blew it again, you worthless fool," or something like that?

**Lowell**: I just start something else. If something doesn't work, change it and do it again. That's kind of an intermediate step-doing one thing, and then another. That's why the ideal solution is a knob. If you have all the knobs under control, then you have complete control over the situation. So if it doesn't work, you need another knob or something that you will have control over. The object of the knob is to get complete control so you can really try everything very quickly. You need to make things happen as fast as you can so you can see, so you get more information, and get more feedback. And this happens on a continuous basis as opposed to an interval basis.

**RBD**: Are there times when you want to be creative, but you find that you have a difficult time doing it? Like you can't just lie in bed and come up with a solution.

**Lowell**: I'm sure there are, but I try not to think about it.

**RBD**: So you concentrate on your successes rather than your failures, which seems like a good strategy. But I'd like to find out how, specifically, you deal with failures or with being stuck when you are trying to be creative. Was there ever a time, say, when you wanted to do something, you thought you had all the information, you lay in bed and it just didn't work?

**Lowell**: Well, I don't think of those kinds of things as failures, what I try to do is categorize those as solutions to other problems that have not arisen yet. There are a lot of times that you can try something that works very well for whatever minor thing it does, but it's not going to solve your problems. So you've got to store it away. Maybe it will be a solution to a problem that comes up later.

**RBD**: So when something doesn't work, you think of it as a solution to a problem other than the one you happen to be working on. That's great.

Let's now contrast this example of creativity with an area where you are not creative to find the differences. Is there an area in your life that you can't be as creative with as you can with your inventions?

**Lowell**: Communicating with people and things like that.

**RBD**: Okay, so how do you think about communicating? How is it that when you think about that, you can't be creative? Think of a specific situation where you wanted to be creative, where you wanted to have more choices in communicating with someone and you couldn't.

**Lowell**: Well, I don't think about being creative when thinking of communicating with people.

**RBD**: So, you don't even think about being creative with it. Okay, so when you think about communicating with other people, what *do* you do in your mind?

**Lowell**: Well, I probably think about the negative aspect. I'd probably say I'm borderline in that, maybe poor, and don't bother to go along with it too much.

**RBD**: Where's the knob on that one?

**Lowell**: I don't think of it that way.

**RBD**: I believe you. Pick a situation where you wish you could have communicated better, but it was just borderline.

**Lowell**: O.K.

**RBD**: I noticed that as you thought about it, your eyes went down and to the left instead of up as they were when you are thinking about creativity.

**Lowell**: Again, this is about verbal things, kind of low level information.

**RBD**: Given that belief and the "low level" of your eye movement, I can see why you have trouble being creative. What kind of thing do you usually have trouble communicating about?

**Lowell**: Usually passing off or transferring some concept, some visual or scientific concept.

**RBD**: How would you know if you'd done it well?

**Lowell**: That's a problem: Usually you have to ask some questions. Usually it's transferring some kind of scientific concept and the best way to find out whether it's transferred or not is to ask some very specific questions, which sometimes makes it sound like you think they're stupid because you ask very fundamental questions. But that's what you're going to need to know. You have to ask them questions to get the right answers back to know if they've understood it.

**RBD**: Think of a concept that you would typically have a difficult time communicating.

**Lowell**: I'm thinking of a specific example of something: It's called *reproducibility* versus *accuracy* of a determination of a mechanical part.

**RBD**: I'd like to set up a little experiment here to find out if we could use your creativity strategy to help you communicate to our audience what that concept is. Would you be interested in that?

**Lowell**: Sure.

**RBD**: What I'd like you to do is to put your eyes up and try to visualize some other way you could know they understood you that did not depend on verbal content.

**Lowell**: I guess one way to look at it would be to make some kind of a joke that presupposed an understanding of those concepts. Then if everybody laughs, it gives you a visual response.

**RBD**: Can you see a way to do that with this concept?

**Lowell**: I don't know. We'll try—it might be two weeks.

**RBD**: Well, what are the variables and knobs we have to deal with in terms of them understanding?

**Lowell**: Probably my explanation of the concepts.

**RBD**: O.K., so you have certain verbal descriptions but I think there are also going to be experiences behind those verbal descriptions that will also affect whether they understand it.

**Lowell**: Usually you have to have some kind of experience that everybody has participated in or can relate to that they can use in understanding the situation; you have to give a concrete feeling to the concepts also.

**RBD**: A concrete feeling. Can you visualize what you'd like all these people to have? You said a concrete example with a concrete feeling to it that you're going to use to explain these concepts. If you could visualize just three knobs, what kind of variables would you have in terms of explaining it to these people, so if you tried it and it didn't work you'd know which knob to adjust. What kinds of things could you adjust?

**Lowell**: The number of examples, I guess. And we're talking about two different concepts, so that would be two of the knobs. And the third one would be reciting an incident or an element, or a further example where everybody understood that as a common occurrence, perhaps.

**RBD**: Well, look up and picture that right now. If you were going to explain those terms, would you be able to adjust those knobs and get any of that information across?

**Lowell**: Yes, I think so.

**RBD**: When you started to work with your lenses, when you had enough of an idea, you'd start to try it. Do you have enough of an idea yet to try it?

**Lowell**: Yeah, I could try it. In chemistry, or mechanics, there's a fundamental concept of accuracy. Let's say you make something two inches long, and you order it and make a drawing and then there's a dimension on the drawing that says "two inches" and then it says "plus or minus .001" and that's one thousandth of an inch. The drawing could also specify "plus or minus a tenth of an inch" or a fourth of an inch. The cost of the part is determined by the accuracy that is required, not by whether the size of the part is two inches or three inches.

Now when you assemble that part into equipment or machinery, you want it to be *accurate*, but what you want even more is for it to be *reproducible*. So if you order a two-inch part, it may come back 2.1 inches. But if every piece in the shipment is 2.1 inches, then you can make adjustments for that and the rest of the equipment and everything will work fine. So the size of the piece is off but it's been reproduced exactly in all the parts. But if the pieces come back between 1.9 and 2.1 inches, that's a real big spread and everything really doesn't work effectively.

So there's a distinction between the accuracy, 2.0 inches as measured against a standard meter or measuring device, and the reproducibility of parts, which is whether every part comes out the same. And that gets to be critical when you're really trying to make things work. Does everybody understand that?

**Man**: I work with airplanes, and I visualize that as an airplane. The airplane might be a foot extra in length because each part was a little longer.

**RBD**: Another possible knob to include might be the degree to which you exaggerate your example. Like using a big change in the length of an airplane to show what you mean.

**Lowell**: Where this really shows up is in automobiles, where you have the concept of accumulation of errors: You can have all these little pieces that are off a little bit and you have a whole bunch of them stacked up, like the airplane example, where you get a tremendous change in the overall length and that's when things don't work. So you don't want to have your errors accumulate. You want to have them stay as close as you can. But if you make everything really tight, then your cost goes way up. An example of this might be a Rolls Royce, where the specifications are very close, very tight on every part and every one works, and they last fifty to seventy-five years. The opposite case is a Chevy or a very economical car which costs a lot less money. The specifications are very, very broad. And some work a lot better than others because they're not all that really tight fit.

**RBD**: I'm sure everybody who owns a Chevy can get a concrete feeling for that.

**Lowell**: We hired a mechanical engineer who came from Ford, and he told us that the way they adjust the specifications is they make them as loose as they can and they don't consider that the tolerances are sloppy enough until one to two percent of the engines don't work. And so they put them together, and if one or two percent don't work, then they disassemble them again and throw them back into the bin and reassemble them again, and then they work fine. They work fine because they have a different accumulation of the variables that might meet the specifications. (Laughter.)

**RBD**: So you finished this and everybody laughed. Are you satisfied that they understand it?

**Lowell**: Pretty much.

**RBD**: Was that different for you that way than you would normally do it?

**Lowell**: Yeah, because of the visualization. I don't think I've ever done it before.

**RBD**: One of the things that's interesting to me in this is that sometimes visualizing things you don't usually visualize, even though you can't think of how to picture them at first, can be really useful. All you did here was a little bit of trying to get a picture, and all of a sudden it got you that much further along.

I also notice that the use of analogy often seems to be an essential element of creativity. For instance, maybe I can't explain to you exactly what a certain concept is, but if I gave you a metaphor, even though it isn't really exactly what I'm talking about, I might be able to get the picture or the feeling or the sounds across that would make it click, fall together, or clear for you.

Your existing creativity strategy has always allowed you to do certain things really well. By eliciting its structure you can generalize it to improve your creativity in other areas as well. You've always thought about communication in a certain way; now you can do it differently. In fact, a major part of creativity is the ability to switch between different modes of thinking. It's not really one strategy; it's the ability to shift strategies. And now you have a way to do that.

Imagine what would happen if you sleep on it one night.

**Note**: Not long after this session Mr. Nobel was able to communicate well enough about his idea to license his three-dimensional imaging technology for five million dollars.

# New Behavior Generator: Developing the Realist

**RBD**: One of the most essential processes of creativity is that of moving from a dream or vision to action. In essence, this is the function of the 'Realist.' How to manifest the dream or vision. In NLP we've developed a kind of all purpose creativity strategy, organized around this process of moving from vision to action, called 'The New Behavior Generator.' The basic steps to the New Behavior Generator were set out by John Grinder. I've added refinements based on some of the elements of the R.O.L.E. Model, T.O.T.E. Model and my study of Walt Disney.

The New Behavior Generator is an elegant strategy that can be applied to almost any situation that involves personal flexibility. It encapsulates many of the principles that Lowell brought up during the preceding interview. While the basic focus of the strategy is on the realist—on generating specific actions and behaviors—it involves an interplay of elements of dreamer, realist and critic. The basic steps involve forming a visual image of a desired behavior (dreamer), kinesthetically associating into the image on a feeling level (realist), and verbalizing any missing or needed elements (critic).

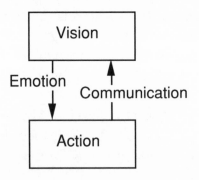

**Figure 4.16. Overall T.O.T.E. for
New Behavior Generator.**

# New Behavior Generator T.O.T.E.

These three steps form a feedback loop in which vision and action interact through the intermediate processes of emotion and communication.

In order to demonstrate this, I'd like to lead someone through the steps incorporating some key T.O.T.E. and R.O.L.E. Model elements.

Who has something that they'd like to develop more flexibility about?

**J**: I do.

**RBD**: O.K., J. We need to start with an outcome. Perhaps something you've been trying to be creative about, but which you've been a little stuck with.

**J**: I want to be able to convince someone they have self-worth.

**RBD**: I can imagine why this is something that you sometimes have difficulty doing. That's a very general outcome statement.

One of the things that is very important for the 'realist' is having an evidence procedure for your outcomes. That is, some way of knowing when you've accomplished that outcome. Therefore, my first question is, "How would you know if you convinced somebody of their self-worth?"

**J**: I would know when he had taken steps to bring income into his life.

**RBD**: You mean monetary income?

**J**: Right.

**RBD**: So there is something you would actually see?

**J**: Right.

**RBD**: Do you have a particular person in mind?

**J**: Yes.

**RBD**: O.K. (To audience) The first step in this strategy is to get a statement of the goal, and then identify some sensory-based evidence indicating the achievement of the goal. You ought to be able to describe something that would indicate some concrete expression of the goal. "Self-worth" is the land of the 'Dreamer'. Monetary income is the land of the 'Realist'. (Laughter.)

(To J.) I also want to find out whether there is anything you can *already* do that is similar to this outcome? Lowell mentioned the usefulness of starting with something that approximates the results you want to achieve. Is there anything you can do that is comparable to convincing somebody of their self-worth? It must be something you can be creative about and which you can do well. Is there an area, in communicating with people, where you can easily convince them of something other than self-worth?

**J**: Yes.

**RBD**: OK. Look down and to the right for a moment. I'd like you to get the feeling of what it was like when you were successful and able to easily convince somebody about something other than self-worth. Do you have the feeling?

**J**: Yes.

**RBD**: Is it the feeling you have when you're able to deal with somebody and do it effectively?

**J**: Yes.

**RBD**: Good. (To audience) So we now have the statement of the goal: convincing someone of their self-worth. We have some external sensory based evidence that would show us when he has reached it: The person would be taking concrete steps to produce monetary security. We have an internal reference experience for the feeling in J. that accompanies successfully reaching a similar kind of goal. These constitute the 'Test' part of our T.O.T.E. Now let's go through the steps for the 'Operation'.

(To J.) I'd like you to look down and over to your left and ask yourself, "If I could already convince people that they had self-worth, easily and effectively, what would I look like?" Say those words to yourself in your mind. "If I were already able to convince people that they have self-worth in a creative, effective way, what would I look like?"

**J**: What would I look like?

**RBD**: Yes, what would you look like? Repeat that question to yourself and then move your eyes up and to your right, and visualize yourself as if you were watching a movie of yourself. I want you to visualize yourself and the other person you want to convince. I want you to see what you would be doing. What do you have up there? Any image at all?

**J**: No. I can get a kind of feeling about what I want it to be like, but I can't see anything. I'm not very good at making pictures. I don't have any skill at it.

**RBD**: Okay, you have a feeling but you don't see any image at all. You're having difficulty getting an image. Can you get a piece of an image? I mean, can you see the kind of shirt this person might wear? Can you see any of the furniture in the room in which you will be seeing this person? Can you see how your own hands might look as you are talking to him? Can you see the shape of his head or mouth?

**J**: Well, yes, now that you bring those things up I can get a sense of myself and that person. But I'm blank about what to do.

**RBD**: That's all right. Look up and over to your left for a moment. Can you remember what it was like when you were able to be flexible and convincing with someone else about a different subject? Take your time.

**J**: Ah... Okay, yes. I have a memory of talking to someone else, where I was confident and convincing.

**RBD**: Good. Now, we're going use that image as a reference picture. Imagine you were editing a movie or an animated film, and you could take the image of yourself as a character and pull it out of the movie of your memory and paste it into your imaginary picture of convincing this difficult person that he has self-worth. In other words, put that image of yourself being effective up here to your right, so it's not a memory anymore but becomes part of a fantasy. Use that image from your memory to help you see yourself up over here convincing that difficult person more effectively. Can you visualize that?

**J**: I have just a concept of a picture.

**RBD**: Well, that's a start. Let's see if we can develop that "concept of a picture" a little more fully by bringing in some of the other steps of the strategy.

I'd like you to step into whatever image you have. As if you suddenly became the character that you were watching in a movie. Put yourself into your fantasy so that you feel as though you're right there. Put yourself inside that experience and get the feeling of what it would be like to be doing what you were just imagining and watching yourself doing up there. Step into it and get the feelings, and as you do so, move your eyes down and to your right.

**J**: (Moves eyes from up right to down right. Blinks his eyes as if confused and then shakes his head.)

**RBD**: What's going on? Did the picture disappear?

**J**: I can't seem to get the feeling.

**RBD**: You can't get the feeling? What happened? You had the picture. You put yourself in and saw it through your own eyes, and what happened? You stepped in and nothing happened?

**J**: I just feel empty. I just don't feel good enough...

**RBD**: I see. It looks like we found the 'Critic.' That's okay, we'll just incorporate that into the outcome.

What I'd like you to do is to look back over to your left and state the following, "If I could already convince people that they had self-worth, *including myself*, easily, effectively, and creatively, so that I could really feel it, what would that look like? If I already could convince people that they were worthwhile, including my own 'critic', creatively, and effectively, and I could get the feeling from that, then what would that look like?" And then put your eyes up here to the right and visualize it.

**J**: (Looks up and smiles.)

**RBD**: In fact, to help you out a little more, look over to your left and think of someone you admire. Think of someone who has been a role model or a mentor for you, that you think is creative, flexible and convincing. Has there been someone like that in your life?

**J**: (Eyes up left.) Yes. A few people actually.

**RBD**: Imagine how these people, these role models, would convince your 'critic' that *you* had self-worth. Maybe choose one in particular, and just wildly fantasize how that person would be creative and convincing with your critic, and how this mentor would handle that difficult person in experiencing his self-esteem.

**J**: (Eyes up left and right. Body relaxes, breathing deepens.) He doesn't need to use so many words. It's something in his eyes and in his face and in the tone of his voice. (Smiles.)

**RBD**: Sometimes creativity involves doing less, not more. Sometimes creativity allows you to do fewer things but more elegantly and congruently.

Now, I'd like to ask you to look over to your right and picture yourself doing some of the kinds of things you just saw these people doing. Edit this movie so you are swapping characters in a way. See yourself using the kind of eye contact, facial expression and tone of voice that you experienced in these role models. Just dream about what it would be like for you to have their flexibility, their wisdom, their creativity. That's right.

**J**: (Eyes up right. Body is still for a while and then he laughs.)

**RBD**: You've got it?

**J**: Well, I don't know if it's going to work, but it sure is different from anything I've done before.

**RBD**: Sounds good to me. Now step into *that* image so that you feel you're right there doing what you just saw yourself doing. Redo the whole thing with yourself inside the image and having the feelings of what it will really be like to do it. Just step into that picture and get the feeling.

**J**: It feels different. It's easier somehow.

**RBD**: I want you to compare it with the feeling of what it was like when you were successful. When you compare it, I want you to come up with a set of words for what is different about it. Notice if there is anything missing in the feeling you got when you stepped into this picture from the one you got when you were successful. What's missing from that feeling that you had when you stepped into the picture of yourself doing what your mentors might do?

Now, silently, to yourself, give a word or set of words to whatever you feel is missing. Name whatever else you'd like to have. I'm sure your 'critic' can be pretty verbose if he wants to.

But once you have those words, move your eyes over to your left, so that they are down and left. Add them into your outcome statement. Say to yourself, "If I could already convince people that they had self-worth, *including myself*, easily, effectively, and creatively, so that I could really feel it, and..." and then just fill in anything else that your critic thinks is missing. Then ask, "What would that look like?"

Put your eyes up and right and get the image of yourself doing it. Then step into it. Move your eyes down and right and get the feeling of doing what you saw in the picture.

Once again, compare that feeling when you step into it with the feeling you've had when you've been successful. Are they exactly the same? Ask your critic, "Is anything else missing or needed in this picture?"

**J**: I think I can do it. Now the feeling is there.

**RBD**: Okay, so now the feeling is there. Now you think you can do it. What I'd like you to do is look back down and to your left, and say to yourself, "If I could already convince people that they were worthwhile, had self-worth, had the feeling for it, and be convinced that I could do it, that I could really 'Go for it!', what would that look like?"

**J**: (Moves eyes down left, then up right, then down right. Smiles broadly.)

**RBD**: Okay, let's check where we've got with this strategy. You had a goal, which was, "I wish I could convince people that they have self-worth." This was something you experienced as being difficult. You felt somewhat stuck and inflexible, especially with certain people, including yourself. Now, my question is: "Do you feel like you could do that right now?"

**J**: I have a map for it, yes.

**RBD**: Thank you.

**J**: Thank you!

**RBD**: A while ago, I read about a study that was with people who had survived airline accidents. Someone had interviewed a number of people who had been involved in serious plane crashes but had survived, often unhurt. They were asked how they had managed to get free of the wreckage, with so much chaos going on, while many of their fellow passengers did not. It is an interesting question, especially in the frame of what we've been discussing about creativity and the realist, because escaping an airline wreck is not something you get much chance to practice. How do you prepare yourself to do something you've never done before?

The most common answer to this question that the survivors gave was that they had run a kind of mental 'dress rehearsal' over and over in their minds. They would visualize the sequence of undoing their safety belts, moving out of their seat, running down the aisle to the nearest exit, jumping down the slide, etc. They would repeat this imaging over and over, feeling themselves doing what they saw in their picture, until it seemed that they had already done this activity many times before. Then, after the accident, when there was total havoc, they did not need to waste any time or conscious awareness thinking about what to do. The program was already in place. I remember one of these people saying that after the crash, he found himself going out the exit and suddenly realized he could hear the person who had been sitting next to him screaming that he couldn't get his seat belt off.

The goal of the New Behavior Generator is to invoke the realist by using language to prompt imaginary scenarios and bringing them to concrete actions by connecting the imagery to the kinesthetic representational system. The strategy is based on several key beliefs:

A.  People learn new behaviors by creating new mental maps in their brains.

B.  The more complete you make your mental maps, the more likely you will be to achieve the new behavior you want.

C.  Focussing on your goal is the quickest way to achieve new behaviors.

D.  People already have the inner resources they need to achieve new behaviors. Success is a function of accessing and organizing what is already there.

The New Behavior Generator is a how-to process that both expresses and supports these beliefs. I would like to go over the steps of the strategy because there were very specific and important steps that might require explanation. The strategy involves going through a set of representational systems and accessing cues that essentially follow the steps listed below:

1. Ask yourself, "If I could *already* achieve my new goal, what would I look like?"
   *(Put your eyes down and to the left.)*

2. Picture yourself achieving your goal.
   *(Look up and to the right.)*

3. To help you visualize:

   a. Remember a similar successful achievement.

   b. Model someone else.

   c. Picture yourself first achieving a smaller part of the goal.
      *(Move your eyes up and to the left or right.)*

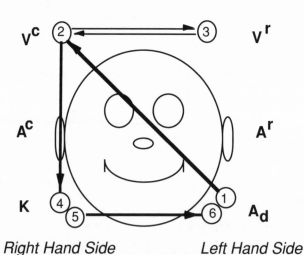

*Right Hand Side*          *Left Hand Side*

**Figure 4.17. Sequence of Eye Movements for
New Behavior Generator Strategy.**

4. Step into the picture so you feel yourself doing what you pictured.
   *(Put your eyes and head down and to the right.)*

5. Compare these feelings to feelings from a similar past success.

   *(Keep your eyes and head turned down and to the right.)*

6. If the feelings are not the same, name what you need and add it to your goal. Go back to **step 1** and repeat the process with your expanded goal.
   *(Move your eyes and head down and to the left.)*

Before you actually start going through this feedback loop, the first step is to define an outcome and establish some sensory-based evidence. How would you know that you could accomplish the goal in that situation or with that person? What would be there? What would you see, hear, or feel? By the way, while this didn't come up as an issue in the demonstration, an outcome should be stated in terms of what you actually want, instead of what you want to avoid or discard.

Then we need a reference experience for the realist. Have you done it before? Have you accomplished this goal or something like it before? What did that feel like? Specify that feeling of success. The actual feeling is what we want to make use of.

This is sort of a preparation stage. You are setting up the 'Test' part of your T.O.T.E. Specifically:

A.  Choose an outcome that you would like to achieve with this strategy. This goal should be something that you yourself will be doing. Fill in the following sentence: "I want to...*statement of goal*." (Ad)

B.  Go back over your statement of your goal and look or listen for words indicating negation or avoidance (i.e., not, stop, avoid, quit, etc.). If you find that you have stated your goal as something you want to not do or to avoid, ask yourself, "What would I be doing instead?" And restate your goal in the positive. (Ad)

For example, if you said, "I want to stop criticizing myself so much," ask yourself, "If I were already
able to stop criticizing myself so much, what would
I want to be doing instead?"

C.   Define how you will know when you reach your goal
by remembering something as similar as you can to
your goal that you can already do competently and
easily. Pay particular attention to the feelings you
have had as you achieve this other goal. Really get
in touch with that feeling and note exactly where it
is and what it feels like so that you can remember it
easily. (Kr)

The operational part of the strategy starts out with a set of
words. You state your goal to yourself in the form of what is
called the "As If" frame in NLP. Lowell claimed that he
thought half in language and half in pictures. The language
is important in that it provides a focus for the imagery and, as
Lowell pointed out, it can be used to represent things that are
not initially easy to visualize. With the "As If" frame you don't
say to yourself, "Why can't I do this," or "Gee, this is a problem." Instead, you say, "If I could already do it, what would I
look like?" You connect the "As If" statement relating to your
outcome to your visual imagination. You say, "If I could already 'X'—which is your goal—what would that look like?"
That is the question. And you begin with your eye position
down and to the left to facilitate your ability to really hear and
record that outcome statement in your brain.

The second step is to look up and to make a constructed
picture of yourself being successful by looking up and to the
right. You might see it on an imaginary television screen in
your mind's eye as Lowell did.

Notice that J.'s initial comment was that he wasn't very
good at making pictures. He said he didn't have any skills for
doing that. So we went through a couple of ways of helping

him to get the picture. If the person you're working with has some difficulty getting to this stage, there are three possible approaches to take. These are like the knobs in Lowell's strategy.

The first is to chunk it down. Break it into smaller pieces. Start with a piece of the scene rather than the whole movie. Walt Disney developed a technique called 'storyboarding' as a skill for developing his films. A storyboard is essentially a series of single images representing key scenes in the movie. This is one method of chunking down. You could try visualizing just the first step of the interaction instead of the whole interaction. You could start with certain details of the image that might stand out or be easier to picture at first.

A second tactic would be to remember a similar situation as a reference experience. If the person cannot construct an image, then ask if he's ever done anything similar to what he wants to do now. What did that look like? That's a potential starting place. Try going to a memory of a similar situation.

The final approach in step two is to have him model somebody else. To do this you ask, "Do you have any role models?" "Do you know anyone else who can achieve your desired goal?" "What do they look like?" "Now, can you see yourself doing what they do?" You have them get an image of this other person being successful as if on a movie screen.

Once you've got an image, even if it's not very clear or complete, you want to step into the picture. This is what Lowell described as trying to "see a three-dimensional exploded view of the final result." You associate into the image you are visualizing, and compare the quality of feeling you get with the remembered feeling from the experience you selected as evidence. You ask, "Does the feeling I get from the imagined scene and the feeling I get from the memory feel the same?" "Do I feel as much success when I step into this new picture of something I want to do as I remember from the capability I already know I have and can remember?"

If the answer is, "No," ask yourself, "What's missing?" "What else do I need to add to my imagined scene to make it match what I already know I can do?"

On our first attempt with J., he didn't get any feeling at all. As it turns out, he had stated his outcome as being primarily directed external to him, at others. But changing the world around you also involves changing yourself in relationship to it as well. In a way the problem J. was having with this other person was the same problem he was having with himself. Very often the critic ends up criticizing the dreamer, not just the dream. What is important to keep in mind is that we got a deeper perception and understanding of the problem by "failing" on our first loop. But that is what feedback is for.

You step into the picture and compare the feeling you get from rehearsing doing what you see in that picture with the feelings you get from the successful reference experience. If the feelings don't match, you have to find out what's missing, and then add it into your mental map—widen and enrich your map of the situation.

To be an effective realist, it's important to put yourself into that image so you feel as though you are right there doing it. Then compare that feeling with the one you had when you were successful in the past. Do they match? Or, does the kinesthetic sensation you are getting from your constructed image feel not quite right? Depending on how they match, you're either done, or there is something missing.

If something is missing, you look down and to the left and name what is needed or what is missing. And then you add that to the goal statement. Remember Lowell's comments that, "If something doesn't work, change it and do it again," and, that he categorizes something that doesn't work as, "a solution to other problems that have not arisen yet."

For instance, if you feel, "Well, I can do it, but I'm uncomfortable doing it." you reformulate your goal as, "If I could do it, **and** be comfortable doing it, what would that look like?"

You simply add whatever is missing to the initial goal statement. Then you edit the constructed image of yourself, as if you were editing a movie. Then, once again, you put yourself into the picture, compare the feeling you get from imagining doing what you saw yourself doing, compare that feeling to successful reference experiences, and again name what's missing or what's needed until you get an image that fits. In the end, you'll have a clear, rich map that will feel as real to you as your own past.

This has all the components of what constitutes a complete and well-formed strategy. It has a goal, evidence and a range of choices for accomplishing the goal. We'll be doing other strategies as we go along, but in this one the goal is, "Can I get myself to have the same feeling about this as I have when I've been successful before, based on an image of something I can do." If J. can picture what to do and put himself into it, and it feels the same, he can say "I'm ready. Let's go for it!" All he needs is the person.

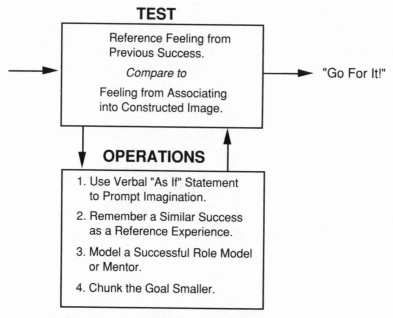

**Figure 4.18. New Behavior Generator T.O.T.E.**

To review, the operational part of the New Behavior Generator involves the following steps:

| Dreamer | Realist | Critic | | | |
|---|---|---|---|---|---|
| 1. | 2. | 4. | 5. | 6. | 7. |
| State Goal | Visualize | Does It Feel | | Name What Is | |
| In Positive | Yourself | Like I Can | | Needed Or What | |
| Form. | Achieving It. | *Really* Do It? | | Is Missing. | |

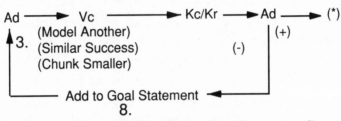

**Figure 4.19 Steps to New Behavior Generator Strategy**

1. Say to yourself, "If I was already able to...(state your goal)... what would I look like?" (Ad)

2. Construct a visual image of what you would look like if you were in the act of achieving the full goal you have just stated. You should be seeing yourself in this image from a disassociated point of view as if you were above or next to yourself looking at yourself. (Vc)

3. If you have trouble coming up with a clear image of yourself, use one of the following strategies:

    a. Chunk down your goal into smaller steps. Ask yourself, "Is there any portion of my goal that I can see myself achieving?" For instance, "Can I see myself accomplishing the first step of my stated goal?" Visualize yourself successfully achieving that smaller part of your goal. (Ad->Vc)

    b. Use an image of yourself from a similar successful situation. Ask yourself, "Is there something similar to my goal that I can already achieve?" Visualize what you do in that situation and edit or modify the image to fit your current goal. (Ad->Vr->Vc)

c. Model someone else. Ask yourself, "Who do I know that is already able to fully achieve the goal I have stated?" Visualize what this other person does to be successful. Then visualize yourself doing what you just saw your model doing. (Ad->Vr->Vc)

4. Mentally step inside of the image you created of yourself achieving your goal so that you feel as though you are doing right now what you just saw yourself doing. What would you be seeing, hearing and feeling? (Vc->Kc)

5. Compare the feelings you have as you put yourself fully into that experience with the feelings you identified earlier from a similar experience in which you are already successful. (Kc/Kr)

6. Decision Point

   a. If the two feelings match exactly so that you feel as confident that you can achieve your new goal as easily as you achieve the goal you are already successful at, then you are done.

   b. If the two feelings do not match then name what is missing or what is needed (i.e., "creativity," "more confidence," "relaxation," etc.).

7. Apply the same rule to this statement of the needed resource that you applied to your initial goal statement. That is, state it positively. For example, if your statement of what is needed is "to be less nervous," ask yourself, "If I could be less nervous, what would I be doing instead?" (Ad)

8. Refine your goal by adding the name of the needed resource that you have identified to your goal statement by simply connecting it with the word "and." For example,

the goal statement may now be something like, "I want to be more assertive with my co-workers (initial goal statement) AND keep in mind their feelings as well." Go back to step #1 and repeat the strategy. (Ad)

**Note**: You may add any number of needed resources to your goal statement so that when you are done you may have refined your goal to something like: "I want to be more assertive with my co-workers AND keep their feelings in mind as well AND maintain a sense of my own self-confidence AND remain cool if someone gets angry." As Lowell pointed out, "The whole process is a series of little steps."

When Lowell is being creative he has a picture and a set of knobs that control that picture. He fills in all the blanks, then he's ready to try it. If his strategy does not succeed, he goes back and loops through all the steps again. As Lowell said, "If it doesn't work, I adjust the knobs." All we're doing here is substituting a set of words in place of dials. Instead of turning a dial up or down, you simply add more into the goal statement; you ask yourself if you can picture it.

Often, when someone can't do something, they ask themselves, "Why can't I do it?" or "Whose fault is it that I can't do this?" or "What stops me from doing this?" and they visualize all the times that they failed before. This strategy is simply saying: "Orient toward success!" Make your words say, "If I could already do that what would it be like?" And make your picture and step into it. So you get a full, multi-sensory representation of being successful. Any questions?

**R**: It makes a lot of sense, but I don't feel that I have a full grasp of it.

**RBD**: I think the reason for that is that you have not done it yet. Engaging in the exercise gives you the kinesthetic dimension of it.

To do the exercise, pair up with a partner and lead each other through the strategy by going through the steps listed previously. State the goal. Make the picture. Step into it. If something is missing, you name it, and just go back in and add that into the statement of what you want.

For example, let's just act 'as if' R. were my partner for a moment, and his outcome just happened to be the ability to 'grasp' this process easily. I'd have him find a reference experience for getting a handle on something that he's learned. I'd ask him, "What is that feeling of grasping something like—when things fall together and you understand them on a feeling level?" That's a specific feeling that you know about, isn't it, R.?

**R**: Yes.

**RBD**: Then I would have R. look down to his left and say, "If I'd already been led through this thing and grasped it, what would I look like?" Then he'd look up and to his right and construct an image of himself grasping this strategy easily and completely. Then I'd have him step into the image that he just saw of himself, put himself into it the way he would be sitting and breathing and thinking if he had *already* grasped it, and find out how that feels.

Now, R., compare that feeling with what it feels like when you know you've grasped something before, when it's fallen together and you've understood it before. Is it the same?

**R**: I think I've grasped it.

**RBD**: I rest my case.

# Creativity in Communication

**TE**: We would like to devote some time to the exploration of creativity in communication. In particular, getting what you want and giving someone else what they need at the same time. We want to talk about being creative in a win-win situation and about what goes on inside your "mind" when that's happening.

When you are creative with material objects you can patent them or copyright them and, consequently, own them. Creative communication cannot be copyrighted or patented or owned, yet, in some ways, it is truly more valuable.

For instance, the psychologist Leo Buscaglia has some wonderful ideas about how to act as humans, and they're very creative: how to interact with each other, about inter- and intrapersonal relationships. But when these ideas come out of his mouth and they go into everybodys' ears he doesn't get a dime for them after that. When you use some of his good ideas, he doesn't get anything for that except the satisfaction of knowing that he did something that possibly made you a better person. The kind of creativity that makes communication between each other possible, that gives people new ideas, the intangibles, are important, too; not just the things you can put on discs or put in a box. All those are wonderful, but there are these other aspects to creativity that are equally as important.

My guess is that most of you readers want to learn how to communicate with yourself and other people better and more creatively. But what does that mean? What does it mean to be able to communicate with others in the world more creatively than you already do? How do you come up with a good idea for how to approach somebody so you can get what you want, and they can get what they want?

To me, anything can be negotiated if you're creative enough, and anything can be negotiated in a way that both sides win. Otherwise, it's not really a negotiation, it's an organized coup. And both sides agree that one side is going to win and one side is going to lose.

You know what happens when one side loses, don't you? They want to even the score. They want to get even with whoever won. For example, think about people that work in steel factories and in car factories. They wanted labor unions. In the beginning, people who were working for a living in industry were getting treated poorly. Then labor unions became really powerful and people were putting radios in cars and getting twenty dollars an hour for it. I knew a guy who was making forty thousand dollars a year in overtime, putting radios and hubcaps on cars. Later he was out of work. Then the unions are going: "We'll give a little of it back if we can only work." And what's management doing? Management's going, "Sure, you want to give it to us, we'll take it back, and when we're done getting it, we might even close the factory."

Now to me, that's not being real creative because what they're not seeing is what's going to happen in the future. I think one of the most creative things that people can utilize to organize their thinking in a way that makes their life and the lives of others around them easier, is the ability to go into the future and take into account all the possibilities that could happen.

We should also become aware of our own programming, how we respond to people so we are not making interpretations or judgments about someone's behavior based on our own unconscious assumptions. It works both ways.

Sometimes, when you meet someone, you feel that you've known them. There may be something about the look on their face or the sound of their voice that reminds you of someone else. You don't even know where it's coming from. Maybe it's someone you knew as a child, maybe it's an aunt or an uncle. There's something about their external behavior that makes you feel that you like them.

And then again, there are other people who match things you dislike. When you were a child and your father was angry with you he may have used his tone of voice, or pointed his finger in a certain way. As an adult you meet some guy, and he comes up to you and says, "I want to tell you something," and points his finger and uses a certain voice tone. All of the sudden, you find yourself very stressed and you can't figure out where it's coming from.

Likewise, you may sit a certain way and someone may come up to you and say, "Hey, you're brooding." But you may respond, "No, I feel fine, I'm just thinking about what I'm going to do tomorrow." And that person goes, "Whew, I thought you were mad at me."

**RBD**: I had an interesting case of this once in which a couple came to see me because of a problem in their relationship. When the guy was in business situations, he had a certain way of acting towards women that bothered his girlfriend. She would feel like he didn't care about her. He said he only acted that way toward people he didn't care about and that it was a show. But she didn't perceive it that way. And she would feel bad. In his own model of the world there was nothing to it, so he didn't think that her feelings counted. To him it didn't mean anything, and he could not understand why she didn't recognize that. The result was that he felt she was trying to force him into something and was upset about it. I said to the woman, "He obviously has strong feelings about what's going on, too." And she said, "Oh, that's not feelings. That's EGO." They were each creatively discounting the other's feelings.

In NLP there is a very important process called "pacing and leading." When you are pacing, you are trying to step into another person's shoes and experience their model of the world. In pacing you want to communicate with someone in their own language and through their own existing way of thinking. Leading involves the attempt to get another person to change, add to or enrich his or her world view or thinking process. The basic idea of pacing and leading is to incrementally introduce somebody to changes or your own world view through a balance of acknowledging and then widening their model of the world. For instance, when people are learning or being introduced to something new, it is best to start with something familiar and then move to something new.

Most people think of creativity as being primarily associated with leading. But often a great deal of flexibility is required to enter into another's world view, and a great deal of innovation can be stimulated by the process of pacing.

For example, I remember one time we were doing a sales seminar for a telemarketing group. There was one guy that no one had been able to sell. It turned out this guy talked very s...l...o...w...l...y... But he was the president of a big company that could become a real key customer. People would call him and say, "Hello, sir, I know you're a very busy man, if I could just take a minute of your time," speaking at about twice his speed.

But that isn't the way that person thinks, or listens. So we had them call the guy up and say, "Hello... (very slow)... I'm from xxx company... and I'd really like to have some time... to talk with you.... when you really have some time... to think about our products... I know it's really important for you... to take your time and think about things... Could you tell me when we could call...." and so on. Instead of saying, "I'll only take a minute." You say, "When could I call you back when you would have enough time to think about this comfortably and thoroughly?" The company president felt so comfortable with the approach that he scheduled a meeting, and the telemarketing group ended up getting the account.

One of the most important outcomes of pacing is the establishment of rapport. When people know you can think as they do and can take their world view into account, they are much less resistant to new ideas.

There are a lot of creative ways of pacing someone. In addition to matching voice tone and tempo, you can match key words such as representational system language and physical posture. One way to pace someone at a very deep level is to speak at the rate which the other person is breathing. You speak in tempo with their breathing rate.

I remember a businessman who came to an NLP seminar and stood up and said, "You say all this stuff! It's too easy. I'm in the REAL WORLD. This stuff is for seminars. I just don't feel that it will work with MY clients." So I said, "Why don't you come up and be a demonstration subject. You pretend that you're one of your difficult clients in the real world, and we'll try to get a hold of how this might put you more in touch with them."

So he came up and sat across from me and we started "role playing." The first thing I did was to subtly put myself into a similar body posture. He said, "Well, I'm a busy man. I have to see a hundred people like you every day. Most of them are full of crap and end up wasting my time. Let's hurry up and get through this." As I responded to him I began to match my speech to his breathing, and I said, "It sounds to me... like you want someone... you feel you can trust... Someone who cares.... about what you need... Think of somebody you have really trusted... in your life... and how you felt... That's the kind of relationship... I'd like to develop with you." I continued pacing his breathing, and finally after about three minutes of this he said, "You know, I was going to try to be as resistant as I could, but right now I'd buy anything from you."

**Man**: I remember hearing a famous lawyer talking about selecting jurors. He claimed there were certain people that he would never want to be jurors because they don't *hear*. He went on to say that Detroit gives the largest awards for cases, because the people there hear-in Miami, where there are Jewish people and Italian people, who are very warm, but who didn't make the same kind of decisions. Does that mean the auditory is closely connected with the judgments?

**RBD**: It is probably more of a statement about the lawyer than it is about these specific people. People who are "warm" are probably more kinesthetic, and the lawyer was probably more auditory. In a way, law is built around the auditory verbal system. What this lawyer was saying is that he likes to select people who fit with *his* way of thinking. Another, more creative approach would be to adapt your presentation to fit the audience you are addressing by utilizing *their* way of thinking.

A classic example of utilization is a story John Grinder tells about a time he had to take someone to small claims court for failing to fulfill a contract. He had to wait in the courtroom for the judge to hear his claim. And as he was sitting there, he heard the judge make a couple of decisions. He couldn't help but notice that there was a consistency to the strategy the judge was using to make his decisions. In one case, the judge said something like, "As I *look* over the facts of this case, I can *see* that this happened and that happened, and as I *look* at that I have to *ask* myself, 'How will justice be best served in this instance?' and I *feel* that I should decide in favor of..." The next case comes up and the judge said something like, "I *see* that I've had to deal with you before. If I *look* to the future, I can *see* that this might happen again and again and I have to *ask* myself, 'What is going to be the best way to keep this from continuing?' And I *feel* that I must take strong action now..."

John said to himself, "Aha! there's a pattern there." When it comes to be his turn, he says something like, "Your honor, please *look* over the facts of my case, and as you *focus* on them, let me paint you a *picture* of the events. I'm sure you can *see* that this happened, and that happened, and as you *look* at that, I know you're going to have to *ask* yourself, 'How will justice best be served in this instance?' I am certain that you'll *feel* as I do, that some recovery is due to me." And the judge said, "Very well stated. I feel that I can see what you are saying," and the decision was eventually made in John's favor.

The point is, if John had gone in and said, "Your honor, I really *feel* that I deserve to get my money back," the judge could very probably have said, "Let's not jump to conclusions. I don't see your point. I think that you're not *looking* at this carefully enough." Feelings came at the end of the judge's strategy not at the beginning.

Likewise, if John had said, "Your honor, please *look* over the facts of my case, and as you *focus* on them, I'm sure you will *feel* as I do that some recovery is due to me." The judge would have said, "Well, I don't know. Something *tells* me there are some important questions that may have been left out here." There was an important verbal step in the middle of the judge's decision strategy. The chain is no stronger than the weakest link.

By the way, remember that this process is at the level of strategy and capability, not at the level of values, beliefs or identity. John would not have been able to get the judge to act unethically against his own beliefs or values by matching the representational systems of his thinking strategy. But the judge would have had to organize the facts of the case accord-ing to his own strategy eventually anyway. With the exact same facts John could have reversed the strategy sequence and said, "Your honor, I know that you feel this way about things, and if you asked yourself this, I'm sure that this is the picture that you'll see." Mismatching that process would serve to create unnecessary delays or damage rapport.

In terms of creativity, when you are trying to sell or present an idea, you're in the same situation. You've got to repackage your ideas into different strategies.

As a way to practice recognizing different strategies you might get a kick out of looking through magazine ads. I remember reading an ad that showed someone who was saying, "I like to feel that I've seen everything. That's why I ask a lot of questions." That will appeal to a person whose strategy is to have a feeling that they've considered all the possible options. I've seen others that say, "I'm the kind of person who knows what I want as soon as I see it." In other words, different people are going to have different strategies for learning, decision making, etc., as they do with creativity.

A very important aspect of creative communication is the ability to wipe clean any preconceptions about a certain issue in order to understand another person. Just because other people think differently doesn't mean they are bad. In fact, a strategy we teach in negotiations is to point out the differences between yourself and the other party. The wife may say, "He doesn't love me because he never touches me in public. I feel he doesn't want to be with me." The husband may say, "I can't think when she's touching me and I've got to be clear about what I am saying to this person." So we point out that he tends to make pictures and when she touches him it interrupts his pictures. And then she says, "Oh, you mean he does this because he's visual and not because he hates me."

And this makes a big difference. The fact that he has a different map does not mean that he doesn't love her. These kinds of realizations can bring about profound changes in people. Some people aren't aware of ever making visual images and some people can't imagine doing anything without visual images.

In general, if you are communicating something to a group of people you want to take a multi-sensory approach. If you are teaching or training you might ask yourself, "How do I demonstrate this visually? How do I demonstrate it so the people get a feel for it? How do I demonstrate this so they hear it?" People learn in different ways and it is important to cover all the bases.

Incidentally, no matter what you do, someone will invariably come up to you and say, "People learn best by seeing demonstrations. People learn by watching. Can you do more demonstrations?" Then someone else will come up and say, "I get confused by demonstrations. People learn by doing. Can we do more exercises?" And, of course someone else will say, "People learn best by listening and discussing. I can always practice on my own. Could you talk some more about your thoughts and experiences?" People have different strategies. Therefore, it's always good to do a bit of talking, a bit of demonstrating, and a few exercises in order to appeal to everybody.

One of the key goals of NLP is to get people to recognize and respect other people's models of the world. If you can do this, you can benefit from diversity-otherwise you will fear it and fight it. Then you will use your creativity in a way that maintains problems instead of solving them.

We have mentioned before that one of the key NLP skills in creative communication is the ability to observe and 'calibrate' the responses of the other person. NLP defines a number of important clues and cues to pay attention to in order to be more aware of and responsive to someone else's model of the world.

The kinds of behavioral cues you get and the kinds of cues you use when you are interacting with people will often depend on the context and the kind of information you're gathering from a person. If you are in good rapport with someone and you are asking about something he is very involved in, his eyes might move around all over the place. When answering questions it is common for an individual to orient his body toward the person to whom he is talking, but to shift his eyes around. However, when he is looking for a response from the questioner as opposed to answering a question, he will look intently at the other person.

For instance, if I'm talking to you and I want to be sure you understand what I am saying, the question is: Am I responding to what I see you doing in front of me or to an image that I see in my mind's eye of what I am trying to get you to understand? Am I telling this person something and waiting until I get all my words out before I look to see if they've followed me, or am I trying to adjust my words based on the ongoing responses I'm getting from that person as I am speaking?

Depending on what my goal is, I might want to be watching you very carefully to see what responses I'm getting. If I were communicating to you and I was really trying to get an idea across to you so it fit into your particular model of the world, I would watch every minute detail that I could see. I would watch for a shift in your breathing or a head nod, and so on. That is a different goal than trying to use you as a "sounding board" for my ideas. When you are communicating with somebody, you have to take into account that there will be different goals and thus different sources for the accessing cues you are observing.

**TE**: There are also cultural conventions related to things like eye contact. Breaking eye contact will make some people more comfortable then having constant eye contact with them even though you are very interested in their responses. Some people don't want to be looked at that closely. They may prefer that you, every once in a while, look away and not look at them.

**RBD**: I know a guy who was born in Scandinavia and moved to inner-city Chicago with his family when he was a child. He had a lot of trouble when he went to school. When people would talk to him, he'd look them straight in the eye trying to be polite and they would get mad at him. They kept beating him up and he didn't know why. He finally stopped looking them in the eye and they stopped beating him up. In that particular sub-culture, that was a way of provoking a fight.

The way somebody pays attention often depends on whether he is visual, auditory, or kinesthetic. A more auditorily oriented person may give you full attention by having his head cocked the side. He isn't looking at you at all. That's one of the interesting things about how accessing cues relate to communication. Some people might say, "Gee, he's not paying attention to me because he's not looking at me." But if the person you are talking to communicates auditorily, they might actually turn their ear toward you without looking at you when they are listening to you. A kinesthetic person might need to be moving around a lot to communicate. They might not be able to listen or talk effectively unless they are moving their hands.

**TE**: They are the kind of people whom you tell to sit on their hands and talk, and they have nothing to say. In NLP you adjust your communication with someone through the process of "calibration." You might watch the person's eye movements to determine whether they primarily access auditory, kinesthetic or visual eye positions. Then you can adjust your mode of communication to fit the way in which it will make the most sense to that person. You try to adjust your communication to the listener. Rather than try to communicate in a way that would make sense to you, you have to find out how things make sense to someone else. Otherwise, you're the only person who can understand what you're saying.

**RBD**: It's like the salesman who ends up selling something to himself. He says, "Can't you see this feature?" And the other person says, "It just doesn't feel comfortable." So the customer keeps wanting to get a feeling from it, and the salesman keeps saying, "look at this" and "look at that." Or he'll say, "So many people have said good things about it," and he'll tell the customer all the things he's heard about the product. And the customer still isn't going to change his feeling. The idea is to communicate through the strategy in which the other person is thinking.

# 5

---

# The Critic

**RBD**: Once you do come up with something creative, the next problem is how to proceed with it. Where do you go from there? Is it a good idea? Can you protect it? How will society perceive it? How do you make it financially successful? This is the domain of the 'Critic'. The 'Critic' is not just a destructive function. In fact, if you can get the critic on your side, you could be unstoppable. When your own worst critic says, "Go for it!" you know you are on to something.

We are all familiar with the negative side of the critic. The critic can block, negate, attack, interfere, resist, etc., if it is turned against you. But if the critic accepts your ideas, it can turn all of those problematic processes in a different direction and protect, support and encourage you. The 'dreamer' and the 'realist' don't provide these functions.

The basic function of the critic is to evaluate the expression of an idea. The critic represents and provides the general filters and positive or negative reinforcements for the products of creativity. As I said earlier, the critic has to do with the general fit of the expression of an idea into a larger system. One of the goals of the critic stage is to get an evaluation of your product from as many different perspectives as possible.

The critic T.O.T.E. revolves around the feedback loop of incorporating or rejecting the responses of others to the final product. It is especially important at the critic stage in the creative cycle, to perceive the responses of others as feedback, not failure. As I point out in the *Strategies of Genius* book:

> I think that everybody already has the dreamer, realist, critic in them. Unfortunately, what usually happens is that the dreamer and the critic get into a fight. If you take a typical business meeting, you can have a dreamer, a realist and a critic in this meeting. Rather than functioning in some organized strategy, the dreamer says something, the critic argues against it, then the dreamer has a polarity reaction to the critic. The realist says, "What about this?" And you get this mass of chaos as opposed to saying, "How can we structure this so that these strategies support each other?"
>
> One of the biggest problems is that the critic doesn't just criticize the dream. The critic criticizes the dreamer, "You made a stupid idea!" Part of the key, part of why Disney could function so well is: he didn't criticize his team or himself, he criticized the plan to accomplish the dream. I think that what keeps the critic and the dreamer from being a polarity response is the realist.

One of the ways to avoid conflicts between the dreamer, realist and critic is through the recognition, acknowledgement and organization of the three different functions. Disney was very systematic in implementing the various stages of the creative cycle. He was very clear about what stage a particular animated film, movie, or project was in, and had specific strategies he used in each stage.

For example, at the critic stage, one of his specific evaluation procedures was the multi-sensory check. There is an interesting example of it that arose when he was developing the *Pirates of the Caribbean* ride at one of his amusement parks. It was supposed to be a New Orleans-type atmosphere, but when he went in and experienced it, it just didn't seem right to him. He gathered a group of people around him. He got the guy who was sweeping the floor and one of the waitresses and somebody else that happened to be in the vicinity. He pulled all these people around the table and he said, "Look, there's something that isn't right here. Does it sound like New Orleans?" They had taken great pains to have authentic music and background noises recorded for the display. "Does it feel like New Orleans?" They had a special system installed to control the humidity and the temperature. "Does it smell like New Orleans?" They had Creole cooking smells and fans in strategic locations to make sure the smells were spread all around. "Does it look like New Orleans?" They had modeled the buildings, complete with wrought iron fences, after the French Quarter in New Orleans and dressed the characters in authentic period costumes.

The guy who was sweeping the floor had lived in Louisiana for a while. Finally he piped up and said, "One thing that would make it look more like New Orleans to me is lightning bugs. I can't imagine a hot summer night without lightning bugs." Disney said, "That's it!" The young fellow got a bonus and Disney had his staff put in 1200 live lightning bugs until they could find a way to simulate them.

Disney encouraged and utilized everyone's perspective. His commitment to quality was reflected in the systematic precision he employed to implement and evaluate his creative products. To avoid confusion and conflict, he even sorted different activities into different physical locations. He had a story room for the dreamer. The story room had walls covered with pictures, storyboards to stimulate ideas. In the realist stage, his animators had their own offices, complete with all the tools they would need to bring the dreams to life. For the critic stage, everyone worked in a small cramped screening room underneath the stairs that his animators nicknamed the "sweatbox."

# Integrating Multiple Perspectives

The following steps outline the general evaluation strategy that I have implemented at the critic stage with numerous project teams.

1. *Determine the specific goals and criteria for the product.*

    For each piece decide what specific response you want it to elicit in the user. For example, do you want the user to think that they are doing something simple, important, fun, etc.? Do you want the user to feel comfortable?

    a. To do this you will want to keep in mind WHO the product is for: a first time user? an experienced user?

    b. When designing your product it is useful to have the input of a number of various groups including: design staff, technicians, marketers and users.

2. *Contrast different people's responses to the idea.*

    Find out what different groups of people see, hear or feel in response to the product. Contrast the response of the people who experienced what you wanted them to experience with the ones who didn't. Find out what the ones who didn't respond appropriately would need to have added, changed or deleted in order to get the desired response (as opposed to what they thought was wrong with it).

Do not critique or evaluate any particular suggestion at this phase. You do not want to stifle or offend anyone. This is important because:

a. People that have been involved in the project and have a lot invested may feel unappreciated and that the evaluators are "picky."

b. Unacquainted evaluators may feel "stupid" or intimidated or that they are not being heard.

3. *Filter the suggestions.*

Figure out if those features can be reasonably added into the expression of the idea given the physical constraints, time limits and goals of the project. Consider each possibility—you may be surprised at how many things may be easily worked in even though they seem difficult at first.

**RWD**: Getting a number of different perspectives is very important to the success of an idea. If you take any successful product—if you look around and you find an invention that is being successfully marketed—I think that the basic invention accounts for perhaps twenty-five percent of the success of the product. There's another twenty-five percent in manufacturing and good design. That is, being able to make the product for the marketplace at a price that is low enough that people can pay for it and high enough that you get good quality.

I think there's another twenty-five percent in marketing. I don't think it's necessarily true that if you build a better mousetrap the world is going to beat a path to your door, because first the world's got to know that you've done it. You've got to let the world know that you've got the better mousetrap or they're not going to beat a path to your door. If you come up with the better mousetrap, or a pet rock, or a Jaqui antenna, and wait for people to beat a path to your door, it might be too late to take advantage of it. The original patent on the Jaqui antenna expired before the FM and television grew to the proportions that they are today. And every antenna that you see on the top of a roof probably infringes the claims of that patent that expired years ago. You've got to get the knowledge out that you have the patent, that is, that you have this product.

A final twenty-five percent is probably in money management—the financial management of the idea. To the extent that an inventor or a team can supply the ideas, the manufacturing capabilities, marketing capabilities and the financial management, they have a good shot at making an idea successful. If you are planning to go out and find money to support an invention, keep in mind that investors do not like to invest in a single idea or a single person. In the creativity seminars we have conducted, it always impresses me that people will often spontaneously and unconsciously form groups of four, and that is typical of what investors like to see, because it indicates that these four areas will be taken care of. It is also typical of project teams that form inside of organizations. In order to effectively develop a new product within a company you minimally need a team composed of people from engineering, production, marketing and finance.

You could get investment backing for a single idea if you have a good business plan and the right team of people. The team usually involves a person who is the driving force—the inventor, the dedicated advocate, the mind behind the idea. But it must also include the rest of the organization, including manufacturing, marketing, and money management. Then you can usually find investment money to support the overall operation, even with one idea.

It's even better if that group has a number of ideas or a number of variations of the same idea already in mind. You are more likely to get support for it. But it's very difficult to get support for a single idea. It's a little bit like the person I talked to once who said he used to sell toothbrushes. He'd go around to different stores and try to sell toothbrushes to druggists.

The problem was, he'd walk into a drug store and say, "Do you want any toothbrushes?" If they said, "No," he had to find another drug store, which might be several blocks down the street. He wasn't making a living until he added Lifesavers, safety pins, and three or four other products. Then, when he walked into the drug store and asked, "Do you want any toothbrushes?" and they said "No," he'd ask, "Well, how about some safety pins or Lifesavers?" He had enough different products that he was selling that there was a good chance that he wouldn't waste a visit.

Inventions are a little bit the same way. Trying to market a single invention is very hard. If you're fortunate enough to have quite a number of different inventions, then every time you talk to someone, if they're not interested in one, they might be interested in another or in putting together a group of them to develop several of the ideas together.

## Packaging to Others

**RBD**: A lot of creativity has to do with how you frame something. Like the "pet rock" phenomenon. How do you take a bunch of rocks and and make a million dollars selling them to people? That's not a function of the content, but of how it's framed. It's the frame that you put around something that gives it meaning.

This also relates to how you are going to market your idea or invention to somebody. It is one thing to generate an innovation. But when you start to say, "How am I going to sell this to somebody?" "Why would someone else be interested in this?" "How am I going to explain its value to someone?," it starts to shift and refine your perception of your idea.

So one of the last steps in the total creative process is the framing, the packaging, the marketing of your idea or product. You may think your idea is great, but how are you going to get other people to see the same thing? A lot of times that doesn't happen so easily.

There's something in the computer business called the "five-year overnight sensation," meaning the product or idea has been around five years before finally somebody recognizes its value, so it becomes an overnight sensation.

**RWD**: Sometimes something that won't appeal to people on its own will be appealing when combined with something else. For instance, this man who was trying to sell toothbrushes had a friend who was also trying to sell toothbrushes. He'd go to the airport and wait for a plane to come in. As people would get off the plane he'd offer to sell them toothbrushes to freshen up their mouths after a long journey. He wasn't selling very many. One day he got the bright idea to have a friend stand up at the front of the line of people leaving the plane and hand each one of them a free piece of candy as they got off the plane. Many of the people absentmindedly took the candy, opened it and, as they walked along, they would eat it. When they got out of the arrival area, there'd be the toothbrush salesman and he'd say, "Want to buy a toothbrush? You probably need one if you've been eating candy." His sales went up tremendously.

**RBD**: Having the idea is one thing, protecting it is another, and getting other people to recognize it is still another. After innovation and invention comes evaluation. After you come up with an expression of an idea, how do you introduce it to the rest of the world? And how does the response of others affect your creativity?

## Filters and Reinforcements

Again, one of the goals of the critic phase is to determine how something will fit into a larger context or system.

On a micro level—at the level of the individual—filters and reinforcements are developed and promoted through personal coaching. The coaching process involves the application of the R.O.L.E. Model tools of physiology and representational systems in the form of mental strategies. We have explored several coaching processes in the form of the utilization exercises and New Behavior Generator Strategy.

On a macro level—the level of social and organizational systems—filters and reinforcements are developed and promoted through environmental and contextual constraints and feedback. In a company this is done administratively. While on a micro level, reinforcement might come in the form of personal satisfaction; on a macro level, reinforcement might come in the form of things like receiving public credit, money, or in some cases avoiding criticism or punishment.

## Social Filters

Macro level filters and reinforcements are generally manifested through the values and belief systems of the social or organizational culture.

For instance, in the U.S., creative spelling is not reinforced the way it was in England in William Shakespeare's time. When Shakespeare's father registered his land, he spelled his name six different ways. Because names had many different spellings, you wanted to be sure you covered all the bases. The people who invented the English language did not initially care about consistent phonetic spelling. We are stuck with their results. That is probably why Shakespeare is spelled with so many extra letters that are not pronounced.

The point is that different social and organizational cultures foster and promote different values and beliefs, and thus different processes of creativity.

Through the 1970's and 80's there was a significant difference in the kinds of filters promoted in the United States and in Japan. The Japanese tended to lack creativity on one level, but they were highly inventive. Rather than concentrating on large scale innovation, they would take something that already existed and make it better through a process of continual and incremental improvement. Americans have tended to value "quantum leaps" and "breakthroughs" more than incremental improvements. Americans also tend to have more identity invested into inventions and ideas. A U.S. company will look at a competitor's computer program and say, "Well, it was not invented here. It's got to be invented by our staff. It's got to be our product." But the Japanese don't care. They'll take a product from anywhere. The two countries emphasize different filters and reinforcements in the process of invention.

**RWD**: I read an article some years ago about the Russian patent system. They did not really have a patent system. What you did was apply for a hero badge. Essentially, that's what you got, an author's certificate. If you made an invention and you were a Russian citizen, you would apply for an author's certificate. It certifies that you're the inventor. And that's fine. What inventors and creative people often want is recognition. If you have created something, you want people to know it. Recognition is important. However, this article I read on the Russian patent system pointed out that in Russia, the people conducting research and development don't care about infringing on the rights of others.

One scientist said, "I like research and development, that's why I am doing it. I also like crossword puzzles. I could care less how many times a particular crossword puzzle has been solved by someone else. The question is: 'Can *I* solve it?' I don't care if the autoworks up in Siberia has been spending millions of dollars a year working on this problem. I want to work on this problem because I like it. And I don't care what they are doing." They're conducting their research because they're doing something they like to do and there is no reason for them to care whether or not the same research has been conducted by someone else. They have no reason to look in the books for the prior-issued patents to see whether someone else has done the same thing. The question is: Are they doing something that they enjoy doing? Is it something that they want to do?

The U.S. system is different than their system because of its private enterprise feature. Nobody in the United States is going to spend a lot of money conducting research on something somebody else has already patented. At the patent office in Washington, there's a sign with a quotation attributed to Lincoln which says, "The patent law added the fuel of interest to the fire of creativity." The patent laws create a profit incentive. The private enterprise feature provides for a monetary reward not only to the inventor, but to the company that's going to back the inventor.

The patent system itself is even more important. Its two most significant aspects are: 1) the encouragement it gives the inventor to disclose his idea in return for a monopoly rather than keep it secret, and 2) the encouragement it gives industry to support the inventor and to invest in the inventor.

Beginning in about 1950, just after the Second World War, the U.S. government began supporting a great amount of research and development. The Department of Defense, the National Aeronautics and Space Agency, and the Atomic Energy Commission all spent millions of dollars on research and development contracts. Out of those contracts came many inventions that were owned by the government.

Originally, the inventions deriving from those contracts were not owned by the government, they were simply licensed to the government. The government had a royalty-free license for any invention made under government contract. But there were a number of senators who said, "Oh no. If the American public pays for this research and development, they should own the results of it; the government should own the patents." So Congress passed laws providing that if the government spends money on atomic energy the results of the research should be owned by the government.

The trouble is that a patent that's owned by the government is owned by the people and something that is owned by everybody is owned by nobody. There was a great deal of research and development work done which resulted in patentable inventions owned by the government. For example, in the chemical field, a certain medicinal drug was developed and patented, but none of the chemical companies would touch it because it would take millions of dollars to get it on the market.

None of the companies were willing to invest that kind of money into the drug if they would not have a chance to recover that investment. As a result, those patents were never exploited. In order to overcome this problem, the government said to the drug companies, "If one of you will take control of this drug and make the investment necessary to develop it for marketing, we'll give you an exclusive license." The idea sounded good, but when it came right down to it, nobody really believed that the government would do anything to enforce that exclusive license once it was granted. If another unlicensed company began to market the same drug, nobody believed the government would sue to enjoin the company, or make it pay damages.

As a result, the government has steered away from giving exclusive licenses. They are no longer supporting nearly as much R & D as they have in the past. Instead, they're giving a tax reduction to R & D partnerships as an incentive for people to conduct R & D. We depend very heavily on R & D to keep ourselves ahead of the rest of the world, to keep ourselves in a strong economic position. If a considerable effort is not made to support and encourage creativity in this country, we may drop behind very quickly.

Look around the USA at some of the big companies. RCA is an example. I left RCA and came out to the West Coast a number of years ago. At that time, RCA believed in gridded tubes, the old kind of electron tubes that had grids in them. I was interested in velocity modulation, which Varian Kleistron had developed and which the Eimac company was building. At about the same time, I remember hearing that somebody at Bell Telephone Labs had come up with something that was supposed to do the same things that tubes did. They called them "transistors." But that was something that was foreign to us. It did not fit into RCA's scheme of things at the time. And it certainly was directly contrary to everything that Varian and Eimac were doing.

This is another example of success standing in the way of creativity. The successful and established company which is selling a product and making money on it is not very interested in the new products. The company ceases to be creative because it was too successful in the line that they were working in. We see that occur in the USA on a corporate basis. We can also see it in the world on a country to country basis. When a country stops being creative and stops striving to stay ahead and wants to continue to live on what they've done in the past, look out. They may be on their way down.

**RBD**: The culture of an organization determines what kind of values are emphasized and creates a context that promotes certain kinds of activity and not others. Values determine what kind of results get reinforced. An organization that values financial success over innovativeness or quality will attract certain kinds of people and encourage certain kinds of creativity. Another aspect of organizational influence on creativity has to do with the source of feedback. In other words, who decides what is accepted and reinforced or not? Does the evaluation come from peers, administration, customers or the general public?

**RWD**: One example of different kinds of cultural and organizational filters and reinforcements is the difference between the kind of creativity fostered in industry versus the university.

I was very fortunate to get a chance to talk to a man named Terman who wrote the basic book on electronics. He was a professor at Stanford, and he happened to have worked with Russell Varian at the time that Varian invented the Kleistron, and started Varian Associates. That was why I was talking to him. I said to him, "You know, we in the industry envy the people at the universities because they do all the really basic research. They're doing the important things. We're merely inventing the gadgets, taking the basic inventions and turning them into something that can be sold to the public." And he said, "Well, we feel just the other way around. Sure, we're studying the stars and the nebulae out there, but nothing that ever touches anybody's life. We're working on things that are so far out there. We all envy the R & D groups in industry where you're inventing the thing that's actually going to go into somebody's house, or somebody's actually going to use it to produce some desirable result."

I don't know which one is the most creative, the university or the industry. Is broad innovation more creative than inventing the specific pieces that make that broad innovation a success?

There's an old saying that "Necessity is the mother of invention." You have to be under pressure and stress, something to force you to make inventions. Maybe in industry there is a greater urgency, a greater pressure to make inventions. But there is a counter argument that nobody invents self-consciously, that if you are put under too much pressure, if there's too much stress, too much of a day to day need to get ahead, then you're not as creative. Therefore, under this argument, the university is the most likely place for creativity. In my own opinion, the catalyst to creativity and to invention is other people with similar abilities, enthusiasm and interest.

If you take a person who is creative and who has ability, and rub him against another person who has ability, you get the exchange of information and enthusiasm about an invention. If you are really trying to force invention, the most important thing to do is to get people together on the basis of a common interest and a common desire to do something new and different. I think you'll quite often be amazed at what goes on.

That may be one of the reasons why there's such a movement of people between companies in Silicon Valley. Every time you go to a company there you don't know who you're going to see. It may be the person you visited last week at another company, who has since changed jobs. Constant turmoil and constant interaction between the people will result in a great deal of creativity.

People invent when they are not self-conscious and when they are exposed to stimulus from other people. People invent when they are optimistic. When I worked at the electronics company Eimac, I knew the two people who ran the company: Bill Eitel and Jack McCullough. They were interesting people, and I have never run into anyone quite like them. Eitel was president and McCullough was vice-president and secretary/treasurer. Their positions gave them equal power. They shared one office and had two desks that faced each other. If you went in to talk to one of them, you talked to both of them. Later on, after the company had grown considerably and a new building was built, they still shared one big office, big enough for two desks. Bill was always the friendly outgoing guy. If you walked into the office, you would think Bill ran the company. Not only that, he was really enthusiastic about your ideas. Jack would sit there very quietly and Bill would lead you on and encourage you to expand on your ideas until, if you were foolish enough to press your advantage and become overly enthusiastic, Jack would ask a question that would cut you off right at the bootstraps. You would think you were doing well, you got Bill to agree that you should hire one man, and he would say, "Oh, I think that's a great idea. We really need to get more patents

234 TOOLS FOR DREAMERS

cranked out, I think we ought to hire a man." "Well, what about two? What about three?" Pretty soon Jack says, "Wait a minute. Do you think you can really support that many people?"

Bill and Jack were joint inventors and there were a lot of joint inventions that they made. Russell and Sigurt Varian made a lot of joint inventions, as did Hanson and Varian. With joint inventors, you will often find that there is one of the two who is the idea guy, the dreamer, the one that has an idea a minute and some of them are good. The second person, the critic, is the one who tells the first one which ideas are good. He is the one who has the ability to filter, to apply his background and knowledge to it. It is not possible to come up with new ideas and to be critical at the same time.

**RBD**: The difference between Activision and Atari in the early 1980's provides another good contrast between organizational influences on creativity. This was at the height of the video game craze and Atari had been one of those big Silicon Valley successes. They were bought by Warner Brothers, a giant communications corporation. Like so many other Silicon Valley companies, Atari went from being a relatively small organization of motivated and creative entrepreneurs to a large company under traditional management practices. They shifted from being a dreamer-oriented organization to a realist-oriented one. They started trying to cut costs and moved their production facilities to Taiwan. They implemented a dress code, requiring people to wear shoes, etc. That is, their organizational culture was no longer congruent with the entrepreneurial spirit that had initially brought the company its success.

Xerox ran into a similar kind of problem at their Palo Alto Research Center. They had some of the most innovative future thinking minds collected there in the late seventies and early eighties. Then they decided to get serious about what they were developing. They made people shave their beards and punch time clocks and stuff like that. Many people jumped ship, took what they had been working on at Xerox and developed the Macintosh for Apple.

Many people left Atari and went to work for Activision. Activision's culture was to treat their designers like prima donnas. The company paid them a six figure salary even if they did not come up with a program for that year. When the designers came up with video games, the only feedback they received was given by other designers. No feedback was given by management or marketing. When a designer finished a program, they gave it to marketing who had to figure out how to sell it. Marketing had to be as creative as they were. Instead of having marketing tell the designers, "This is what sells. You guys write something that sells this way," they had to both be creative.

In Activision's first year, they had fifty people and they made fifty million dollars. A million dollars per person is a much better average than they had at Atari. Atari had a different attitude and a much different reinforcement for creativity.

Of course, while Activision's strategy might work great in the short term for four or five inspired designers, it runs into some obvious difficulties in the long term. Their success led them right into the same dilemma that had caused problems at Atari. As more designers were brought into the company, they were flooded with "an idea a minute—and some of them were good." In other words, they had to implement more filters on the games that they were choosing to spends thousands of dollars to on promote. Naturally, they initially gravitated toward the standard approach—emphasizing the new games that were most like what had previously sold or were currently selling well were marketed. The primary filter was monetary feedback from the marketplace. And, while this is a naturally effective initially, it runs right into all of the issues we've been discussing about success leading to problems. What has sold well yesterday and what sells well today may not be what will sell well tomorrow. The problem with this strategy is that it might prevent you from innovating something that will be tomorrow's success—even though today's market and technology are not prepared for it. And this was happening at Activision. They were beginning to lose ground to other smaller and more innovative software companies.

The solution that John Grinder and I suggested was that they implement two kinds of incentive strategies; one based on marketability and one based on innovation. We suggested that they give a quarterly bonus to those designers who had produced the most marketable game, and also a bonus for the most innovative game concept. The marketability bonus would be determined by the marketing managers. The innovativeness bonus would be voted on by their peers, other designers. This would provide a dual reinforcement system.

In a way, since creative people will push to be creative whether you reward them or not, this is not really a "reinforcement" in my opinion. Rather it is a kind of "meta message" from the organization about their values. It was really intended more as an evidence procedure about the larger T.O.T.E. or identity of the company than a reward. It also created more explicit feedback loops between the marketing and engineering people and between the designers themselves.

Another example of cultural change is Apple. John Sculley gives a good description in his book *Odyssey*. Before Sculley came to Apple it had a culture that emphasized revolutionary, renegade approaches. Steve Jobs epitomized the desire to have a very high innovation rate and come up with something completely new and different every year. As the company grew, however, and the market expanded and changed, they couldn't keep it up. Sculley implemented an incremental innovation approach, and rather than trying to develop new computers each year, established a strategy of constantly improving their existing product line as different versions. Jobs was a technological entrepreneur. Sculley was a marketing manager. Their values and filters were different and created different kinds of environments for creativity.

Our next interview illustrates a number of important points about managing some of the issues relating to social and organizational culture. Bjorn Rorholt is a famous Norwegian scientist and inventor who is very familiar with social and organizational filters and handling the critic.

# Interview with Bjorn Rorholt
# Oslo, Norway 1987

**RBD**: What I would like to do is find out a bit about how you think, and primarily about what is unique about your way of thinking. As a scientist and inventor you have been able to find innovative ways around problems that other people were unable to solve. We'd like to find out if there are any principles or structures to what has made you special.

If you could think of three different problems that you have solved that involved creative or innovative thinking and tell us about them, I think we'd have a good starting point in our exploration.

**Bjorn**: Yes, I could take a problem which did occupy me for a while during the war, concerning cryptography. I picked up knowledge about technology that could be applied to solving this problem but I didn't realize it at the time. One day, I met a man at a military mess hall who told me that he was bothered because he couldn't solve this cryptographic problem. We continued to talk about that over coffee, and all the time I was thinking that here is something—some connection, and all of a sudden—I had the connection! Because the crypto-graphic problem that he talked about, I had labored with during the war. We were in occupied Norway and ciphering messages to be sent by illegal means to the United Kingdom, and received and deciphered. I think it stuck in my mind, the problem as such.

Then, when I was in England I tried to convince the British Secret Service that there was a solution to this problem which was much simpler than what they were doing. Of course, nobody listened to me.

**RBD**: That is what usually happens when someone comes up with a brilliant idea.

**Bjorn**: This is what happened, and I was relieved of that job because I gave them too much trouble. So I found another job, it was not so difficult to find jobs during the war. Afterwards I went to school in the United States. I was interested in large scale digital calculators. In fact, I delivered the first major paper on large scale digital calculators at Harvard University in 1948. I always like to say that I learnt to calculate at MIT. I learnt to *think* at Harvard.

**RBD**: And you learnt to be a genius on your own.

**Bjorn**: Not quite.

**RBD**: Before we go on, I'd like to to backtrack over what you've said so far and make sure we have the important elements. You said that, by chance, you had picked up knowl-edge that led you to a solution to this cryptographic problem that was much simpler than what was being done. Only you didn't make the connection that it was a solution until someone told you about the problem.

**Bjorn**: Yes, this fellow, who really should have had more credit than what he ever got, defined the problem for me. That is important. So I said, "OK, I will make you a machine in three weeks which will do just that"—and I did. Being a dutiful military officer I wrote to the Chief of Defense Staff and the Ministry of Defense and reported that I had made what I thought myself was quite an important invention. The people from the Defense Research Institute, who are the top, were the first to answer, to say, "It's impossible; you cannot do it that way." I explained the device to them, and again I got an answer "No, no, you can not do it that way."

The machine worked. I knew that. So I said, "Why can't they understand it, it's so simple."

**RBD**: You started from the belief that it was simple.

**Bjorn**: Yes, the belief that it is simple is absolutely essential. The thing was that I made the machine and it worked and I was of course quite pleased and I said to myself "Now here we are, it works!" And the defense staff came back with a nice solution, and that was: "If this had been possible, the Americans would have done it a long time ago." I hear that every time I think of something new, that "If this had been possible, the Americans would have done it a long time ago."

**RBD**: Actually this raises a question I'd like to go into more deeply later on which is, "When you get that kind of negative feedback, how do you keep it from getting in your way?"

But before we get into that aspect of creativity, I wanted to explore a little more fully how you made the "connection" between this problem and your solution. You were saying that one of the things that always stumps you is how people fail to connect different things together. It seems to me, that is something that you can do that other people could learn from. How, specifically, did you do it?

**Bjorn**: It is not difficult. It is more difficult not to connect things together. I do find that there is an inner consistency between things that happen in nature. Whether you explain it in words or in mathematical formulae does not in fact change the nature of things.

For example, in this cryptographic problem, to cipher a message they needed to use something that was random. So, how do you know that the thing is random? I just ask the question—"How do you know that something is random?" "Can you prove that something is random?" You can prove something that is systematic, but the nature of being random is that you can't prove it, you simply can't.

The most perfect way of making a random thing is to take away completely the possibility of memory, because if you have no memory you cannot make anything *but* random.

**RBD**: So what you are saying is that non-random involves memory of some sort and random involves no memory. That is quite simple and quite profound. To make connections you need memory. Take away the memory and no connections can be made.

Another thing you said that seems quite profound is that there is an inner consistency in things that happen in nature that goes beyond words or mathematics and that you trust the "nature of things" more than words or formulae. (Perhaps it's just that nature has more memory than we do.)

One of the limitations to creativity often seems to come when people confuse the "map for the territory." If something isn't in the map, it can't be in the territory. You, on the other hand, tend to learn from the territory first, and then adjust the map to fit it.

**Bjorn**: Well, since I was a boy scout, I know that when there is an inconsistency between the terrain and the map then the terrain is usually right. It amounts to a belief.

One of my professors at Harvard, Professor A. Purcell (who was a Nobel Prize laureate), opened up his course in electron physics by saying, "Gentlemen, I'm going to teach you something that's called electron physics. You may think that the electron is something that exists, but I will tell you that an electron is solely a product of the human mind. It serves it's purpose solely because it correlates theory and observable facts. We have come to a point where every week we can subject the electrons to an experiment and we can predict what they will do and whenever we observe them they do just that. But what they do when we don't observe them, we don't know." He had intimate knowledge of electrons and I'm sure that some of the people in the Nobel committee would have been shocked to hear him say that an electron does not exist.

But it was this kind of belief that helped me to be not so intimidated by maps like science and math. I remember taking a very important math exam. One of the questions was, "Discuss and explain the following non-linear differential equation." Now most people see "non linear differential equation" and think, "That's too complex, too difficult. I won't even try it". But, because mathematics is a language, I thought, "What is this equation trying to tell me in plain words?" Then I saw that when I switched around $x$ and $y$, which was just put in there to make it complicated, I saw, in front of my eyes, this little mass point move back and forth. When you looked through it, it wasn't actually a non- linear differential equation. At least as long as $n$ was a large number. If $n$ became small enough, okay, so it was non-differential. But it was describing hyperbolic tension, which is a thing that goes like that *(draws shape in the air with right hand)*:

It behaves in a very orderly manner. Therefore, even though it is a non-linear differential equation you can still make a general discussion of what happens. This mass point that was moving around was the famous $n$ in the equation, which

**Figure 5.1. Hyperbolic Tension Curve.**

was the parameter I was going to discuss. It does disappear into infinity, but does it have a finite velocity when it gets there or doesn't it?

**RBD**: So you move back and forth between the map, "words and formulae," which is digital, and the territory, or the "nature of the thing," which is analog.

**Bjorn**: Exactly. In this cryptographic machine, I was fortunate to make some approximate tests to show that something was random. The key was just to use something I knew was random "in the territory." I used radioactive cobalt and a Geiger counter. I did a mathematical series that showed quite clearly that the probability of an odd is equal to the probability of an even number of strokes if the average number of strokes in a test period equals seven or more. After that you can no longer distinguish. So consequently, since you have thirty milliseconds, or twenty anyway in an ordinary teletype, all you need to do to solve the problem of making a random letter is to, within those twenty milliseconds, make a decision between one or zero. That's all you have to do. There's not enough time in twenty milliseconds to have any appreciable memory. So the result will be random.

**RBD**: Let me see if I understand this correctly, because this is an important part of what we are after in terms of your strategy. You took something in a territory that you knew was random—radioactive cobalt—and you said, "OK, how can I make a description of what this is doing?" "What can I find about this?" And by making some descriptions of how the cobalt was acting you found a pattern that allowed you to make a machine operate in an analogous manner.

**Bjorn**: Yes, and instead of making a very complicated machine, I made a machine that made a one or zero decision every twenty milliseconds—just like radioactive cobalt. That was all that was required.

This sat on the shelf in the radio laboratory of the training center for one year. Then, a NATO officer who had many good qualities—he played organ in a church, and he drank a lot (laughter), a very jolly fellow—he asked me, "What's this?" I explained it to him and he immediately understood. And this Englishman went back to the Norwegian Defense Staff and he said, "Look what you got there, you have exactly a machine that does what we want." And then they came up with limousines. And then all of a sudden it was manufactured.

It was standardized within NATO. The proudest moment was when I saw the opening of the hot line between Kruschev and Eisenhower with Eisenhower standing in front of my machine. And so it was, for once, the Americans who learnt something from the Norwegians.

**RBD**: It looks like you are setting that precedent again today.

Incidentally, you said you were "relieved" of your job over this invention earlier on, but I understand that you were the youngest Colonel in the Norwegian Army. Does that require any special creativity?

**Bjorn**: Not really. In the army it is quite easy. The prescription is to pick an understanding chief. Because if you have an oppressive and terrible man to work for you can't do anything. Picking the right chief has been the underlying part of my success.

For instance, we built a large communication system for NATO. Of course, the telegraph administration said that this was "toys for military boy scouts." "Radio links? No, that would never be. Go up to these mountain tops with radio equipment, difficult radio equipment? We can't do that."

**RBD**: So naturally you said, "Oh, yeah?"

**Bjorn**: They had the idea that, because an airplane needs preventive maintenance, electronic gear full of transistors needs preventive maintenance. In fact, this is nonsense. Electronic gear likes the wear. I don't know them personally, but I think they like to work. You switch them on and they work. The only time we had trouble with this radio relay station up on the mountains was when there were people there. The majority of the faults have occurred within half an hour after someone has visited the station, either whilst they were there or immediately after they left (laughter). This is an actual statistic. I'm not making it up.

So we did achieve results. But, again, it was because I had picked a chief who never stopped me. It's almost impossible in any official organization to get that.

I have, in fact, got acceptance for a Doctor's thesis which is going to be titled, "A rational approach to bureaucracy," because I do actually believe that bureaucracy is rule governed. If you take bureaucracy as a big calculating machine you will find that there is one decision cell that has been allocated all the authority. The others are all jealous of it because they think that they should have authority to make the decisions but, since they don't, they are afraid to take responsibility for anything because they might get criticized or punished. This is a very inefficient calculating machine, because everyone in the computer knows that this one cell is the only one that is going to make the decision, and information just keeps incessantly migrating around through the system until it reaches that particular decision cell or gets stuck in one of the other cells and disappears.

Now, with this type of structure you have the overriding law of "the decision of least responsibility" which will always prevail in bureaucracy, otherwise they couldn't survive. According to this law, the only decisions that will be made by the other cells in the computer are those that they perceive as involving little or no responsibility. Therefore you have to design several inputs and put them into particular input cells to this massive computing machine such that they migrate through the computer in the right pattern. You design your inputs so that they all migrate to one of these cells at the right time. They think, "three or four coincident inputs couldn't be wrong," and it appears that the least responsibility is involved in that cell making the decision you want.

**RBD**: So, instead of having to wait until you can get the right chief, you can use the way the system naturally works.

It seems that in this case you are using the process of metaphor or analogy again, as you did with the radioactive cobalt. You make the connection, "A bureaucracy is like a digital computer." Instead of being angry at it for being inefficient, you use the properties of the machine in your favor. Since, as a machine, it thrives on redundancy and repetition, instead of letting that bog you down, you utilize it in order to get the machine to work the way you want it to. If someone gets the same message 3 or 4 times from different sources then it is perceived as familiar and safe, and not a question of authority or responsibility. That's kind of nice.

So that's what you need to be successfully creative in an "official organization?"

**Bjorn**: That, and a resistance to the word "impossible."

**RBD**: Let me ask this question: What do you think is the most creative thing you've done? Would it be the figuring out about the cryptographic machine?

**Bjorn**: If you were to say "inspiring," maybe it is easier to answer. I think it has to be the radar for the blind because it is potentially useful for people who are not so fortunate and it is inspiring to the extent that they would use it, of course. I get terribly tired of people who postulate that the thing is not possible.

**RBD**: Right, you have to get the Englishman to convince them. They're stuck over there in the map and not in the territory.
  How did you conceive of this "radar for the blind?"

**Bjorn**: It was actually stimulated a long time ago by Percy William Beckman, who was my professor in several classes at Harvard. He was a very inspiring man, a very good man. He won the Nobel prize in 1946 for creating 3000 atmospheres of pressure to study some nuclear phenomena. His daughter was very angry with me when I said to her, "I'm told your father had to apply a lot of pressure to get this Nobel prize." (Laughter.)
  Anyway, he had received a grant and he wanted to discover how the bat could navigate without sight. The wire recorder had just come out in the market and we ran them very fast and took up the shrieks of the bat and then we slowed them down so that we could hear them. I sat at the monoscope and found out that the bat has a very versatile system for supersonic guidance. I immediately thought, "How can we do this to help the blind?" Professor Beckman said, "You can do it, but it would weigh about a ton and it would cost about $100,000. It

would not be practical to do it today." But he suggested that since electronics are getting smaller and smaller it might be something for me to take up when I retired. And this is what I did. So I guess this idea also came from an American professor.

The Professor intended to find out how the bat navigates and he, of course, saw the vision of it being used by blind people. I don't think that he did the research for that purpose because I knew him quite well and he didn't work that way. He wanted to find out the physical way that the bat navigates in order to be able to store this and use it for something else. He was very happy when I said that I would pick this up when I retired.

That was in 1948. Ten years ago I started picking up the physical realization because at that time I knew that electronics had advanced to highly integrated circuits and therefore I knew that I could get it within a small box. It would be small enough so that the person could conveniently hold it and direct it and, a very important thing, put it away when he didn't want to use it; because I realized that the blind person needs to switch it off and put it away easily. These conditions were met only after the highly integrated circuits became available a few years ago.

**RBD**: Let me backtrack what we have so far and start to make some observations about a few of the more subtle things that I have been observing. Your ideas seem to come in from your right hand side. You gesture in that direction with your right hand whenever you describe one of these questions that stimulate you to be creative. The idea seems to form out of something you've observed in nature—cobalt or a bat or something that produces a unique ability. To get at the principles of the thing from nature, you make a change in a particular "submodality" and then overlap it into another representational system. In this case of the bat, for example, you recorded the bat's shriek, changed it by slowing it down, and shifted representational systems by viewing it visually on a scope. It was then that you could begin to find the pattern there. In the case of the cobalt, you also listened to it first, on a Geiger counter, and translated it through a mathematical series into a visual expression as well. Then you could find the principle or pattern. Even with the math test you described there was a picture and you could see the lines of the parabolic curve.

While the idea from nature, from the territory, comes from your right hand side, the map, the 'problem' seems to always come in from your left hand side—you gesture in that direction when you talk about machines and theories. There also seems to be a lot of pictures and imagery that you refer to in this area to your left.

Then, you find a way of emulating this naturally occurring ability with a map or a machine through the discovery of some kind of connection or pattern that usually comes through analogy. So you have a way of talking about or mathematically representing these natural principles. These two things, the map and the territory, literally seem to "meet in the middle" on a kind of "mental workbench" that is directly in front of you. Does that fit for you?

**Bjorn**: Now that you say it, it does. Although I've never thought about it in that way before.

**RBD**: In a way the "sonar system for the blind" seems to be a very interesting and deep metaphor for your creative process in a couple of ways. One, you are constantly giving guidance to people who are 'blind' and don't see the vision you see, and, two, your strategy seems organized around connecting the auditory and the visual representational systems. This, to me, is an interesting parallel.

So, to proceed, now you've taken on the problem of making a device for the blind to be able to navigate via sonar. How are you doing it? What is the creative process you are using to develop it?

**Bjorn**: Well, now I try to speak your kind of language. I was thinking through the various forms of sensory inputs to the human consciousness.

**RBD**: Aha!

**Bjorn**: You like that, I know that, but this is true, I do that. You have eyesight, which is some megacycles wide, and you have hearing, which is some kilocycles wide and you have sensory touch which is a few cycles wide. Now, this does not tell the whole story because we must take into consideration all the information we waste. A human person wastes so much and he has a short term memory, very short, in which time he can make use of the full range before storage becomes necessary. To do this he has to do a sort of a band width compression—that is, he has to filter these sensory inputs. A band width compression can never be accomplished in nature or in mathematics without making a choice.

So we have this sensory input to the human consciousness where I believe even a few cycles is a great input. I do not think that we have the capability in a lifetime to store more than one bit a second; I think that's about the size of it. Of course, this particular figure is my own estimate. If somebody says multiply it by one hundred or one thousand I can do that; it doesn't change my principle. I feel that the way to try to help a person who has lost one of these inputs is to try to use one of the other input possibilities and usually in an analog form. If I go to a digital form I have taken away some of the perception of the human person.

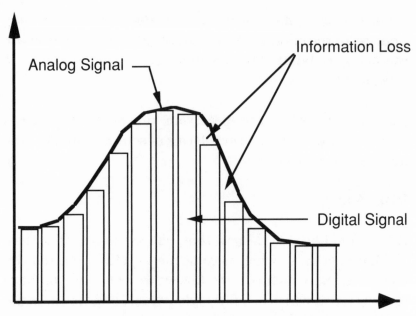

**Figure 5.2. Information Loss Due to Conversion
of Analog to Digital Signal.**

What you come to first is obviously the sense of hearing. But the sense of hearing is very valuable to a blind person, so I try to save that for his own use. If he is only interested in a warning of an obstacle, then I want to have a sensory input which will give you a limited warning of an obstacle which is a one or zero situation. For this I am using tactile stimulation.

So I am trying to use the two remaining input values, and combine them in what may at present not be the optimal manner, but it will get there. I have determined that the present model is good enough to begin with. Apart from that I have no more money to do anything more. I could seek official aid, but official assistance is designed primarily to keep a number of bureaucrats busy and secondarily to help whatever is the nominal thing. So for the time being I will stay away from that.

**RBD**: Let me summarize what I've got so far. It seems to me that what you do as you begin to develop a device is find where the limits are of the parameters you are working with. Where does it get to a point that it changes? For instance, you said that human consciousness can handle about one bit per second. You're looking at the ranges of things you have to work with.

Another thing you are doing that is very common among people who are good problem solvers, is trying to take the problem and put it in plain language, as you did with the non-linear differential equation. You try to simplify it as much as possible. You are not trying to handle all the complexities; you are trying to simplify it. So you take this problem and you ask, "What is this saying, in the simplest terms possible?" Then you ask, "What in the territory, what in the terrain, gives me an example of something that I can use?" It's in the terrain, so I can start to maybe make a map of it and I can then find the connection between this and something else, like the machinery I'm trying to use or the technology that is available.

One very specific question I have, though, is, "When you are actually being creative, and coming up with an idea like this, do you think more in words, in pictures, or in feelings?" Because you've talked here about certain feelings or intuitions that lead you to believe certain things. You talked about using language and you use the tools of language and linguistic structure. But you also definitely used imagery. I'm sure that they all coordinate together. What are you aware of in relation to how you use your own sensory inputs in this process?

**Bjorn**: In physical phenomena, no doubt the physical picture. I was expecting this question, and I was in fact thinking about it, and I couldn't give you a better answer than that. When it comes to other kinds of thoughts I can say very little about what imagery, what kind of pictures I make, except with physical phenomena, definitely pictures of the physical object.

**RBD**: When you talk about these pictures you gesture in front of you to what I was calling a "mental workbench." Is the picture something that you are forming over time and keep going back to over and over, or does it sometimes just pop in to your head? And when you picture it, is it clear and vivid as if you can actually see it, or is it a kind of vague image?

**Bjorn**: I know the physical picture of it, it has formed itself over maybe a year's time. It is just a little lighter than a pack of cigarettes. (You shouldn't say this in Norway because you can't advertise cigarettes here.) It is a small thing, but this is a particular kind of creation where the idea and everything had already been worked out but the physical thing waited for technology. You can see the same thing in painting—Michelangelo just happened to come on the stage after the paint brush had been invented.

For instance, for this little hand radar I need a more efficient vibrator to stimulate the fingers and now I know exactly how I will make it. I was in Radio Shack about a week ago and I saw a little buzzer that will do it if I can just fish it out and fix it a little bit. This happened just as I saw it first in a catalog and then in a shop—you can't get very much more physical than that. You have to place it inside this little box and I checked it, I can do that. It is not in principle an innovation, but it is a great practical improvement.

The only problem I've reached here, at the same time, is that I have no money to make it. So I will wait until I either get more money or die.

**RBD**: This brings us back to a question that we touched upon earlier that I'd like pursue a little bit. You were talking about the response that you have when other people have told you something was impossible. When you're working with something, you cannot always be successful at first. One of the big problems for many people with creative ideas is that when they try to invent something and it doesn't work they feel, "Oh, I failed." When you're working on an invention, like the sonar or the cryptographic device, how do you deal with the lack of success, or what other people would call a mistake or a failure?

**Bjorn**: When I was much younger I used to sulk but I've advanced and have a much more mature reaction to it. But of course I think you have to accept a fair amount of frustration. My perception is that I try to put it away for a while because the subconscious will work on it and maybe a year or two years from now you can take it up again or maybe the next week. But it is, of course, necessary to cope with a certain amount of frustration.

We are getting into very difficult things because I think there are masses of ways whereby you can sublimate your frustration. You can blame it on somebody else, you can say, "If that hadn't done this, if this hadn't done that," etc. But in putting the blame on somebody else you actually take away from yourself the control and I don't want to do that. So I think that you find that perhaps one of the most important things in persevering is to find the way of dealing with frustration in an honest way.

One point which I think is very important is that there is a certain timidity, even, should we say, a reverence for authority which I'm sometimes unfortunately free of. But there is a reverence for precedence. If I feel that the actual process that I'm trying to seek and to solve is a possible, natural process, than it is no longer a question of *if*, but a question of *how* and *when*. Then you can't get stuck by the fact that somebody else says that it is impossible. In fact, that is an inspiration.

I think that this absolutely unwarranted reverence for formulae, authority, precedence is something that one has to relax about and say that obviously, if this is so then it is possible to do it and trust oneself to the point where you are able to admit, "Yes, this is right."

**RBD**: You talked about being able to put something away because the unconscious would work on it. One of the things I also know that is very important about people who are creative is that, because there are these conscious filters, there has to be a way of communicating or interacting with the unconscious. Some people say, "I put all the information in, I go to sleep and when I wake up in the morning I go back to it," Or some people say, "I meditate or I speak with my unconscious." There are various ways. What kind of a relationship do you have or how do you get access to acknowledge or utilize information from the unconscious?

**Bjorn**: I discussed this with Professor Nespakin who is a well-known neurosurgeon. (I keep asking him if he has found a soul yet.) The question is, "Are all our experiences there, only we can't get at them, or are they not there?" Well, Nespakin cited people who in a very tight situation, some very dramatic situation, could much later recall and recite word for word what had happened. He held the opinion that it is all there and it is our communication with the subconscious that fails, and I tend to agree with that. If this is so, it would help the creative process because sometime later, you see something which is in fact the solution to the problem that you had to give up two years ago.

**RBD**: So, do you do any things to cultivate in yourself that relationship, or is it mostly just that you trust that it is there, believe that it is there, and that it will be there for you to recognize?

**Bjorn**: Not that I know of. I don't believe in any particular form of meditation or any other prescribed method.

**RBD**: We have gathered a wealth of material and I appreciate your participation. I hope there has been some new insights for you into your own thought process and the process of creativity.

**Bjorn**: Yes, almost everything. Really, I don't know nearly enough about it. I think you have pointed out a large number of characteristics and I'm sure that this conversation we have had is at least as useful to me as it is to you. I would certainly like to know more about it.

**RBD**: What do you think are the most important things left to explore?

**Bjorn**: I would like to know what the filters are inside the brain which prevent us from seeing the obvious. What are the filters that protect us from dangers? Because we recognize danger in many forms, and fear is something we should not get rid of—fear is something we should use to protect us in an intelligent way.

We have so many filters and I wish I knew more about how they work. For instance, with regard to this sonar thing, the ear has a longer filter, the muscular reaction to a warning is longer for some reason. The neurologists are not quite able to make sense of it.

I have a friend who lost his reflex in his right leg from a car accident. He can direct his right leg with the use of his brain, he can tell it to do something but he must do it consciously. When he goes skiing he can turn to the right because then he has his weight on the left leg which is intact but he cannot turn to the left, he falls over because the reaction time is not quick enough for him. Although he knows what to do he just cannot keep up with the speed of skiing and he falls over. He insists on skiing anyhow.

**RBD**: I'm sure someone told him it was impossible for him to ski.

**Bjorn**: Probably. But you see, the balance sensors in your foot, are immediate when you ski. That is obvious because otherwise you would fall. But for the ear, the time delay is much longer. I asked the neurologists to tell me why but they haven't come up with a good answer yet. They use a lot of medicalese, but this is "territory" not the map. They cloud the issue, but they can't explain.

**RBD**: Any final comments? We've spent about an hour and I've got a lot of very valuable observations. My goal has been to find the important and exciting things about the way that you think. I think we have found some very fascinating ones. Are there any other final things that you would like to say that come to mind about your creative processes?

**Bjorn**: I can isolate three things. One is the sonar invention, if you call it that. Maybe it was done by my professor. I think I could not have done it without his aid. You can either take the credit or you can make the thing happen but you can't do both. The invention was made and it waited for the technology to catch up. Another is the cryptographic machine where somebody stated the problem and he stated it very clearly, so that he deserves credit, but that was another process. A third process was what happened when my friend came to me and wanted to do this expedition across the Pacific. He said he needed communications. He didn't even know how to state the problem. So I had to synthesize a requirement and then fill it.

**RBD**: What you are saying is that your way of processing allows you to operate at all of these different levels. Some, innovation: coming up with the synthesis of the thing to invent to begin with, as with your friend's expedition. Some, invention: making a creative idea happen, as with the sonar device. And some to discover what was already there, as with the cryptographic device. That demonstrates a lot of diversity.

**Bjorn**: Could it have something to do with an almost subconscious fear of being conventional?

**RBD**: It could be. You said earlier, "If I blame somebody else then I'm giving up control." One of the things that keeps you going, is that you get a feeling that something is possible. Another thing is that there is an irreverence for authority. Maybe it's connected to a sense of identity—a person who is not going to be just another brick in the wall, or something like that.

**Bjorn**: I have a saying, which is, "If you want this thing done in an ordinary way you can hire much cheaper labor than me." It's not really true, of course.

I think it is also a valuable observation that there are a very large number of inventions in daily life which are never announced as such. We are too modest or unaware. But if you really go back and look at your daily life I bet that each one of you have made a number of inventions.

**RBD**: That's nice. Well, thank you very much.

# Tools for Turning Problems into Opportunities and Failure into Feedback

**RBD**: One of the things Bjorn mentioned was the ability to deal with a fair amount of frustration as a creative person. Some of the biggest barriers to creativity come from the various forms of the critic. We have previously explored strategies to handle interruptions, distractions and creative blocks at the realist stage. However, barriers to creativity involving the critic often involve a different level of problem solving.

The kinds of limitations people experience in relationship to the critic have to do with expectations, limiting beliefs and incongruency at a "Want To" level, as opposed to a "How To" level.

Blocks at this level often involve fear—fear of failure, fear of criticism, even fear of success because of increased expectations of your performance on the part of other people. Sometimes people fear the "unknown." There is insecurity associated with the new and unfamiliar. Other common types of blocks at this level involve the lack of payoff or incentives for creativity due to cross purposes coming from politics, hierarchy or "pecking order," conflicts and confusions of values, or ecology issues coming from a threat brought about in the existing system or organization. Oftentimes these kinds of blocks are created by a lack of understanding or respect for different world views. Either type of block can create resistance or incongruity with respect to creativity.

While a number of the tools we've presented and explored so far can be applied to these kinds of blocks, these higher level "Want To" issues often require a shift of strategy from innovating and inventing to "problem solving." In this case the problem itself becomes the focus of the creative effort rather than specifics of the product or expression of the idea.

## Creativity and Problem Solving

Probably the majority of creative activity goes into problem solving. In NLP the word "problem" falls into a class of language known as "nominalization." A nominalization is a process or relationship that is being talked about as if were an object. In NLP, no particular thing or object can be a problem. A problem is a relationship. Specifically, NLP defines a problem as the difference or the gap between your present state and your desired state.

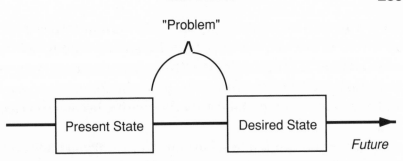

**Figure 5.3. Problem Space Flowchart.**

If there is no difference between where you are and where you want to be, you have no problem. If there is a small gap between where you are and where you want to be, you have a little problem. If there is a large gap, you have a big problem.

In fact, given this definition, you could say that almost all creativity and innovation is directed toward solving or *creating* a problem of some kind. It is important to realize that as soon as you set an outcome, you've created a problem for yourself. As soon as you define a goal or desired state, you have made a problem out of thin air, because you are not at that state yet. That's why so many people are afraid of their 'Dreamer'—the dreamer creates problems by thinking up outcomes.

Of course, it's the map or model that you make to represent a problem that will determine whether it stays a problem or turns into an opportunity. How do you involve the 'Realist'? How do you involve the 'Critic'?

**TE**: When you sit down and go, "What am I going to do about X? I have a problem. I have something I need to solve." How do you think about it? How do you organize it? The first thing is to take your problem and make it into a question. It's a lot easier to figure out an answer for a question than a problem. But, of course, answering your question can create more problems. "Is it the right answer?" "What do I do now that I have an answer?" "Is one enough?"

Of course, some people jump on the first answer they come up with and just go, "Aha, I got a gut response. I know this is what I should do," and go for it. Others sit and go over endless scenarios until the time they have to do the thing has passed and now they no longer have to bother with it because it is too late.

Let's say you wanted to solve a problem and you had three or four scenarios you came up with. How far do you run the scenarios out into the future? How much of past history do you include? How far back do you go? How many people do you include in the way in which you're going to impact them? For instance, do you make decisions creatively for yourself, or creatively in relationship to how many other people this decision is going to impact directly?

## The S.C.O.R.E. Model

**RBD**: The S.C.O.R.E. Model is a model that Todd and I developed to describe the process that we were intuitively using to design interventions. It arose as a result of a supervision seminar that we were leading. We realized that we were systematically organizing the way we approached a problem that was different from even our advanced students, and this allowed us to more efficiently and effectively get to the root of a problem. We noticed that what we were doing intuitively was not precisely described by any of the existing NLP techniques or models.

Most NLP is oriented around defining a present state and a desired state, and then identifying and applying a technique that will hopefully help someone get to their desired state. We realized that we were making some additional distinctions. S.C.O.R.E. stands for **S**ymptoms, **C**auses, **O**utcomes, **R**esources and **E**ffects. These elements represent the minimum amount of information that needs to be addressed by any process of creativity or change:

1. **S**ymptoms are typically the most noticeable and conscious aspects of a presenting problem or problem state.

2. **C**auses are the underlying elements responsible for creating and maintaining the symptoms. They are usually less obvious than the symptoms they produce.

3. **O**utcomes are the particular goals or desired states that would take the place of the symptoms.

4. **R**esources are the underlying elements responsible for removing the causes of the symptoms and for manifesting and maintaining the desired outcomes.

5. **E**ffects are the longer term results of achieving a particular outcome. Specific outcomes are generally stepping stones to get to a longer term effect.

    a. Positive effects are often the reason or motivation for establishing a particular outcome to begin with.

    b. Negative effects can create resistance or ecological problems.

"Techniques" are sequential structures for identifying, accessing and applying particular resources to a particular set of symptoms, causes and outcomes. A technique is not in and of itself a resource. A technique is only effective to the extent that it accesses and applies the resources which are appropriate to address the whole system defined by the other S.C.O.R.E. elements.

One effective way to use the S.C.O.R.E. Model is to organize these elements on a "time line." Typically, symptoms are something you are experiencing in the present, or have experienced in the recent past. The causes of those symptoms tend to precede the symptoms. That is, the cause of a symptom comes before a symptom in time—either immediately before the symptom, or potentially much earlier. Outcomes occur in the same time frame as the symptom, since the outcome is what you want to replace the symptom with. So if the symptom is in the present, the outcome will also be in the present or in the very near future. Effects are the longer term results of the outcome. They are usually in the short term to long term future. Resources can come from anywhere in time. A resource can be something that just happened to you, happened to you a long time ago, or it could be something you are imagining that could happen in the future. In creativity especially, a majority of resources come from asking "what if?" and acting "as if."

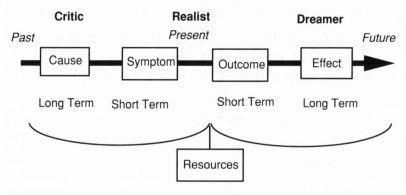

**Figure 5.4. The S.C.O.R.E. Model.**

Effects are the macro goals that shape specific outcomes. We are not always going to know what the effect of some outcome will be, could be, or even should be. Sometimes you have to apply a resource and reach an outcome first, before you can explore its effects.

In a way, the short and long term future is the arena of the 'Dreamer'; the ongoing expression of symptoms and outcomes is the field of the 'Realist'; past causes and problems is the space of the 'Critic'.

The most powerful way to implement the the S.C.O.R.E. Model is to interface it with the R.O.L.E. Model distinctions. Which representational system is most associated with the symptom? Feelings? Words? Images? What about the cause, the outcome, the desired effect, the resources? How might it help you to overcome a creative block by changing the representational system you are using to perceive a particular symptom or cause?

How are causes and symptoms linked? Is it a synesthesia, a trigger? How could you link new resources to a cause or a symptom? Which parts of the T.O.T.E. are involved? Which parts need to be changed? The goals? The evidence procedures? The steps of a particular operation?

What kind of physiology goes along with the symptoms, outcomes or resources?

One way to think about how the two models go together is that the R.O.L.E. Model is a description of structure and the S.C.O.R.E. Model is a description of functions. The R.O.L.E. Model is a way of describing what something is made out of and the S.C.O.R.E. Model is a way of describing how it affects you. (*See* Appendix F for an overview of the S.C.O.R.E. Model.)

**TE**: I'd like to bring this model to life and demonstrate how to address some of these questions. I want to bring this map into the territory and illustrate how to use the S.C.O.R.E. Model to enhance creativity by dealing with creative blocks. Specifically, I want to explore symptoms that relate to being creative with other people. Can I have a couple of volunteers?

M., J. Sure. Why don't you both come up and stand over here?

All right, now this issue we will be working with could be either interpersonal or intrapersonal. That is, either checking out what's going on inside with you (intrapersonal) or it could be about communicating more effectively with other people (interpersonal). M., which would it be for you?

**M**: It could be either. But I guess the thing that concerns me most during the day is selling to people—so dealing with people.

**TE**: Do you sell in the situation where they walk in the storefront, or do you call on accounts?

**M**: Usually I call on accounts or try to make appointments. The thing that bothers me most is when people shut me off, and I don't have a good comeback.

**TE**: How do they "shut you off?" How do they accomplish this? How do they keep you from using your "comebacks"?

**M**: Well, they just say, "We already have a vendor."

**TE**: So, they communicate to you that somehow they've already got what you're selling, or what?

**M**: Yes, or I get some reaction from people that's not the result that I want. You know, that they're turned off by something that I do.

**TE**: So it's not that they turn you off, it's more that you turn them off. Do you believe that the fact that they were turned off by something that you do is a function of your ability to be creative on the telephone?
   Here I've begun the process of defining M.'s symptom in the S.C.O.R.E.

**M**: Oh yeah, I'm sure there is a solution for it. I just don't know what it is.

**TE**: I appreciate that. If you knew what it was, you wouldn't be here with to me right now. What about you, J.? What is the symptom that you want to work with?

**J**: I get stuck working with other people.

**TE**: What do you mean by stuck? In what context? One to one, or a group? How do you get stuck? Does something stick you?

**J**: Group and one to one (looks up and left). One of my problems is that I can see what the issues are and I begin to identify the issues, but I have a hard time communicating them to others.

**TE**: (To audience) I am going to ask some questions now, and I'd like you to listen to my language and the kind of questions I ask in relationship to what kind of response I elicit. Think about what is happening in terms of the R.O.L.E. Model elements we've been working with. Remember working with the S.C.O.R.E. model involves a different chunk size than the T.O.T.E. or the R.O.L.E.

First we're going to find out what M. and J. perceive when they interact with people in these contexts. J. is saying he can see clearly what the issues are—and you notice by his accessing cues (eye movement up and left) that he's not lying to us, that he has remembered some visual image. Something occurs between his understanding of the issues and his communication with other people. Let's explore the structure of this symptom a bit more closely. Let's find out how J. represents his evidence that this problem is occurring. Simply put—how J. knows he has a "problem" or "issue." The perception or belief that something is a "problem" or an "issue" can itself be the block to solutions.

(To J.) Obviously, you've tried many different things to communicate your ideas. When you think about it right now and you go back to that picture of trying to communicate something to that group or to an individual, what do you see? Do you see yourself talking to other people? Do you see their response?

**J**: Yeah.

**TE**: How do you know what to do at any given time when you're speaking? If you're starting to lose them, how do you know what to do to get them back?

**J**: I see if they are agreeing with me.

**TE**: What do you do if you believe they are not agreeing with you?

**J**: Say it in a different way, and see if that helps.

**TE**: O.K. Let's see. Where does it become a problem? If you keep saying it in different ways and it still doesn't help?

**J**: Usually what happens is my voice continues to drop.

**TE**: What do you mean by drop? Tone or volume? Does the tone get lower or do you get quieter?

**J**: The volume and tone tend to drop, like I'm not confident, like they're beating me down.

**TE**: OK, I think we have a pretty good idea of how the symptom manifests itself. Let's organize this problem on a time line and then see if we can find out something about the cause. I wonder who it is that's really beating you down?

J., can you remember a time when this happened? It's a bitch to get beaten down, isn't it? In any way, shape, or form. Can you remember some time when this occurred? And what I want to ask you to do, if this is possible, J., is to remember what happened. You started talking to them. Then you noticed you didn't have them in some way. In this scenario you keep trying to explain it in different ways to them, and you start losing your voice. And you seem to be losing your sense of confidence. Remember that as if it were a movie. And see, at the beginning of the movie you were up there speaking and at the end of the movie your voice was dropping, you weren't getting the response you wanted.

As you review that, I want you to search for what causes that symptom to happen. What is it that's going on there that begins to make you feel that you're losing your confidence? What gets you to begin to have your voice drop, and to not have the confidence? How do you know when to begin to start to drop your voice?

Just review that, go through that a couple of times, if you can. Start at the beginning like a movie. Run it to the end. Run it through a few times. Maybe stop it in between and figure out if there is anything that really sticks out to you. Is it something someone says, a way that they look maybe, something you say to yourself? Just review that. Slow it down so you can see clearly what it is.

(To M.) Now, I basically want you to do the same thing with the symptom you keep confronting. I want you to take one of these experiences where you were talking to someone on the telephone and you begin to notice you're not getting the response you want. What happens when you don't get the response? Do you become frustrated by it? Angry? Fearful?

**M**: I become tense. The thing that worries me, or the panic that happens, is that they are going to shut me off, you know, turn off the phone, or hang up the phone. I don't have time. I need time, that's what I'm always playing for. If I have time I have a shot at it, at least I have a chance to reach them. Time is what I'm trying for.

**TE**: I think if you really played at it more perhaps it wouldn't be an issue. What I want you to do is find one of those experiences and lay it out on your time line. Given that time is one of your issues. Think about when this occurred with you. Pick one that's not too devastating, one that you can review in your mind, perhaps you can see as a movie, like I asked J. to do. I want you to review it in your head, slow it down, speed it up, stop it in sections to listen to it again.

Find out what causes it. Where are the points along the way; where does it start to begin to go, "I don't have enough time!" If you didn't have the sense that you were running out of time you probably could come up with a whole lot of other alternatives. But the time starts to close in on you and that seems to be the focus of the tension, not alternative ways to keep this person on the telephone. So, what I want you to do is just review that, and take note of anything along the way that you hear or see that would indicate to you: "Hey, that's when I start to have a sense of losing time, that it's closing in on me." Just run through that, and I'll come back to you in a minute.

J., how'd you do? Did you find anything in particular that stuck out as a demarcation or a signpost, that this is where it begins to happen?

**J**: I would say that basically I don't feel good about this happening. Somehow, it seems that the harder I try to get my thought over, the more I feel confidence leaving me.

**TE**: How do you know you are losing confidence?

**J**: By the way they respond, actually.

**TE**: Perhaps you noticed J. was looking straight ahead as if he was really looking at someone else. He is telling us that at this point, anyway, he is using an external reference as part of his evidence for the cause. I'm curious, J., do you know that by the looks on their faces?

**J**: Yeah, the looks on their faces.

**TE**: Are you ever wrong about that, by the way? Have you ever had the experience where you think that they're not understanding and they really are? How can you be sure?

**J**: I go back and test it out. You know. They would be agreeing with me.

**TE**: This is a group of people you are trying to talk into something?

**J**: Seeing what the issues are. I'm not trying to persuade them to look at it in a certain way, just taking certain data that we clearly look at and see illustrations. We had a deficit last year and I was able to say that in September: "We're gonna have a deficit if we keep spending this way." There was no way we could have a deficit and keep operating.

**TE**: And this group of people that were listening to you were doing or saying, what?

**J**: "There's no way J."

**TE**: They're saying, "There's no way, J.. There's no way it's going to be that way." Now, let's see if we can isolate the cause. At what point did you feel that you were running out of alternative ways of approaching this? In other words, there was a point where you went, "I'm just not getting it across. They're not following me."

**J**: I think it was at the point where they could not see how I could understand what the figures meant, what we had guaranteed coming in: accounts, receivables, pure hard money.

**TE**: Basically, they didn't see what you saw.

**J**: The figures, yeah, the soft figures.

**TE**: As you now, in your mind, see that picture of you trying to explain this to these people, what feeling does it elicit in you? What emotion, if you were to slap a name on it, what would you call it? You can call it "whitterfitter" for all I care.

**J**: Anger!!

**TE**: Anger? So here you are, you're beginning to feel this "anger," and the harder you try to get your idea over the more your confidence is replaced by this anger—the more the critic takes the place of the realist.

Let me ask you a question: "What feeling would you rather have?" Let's define the outcome. Let's get the dreamer involved in this. If I had a treasure chest down here that I could open up and give you any feeling you'd rather have, to give you right at that moment some other internal state that would allow you possibly to come up with another alternative, or another way of looking at it, what feeling would you rather have?

**J**: Probably relaxed, comfortable.

**TE**: O.K., do you ever have that at any other time? Are you having it now?

**J**: A little bit.

**TE**: Well, what would you have to do to be a little more relaxed? What resources could you bring in that would help you to achieve that outcome?

**J**: It'd probably help to take a deep breath.

**TE**: Well, you take a minute and do that. And then I want you to change your orientation from outside to inside. Let's really make a full rich representation of this outcome. Just search for a minute inside and find that feeling of being relaxed, it's part of that relaxed confidence. It's like, you walk in, you know, things are all right. There's no hurry, there's no rush. You know what you're going to do. There have been times when you've been totally prepared to do what you're going to do, when you had that relaxed confidence. Think about all the inner resources that you have that you can be proud of and confident about. Can you do that?

**J**: Yes. It feels like I'm reconnected to myself.

**TE**: Back in touch with your identity, your mission. That's an important resource. Where do you feel that relaxed confidence, as opposed to the anger?

**J**: Up here in the chest.

**TE**: O.K., good. Let's bring that resource into the place that you need it. Take a nice deep breath. And I want you to go back up to the picture of you in front of the group, before you became angry. Just a little bit before. Let's run the movie back a little bit before you became angry. Then watch the movie run along. As you get to the point where you would have become angry, just stop for a minute, stay connected with yourself, your mission, take a deep breath, and feel that relaxed feeling up here. Just stop for a minute right there. Freeze the frame, O.K.?

Now, look at that freeze-frame: Can you see yourself in it? O.K., What is the effect? If you have the feeling in that picture that you have right here sitting with me, what would you be doing differently? Now, we're not talking about real life for the moment, we're talking about the picture in your head. We want to edit that picture in your head so that what you would be doing, what you would be saying would be congruent to this feeling here of relaxed confidence.

**J**: I would just pause a moment.

**TE**: Then how would that begin to allow you to come up with a new idea?

**J**: That would give me time to figure another way to say it.

**TE**: O.K., good, let's run it up again and stop it when it gets there, right before the anger. I want you to take a deep breath with that pause. I want you to run a scenario out into the future in your head. Run a whole other set of pictures out that go, "Here's something I could have done differently." In other words, I want you to come up with alternatives, even though it's only in your mind. I want you to come up with another alternative in your mind.

**J**: (Pause) O.K.

**TE**: All right, there's one. Now, let's look at it again in that freeze-frame with this feeling. And now let's find three because one choice is not a choice at all, two's a dilemma, but with three you begin to actually have a choice about things. So come up with a third thing you could have been doing differently and use that feeling in that picture. All right?

Good. Now, I'm going to leave you for a second, and I want you to run through those three and explore the effects. Find out if there are any small adjustments you'd like to make in them. OK? Because you might want to include those other folks and find out how they would have responded if you had said this, or if you'd acted this way. Just dream about all the possible effects. If any of them create ecological problems, just continue to stay connected with your identity and mission and make the appropriate adjustments.

(To M.) M., did you gain insight into the cause of your symptom? Did you find a spot in which the telephone call kind of went in the wrong direction?

**M**: I had a sense of urgency.

**TE**: How did you know that?

**M**: Sound of the voice, the way their voice rises; it speeds up.

**TE**: It speeds up? O.K. We know the representational system and orientation—it is triggered by some external auditory quality. Let's explore the linkage a little more fully. What is it about someone's voice rising and speeding up that leads you to believe that they're either not interested anymore, they're about to close the conversation?

**M**: Experiences I've had.

**TE**: That sounds to me like the 'Realist' talking.

So you say experiences from the more distant past are what you have built that belief upon. What in these experiences would get you to make that connection, that link? Because I think that, realistically speaking, most behaviors are learned. I mean, there's a few of them that we come out of the womb with, but a lot of them are learned. And I think because they're learned they can be re-learned—they can be re-linked. And so I'm assuming that this is a learned behavior. It's the way you learned to respond to a certain tone of voice. Can you remember some of the experiences that might cause you to respond that way to that tone of voice?

**M**: Oh yes...face to face with the 'Critic'.

**TE**: Now in those situations, when you hear that voice, and you know you're running out of time, how do you know to respond that way to the 'Critic'? What feeling would that be? What would you call that feeling?

**M**: Tense.

**TE**: Where do you feel that? In what part of your body do you experience that?

**M**: My stomach and my arms.

**TE**: I noticed that you almost stopped in mid-breath, maybe you even hold your breath for a second while you're waiting.

**M**: Yeah, and to try to search for something to do.

**TE**: I would image that it's difficult, because it seems that things are jammed up inside. They won't come up for you. So you get "choked up" about it, so to speak.

**M**: Yes.

**TE**: O.K. It's 'Dreamer' time. You know about magnets, don't you? A magnet's got a North and a South Pole? Take the feeling you have when you get to the phone call and you're just starting to get tense in your arms, and let's call that the North end of the Pole. What would be the South end of the Pole? What is the outcome of the feeling you'd rather have?

**M**: One of the things I was thinking about is just a friendly and relaxed feeling, not responding to pressure. Normally, when I'm talking to people I'm relaxed and friendly.

**TE**: O.K., let's recover some of the resources you have in those situations where you do not perceive there is pressure. Let's remember the last time you were in a comfortable situation, where you were able to talk to people like that. Think of which resources you had available to you that allowed you to be that way. Pick one that's a real good one, where you can really perceive those feelings.

Now, where do you feel those feelings of comfort, as opposed to where you feel the tension? You had that nice, warm, relaxed feeling—call it "warm fuzzies." When you have those nice warm fuzzies, where do you feel it? Is it possible for you to remember what that feels like?

**M**: Yes.

**TE**: O.K., good. I want you to notice what it feels like when you feel it all over. Notice it when you feel it in your face, your arms, notice what it feels like when your muscles are relaxed, and how you breathe, and I want you to contrast that just for a second with that feeling you get when the voice begins to speed up and the tone rises. O.K. Now, you notice the difference in where it's located?

**M**: There's two things: I'm not relaxed, I'm tense all over when I have a sense someone's going to hang up, or I'm not getting through; and the other way, I'm just moving and free and easy, and breathing easily.

**TE**: Especially breathing easily, you can get things out. That's an important resource to remember. When you're breathing, things come out more easily. Ideas come out, words come out. Everything. That's just the way it is. If you can't breathe, it's kind of hard to talk. Hold your breath and talk; it's difficult. Physiologically it's difficult.

Let's see what happens if we bring those resources into these problem situations. What I'd like you to do is this: Try a little experiment. Let's go to the phone call. Let's go back, though, *before* the voice sped up. Let's go back to when you first connected with the person on the phone. And stop the phone call just before the voice begins to get too tense.

**M**: Ah ah...

**TE**: O.K., you're right there? Now back it up just a little bit towards the beginning. Good, now take a breath. Notice where you would be feeling that relaxed feeling, how you'd be breathing, how your voice would be coming out. O.K., I want you to take that, hold on to that feeling, go back to the phone call, and tell me, if you had that feeling in that phone call, what would the effect be? Would you be able to do something differently?

**M**: Oh yes, sure.

**TE**: O.K., what I'd like you to do now is to start back at the beginning of the phone call, run it up to that spot, and when you get there, use that resource again and come up with a whole new alternative, a whole new conversation. Do that right now. Just take your time and explore all the effects of bringing that resource into that situation. There's no rush. We're not under any time constraints here, all right?

(Pause) How would you feel about trying those resources out with those people in the original context?

**M**: I'd feel good about that.

**TE**: O.K., is there anything you can think of that would stop you from being able to do that again next time you're in that situation?

**M**: Nothing.

**TE**: Great. Now let's take this process another step. Is it possible for you to visualize what that would look like, sitting at your desk in the future? I want you to just look at that picture for a second. Just look at that desk, the telephone in front of you. You can feel the headset. And when you pick up the phone to call somebody, remember to breathe. Remember where that feeling's located. And when you hear someone's voice begin to speed up, the tonality on the other end of it come up, what's going to happen?

**M**: I might get up a little nerve just to stay relaxed.

**TE**: (To J. and M.) Thank you both very much. (Applause.)

In order to be creative you have to be able to get in a frame of mind where you can come up with alternatives. Earlier you learned a strategy with which you could generate new behaviors. That's wonderful, but how are you going to know *when* to use it? At the time when you need it, what should trigger the use of that strategy? What should trigger you to come up with another one, if that first one doesn't work?

Creativity is something that you do all the time. When you wake up in the morning and you go to put on your favorite shirt or your favorite dress and the button's not on it and you don't have time to sew a button on it, and you kind of fold it in behind and you kind of wedge that little pin back there so nobody can see it and the dress or the blouse is straight— that's being creative.

If you woke up in the morning and the coffee filters are all gone and you want to make coffee, and you run over and you go, "Well, why don't I just pull up a paper towel and put it in the coffee machine to make coffee?" That's being as creative as anything else. The difference is people don't consider themselves as being creative. If you have children who come home and they're having a problem in school and you solve it for them, that's being as creative as inventing something that's going to take somebody to the moon. I want you to be creative all over, in every part of your lives with every fiber of your being.

# Exercise: Using the S.C.O.R.E. Model

Try this yourself as an exercise. Here are the steps:

1. *Identify the symptoms of the problem state.* Pick some inter- or intrapersonal relationship. You could be dealing with a family member. It could be dealing with a close friend or business associate. It could be anything where you're either dealing with a group or one-on-one. I'm sure that if all of you made it this far in your life you have several examples of places in your life where you'd like to have been more creative in the way you communicate. Pick that experience and then find a partner to be your guide.

2. *Explore the structure and causes of the symptoms.* Start with the realist. Put the symptom on a time line. As the guide, have your partner review that experience and find out whether it's primarily represented in pictures or sounds. Then have your partner tell you what feeling is connected to that point, that picture or that set of words that let's them know something is going wrong. Use the R.O.L.E. Model distinctions to help clarify the structure.

   It's that point at which you've run out of alternatives because of some response you're having to that situation where you want to explore the causes. It isn't that you can't be creative; it's just that something is blocking that process. Find the links. Find the triggers. What experiences occur just before the symptoms? Maybe they occur immediately before the symptoms, maybe the symptom is caused by something that happened a long time ago. It is here that you will most likely find the 'Critic'.

3. *Define the desired outcomes.* Release the 'Dreamer'. Have your partner identify the desired response for that situation. You could use the analogy of a magnet. If one end is North and the other end was South, one was positive and the other was negative—what would be the opposite feeling of that limiting one? Perhaps it's a feeling you get sitting at home, or sitting in a bar, sitting in a restaurant, playing guitar for your friends. And you go, "God, if I could only have done this an hour ago, I could have had a record contract." But when I was sitting there in the office in front of the guy from the recording studio, I froze up because the feeling I had wasn't the one I have right now.

4. *Identify the resources that make that outcome possible.* Explore the representational systems and physiology for potential resources. When they get this opposite feeling, ask them, "What allows you have that outcome?" "Where do you get that feeling?" "How are you breathing?" One of the things you can do is to notice the difference in location, if nothing else. Maybe in one case it's in the stomach, in the other one it's in the chest. That location lets you know which one you're having and can be the missing link to a whole set of resources.

   In J.'s case his breathing linked him to higher logical level—his identity and mission. In M.'s case his breathing linked him to a belief about having time.

   One of the core presuppositions of NLP is that people already have all the resources they need, in some form or another. The key is to find the structure and links to these resources so you can get them to occur at the times you need them.

5.  *Bring the resources into the problem state.* Once you've established what the differences in location and physiology associated with the limiting and resourceful feelings are, run either the movie or the soundtrack up to the point where the limiting feeling would have emerged. Not fully into it, but just before. If it's a soundtrack, stop the soundtrack right there. If it's a movie, freeze the frame. Then go back to the beginning of the movie and remember the resources associated with the desired outcome.

6.  *Explore the effects of applying your resources to the problem state.* Use your resources to generate some new alternatives. Ask, "If you had that resourceful feeling what else could you have done differently? Run a new scenario out into the future. What is something you could have done differently and how do you think you might have been able to have it come out differently?"

     Then ask, "What else could you have done differently?" for the second time. Then, "What is a third alternative?" Have your partner rerun the experience with the new feeling, and generate three alternatives. Each time, stop the memory right before it elicits the limiting feeling. We want to "nip it in the bud," so to speak. Because that's the point where you can be creative. We want to be able to go, "Hummm, that's interesting. I wonder how I can take care of this in a new way?"

After you've reprogrammed these new options, extend those experiences in your mind out to the future. That helps to lay down the new program more fully.

## Discussion: Generating Alternatives and Choices

I was involved with a set of studies that had to do with basketball players in high school. We had two sets of people from the same team. We mixed the sets so there was an equal number of players from the first string and second string in both groups. We took one of the groups and had them practice on the court all the time—normal basketball practice for two hours. The other group we put in a room. And for one hour, we had them imagine all the alternatives in their minds, all the different moves, all the different blocks, all the different picks, all the different things that can happen when you're out on the court. Then we had the two play basketball with each other for an hour. The players who sat in the room imagining the future for an hour played basketball as well if not better than the people who practiced on the court.

One of the players, the center, didn't know what to do with his body. He had no alternatives. He just was at that point where his body had not caught up with himself. So we showed him films of Kareem Abdul Jabar playing center. We slowed them down and had him make those pictures on the inside of his mind. We had him imagine what it would be like if he were moving his body in that way. What muscles would move first? What muscles would move second? How would he have to feel in order to be able to move like that? And you know, we got him to begin to move like that. Instead of being the tall, gangly high school senior who could barely move one arm and a foot at the same time, the guy became extremely coordinated, because he had something that let him know how he was supposed to be acting. He had a well defined, clear, outcome and choice about how to achieve it, as well as a way of checking his progress.

Creativity is all over the place. It's under the chair, it's in your bones, it's in your hair, it's in your head. It's in the universe.

The intent of this exercise is to show you one method to come up with alternatives based on changing a limiting feeling that you have in certain situations. To me that is being creative. Whether it's coming up with something new or it's coming up with something that you've been doing for a long time only it just never occurred to do it in that situation. To me either one of those is being creative.

As a matter of fact, I think we sometimes limit ourselves with the word "creative" or "creativity." To me it's all about alternatives, or better yet—choices. When someone is trying to solve a specific problem, what process do you use to solve the problem, to generate choices? In the frame in which we're dealing with it here and in society in general, this process is referred to as creativity. To me it's just another way of coming up with more effective choices—that's the more encompassing classification—especially in relating to critics.

Creativity in the sense I am using it is not just about coming up with something completely unique or brand new. A person can be creative by doing things that they've done before but in a new situation or context. A lot of creativity has come from that kind of strategy. The essence of creativity is building a new map.

While tension or frustration may limit some people in some situations, those feelings can also contribute to motivating creativity. It's not that there are any particular feelings that are inherently limiting to creativity. Having an argument with somebody, even if it's not what you want to do, can be a very creative activity. In order to keep arguing with somebody and not agree with them at all, you have to be really creative. You've got to be very creative to hold your side while they're holding their side. The question is, in the context of what's going on, is it getting you the OUTCOME that you really want. If your outcome is to have an argument with this person, then you've succeeded beautifully and you're being creative. If, on the other hand, your outcome was to get them to see a different perspective, not argue with them, then you've encountered a symptom. But in either case you are still being creative. And the next time you want to argue with somebody that way, you've already got the template for it. You've already got the creativity for it. The issue is, "Is your creativity working for you or against you?" Borrowing from what Lowell said, "A failed argument is just a solution to a different problem than the one you are trying to solve at the moment."

This exercise is about generating new alternatives to any situation. The term "new" in this case doesn't only mean that the specific action has never occurred in your behavior before— it means you have not used that behavior in that situation before. Either one can make it a new alternative. The essence of NLP and creativity is adding more choices. Knowing what feelings limit your ability to generate or select alternatives gives you the choice either to continue with what you already are doing or to try something different.

I think there probably is very little that we haven't done before. We've made movements, we've made pictures, we've talked. There's probably very little in the way of words, pictures, or feelings that we haven't already experienced. It's just a question of reorganizing them. Then they become something different.

The question addressed by this exercise is, "How could you get those ideas that just pop into your head sometimes to pop into your head at the times that you need them most?" That to me is the quantum leap: not just having the alternatives— it's having them when you need them. The creative leap comes when you have the choice. "What can you do to insure that you are going to be creative when you need it?" On the spot creativity, so to speak, and not when you sit down and have lots of time to mull over it. But here you are in the situation and you're beginning to get a feeling: What do you do to make that be different?

The other issue the exercise addresses is, "What makes that the best option in the circumstance?" "What alternative will be most likely to get you to the outcome and effect you are really after?" This is why you want to play each alternative out into the future. If you do choose that as an alternative, what impact does that have on the rest of the system?

For instance, if you are staying at a hotel, and you get angry at the clerk who's checking you in and he gets angry at you, then he passes it on to the busboy who'll pass it on to the houseman, who'll pass it on to the person who makes up your bed, etc., etc. In other words: How many people does it affect? So, if you have a bunch of alternatives, you want to figure out, "Which one is going to get me what I want, not just right now, but throughout the larger time frame that will be effected by that alternative?"

There's an old saying that, "You get what you deserve." That is, in any system of interactions, you eventually have to deal with the repercussions of your own previous behavior in that system.

By the way, another interesting variation of this exercise is to give your partner your problem and ask what feeling your partner would use and what alternatives your partner might generate. Have them tell you what they feel, how intensely they feel it and where it's located. You try and get their feeling and come up with something as an alternative. Even try their alternatives on. It's endless, the things you can do with this. You've just begun. This is just the tip of the iceberg with this kind of creativity.

My goal has been to help you be more creative inside. You have to talk to yourself and look at your own pictures when you think, learn, make decisions, and so on. I want you to be able to change them if you don't like them; to be able to use the voice if it's telling you to do things that you don't want to do. To be human is to be creative; it's hard-wired into what makes us who we are. There is not way you cannot be creative.

# Safeguarding the Results of the Creative Process: Patents

**RBD**: While 'critics' come in many types and forms, the 'Law' is probably one of the most direct and concrete expressions of the critic.

It is certainly an important "tool" for dreamers.

**RWD**: It is important to be aware of the patent and legal protection available to people with creative ideas. Like all functions of the critic, it can either work for you or against you—depending on which side you end up on.

Not all creativity is recognized in the same way by society. The law, or legal procedures, give certain inventors more favorable treatment than other inventors.

I should start off by saying, "An idea is not protectable." You cannot protect an idea. We've been talking a lot about creating ideas. But ideas as such are not protectable. A manager may be extremely creative in taking a group of diverse personalities and putting them together and getting them to work together. It may take a high level of creativity, the kind of creativity that we are talking about here: use of communication skills, different kinds of skills that it took a long time to learn, a great deal of effort to apply these kinds of skills to this particular management situation and get the company going, make it operate well. But it is nothing that you can patent. You can't patent, you can't protect, you can't copyright and you can't trademark a way of doing business. That's one of the things that's not protectable. You can't even protect the specific arrangement of people.

Only a particular expression of an idea is protectable. There are three kinds of legal protections for the expression of ideas. One is *patent*, one is *copyright*, and one is *trademark*. They are different kinds of legal protection. They have different histories. They are based on different philosophies. But they are the three basic legal tools that are used to protect ideas, or the results of creativity—where you have come up with the specific expression of a certain idea.

## Patents

The first patent law was established in England in the time of Queen Elizabeth I. It was called the "Anti-monopoly" statute. Queen Elizabeth I was granting "patents" in the form of "letters patent." *Letters patent* means letters published for everyone to see. She was publishing these letters patent granting certain rights. For example, she granted Sir Walter Raleigh the exclusive right to sell salt in London. No one could sell salt in London unless they got a license from Sir Walter Raleigh. It was given to Sir Walter Raleigh as a royal favor.

Of course, this made the people who had to buy salt and live in London very unhappy. Eventually, it resulted in an act passed by Parliament that "the Crown shall no longer have the right to grant monopolies." But somebody stood up and said, "Well, the Queen has been granting monopolies for new inventions. We think that if somebody contributed something new to industry, not salt, not a staple, but something new, they ought to be protected. They ought to be given encouragement to sell it, at least for a limited time."

Somebody made the argument that there had been a midwife operating in London at that time who had been highly successful. With this particular midwife, the chance of the baby being born alive was 80%. If you had any other midwife, it might have been quite a bit less. This particular midwife died after a period of time, and his son took over with the same results. It was eventually learned that he had invented the first obstetrical forceps, so that if the baby was in the wrong position, the forceps could be used to put it in the proper position and the net result was that this midwife had a much greater live birth rate than anyone else. In those days, the midwife would come in and everybody else would be sent out of the room. The midwife would do whatever was done in the secrecy and privacy of the birthing room. So he was able to keep it secret for two generations: his and his son's. And the argument was made that if he had had a better way of profiting from his invention other than keeping it a secret—if he could have patented it and obtained an exclusive right on it, in return for him having to tell people about it—many more babies would have been born alive. The net result was that monopolies on inventions were excluded from the anti-monopolies act.

This exclusion was also written into the United States Constitution, but not without considerable resistance on the part of people like Thomas Jefferson, for example. Thomas Jefferson was quite an inventor and had a number of patents. But he was not in favor of the provision giving Congress power to set up a patent law. His attitude was that "ideas should be free as the air. And if I come up with a good idea, it ought to be made available to everybody." He said, "If I light a candle because I have a new idea, and if someone else comes and lights a candle from mine, they haven't taken anything away from me." In other words, he believed, "If I have an idea and I can pass it on to other people to use, nothing has been taken away from me, and my passing it on has given greater light to the rest of the world." And that is good reasoning—on one hand.

On the other hand, I think he ignored the kind of reasoning that led to the patent of the midwife's forceps. Jefferson's reasoning fails to give any incentive for inventors to disclose. In many cases, the inventors would still keep some ideas a secret. And they could profit from them as much as possible before their secret is finally learned. The ability to obtain a patent does give an incentive and it encourages people to make disclosures.

What can you protect with patents? Basically, patent coverage is provided for something that is concrete, something that you can touch with your hands.

U.S. patent law, as I said earlier, is based on the Constitution of the United States. It is written into Article One, Section 8, of the Constitution, which says, *"Congress shall have power to promote progress of science and the useful arts by securing to inventors for a limited time exclusive rights to their inventions."* Patent law says whoever invents a "new and useful article of manufacture" is entitled to protection.

An "article of manufacture" is something concrete, something you can touch. It is a composition of matter: a drug, a chemical composition, a "machine"—something that's made up of physical parts.

You can also patent "a method of making an article of manufacture, or operating a machine." Now the method-type patent coverage is the thing that comes closest to protecting ideas. However, only the method of making an article of manufacture, the method of making a composition of matter or the method of operating a machine or assembling a machine may be protected.

So there are really two kinds of patents. One is the patent on an article of manufacture, machine or composition of matter. The other is a patent on a method of making an article of manufacture, machine or composition of matter.

In considering a method of making a "composition of matter," the first thing you might think of is a recipe. Can you patent McDonald's hamburgers? Or can you go into your kitchen and make a new cookie and patent it? Probably not. There's a 99.9% chance that you could not patent any kind of recipe. I doubt that you're going to be able to show that you have taken any new step that has not already been taken.

For instance, somebody like Colonel Sanders may have a patent on the method of making Kentucky Fried Chicken that involves certain specific equipment, like running it through a microwave heater or something. You can get a patent for that. You could come up with a method for cooking something that would involve some complicated machinery. They cannot patent the idea of Colonel Sanders' Chicken, but they may have patented a very specific expression of the idea, including very specific equipment.

There is a difference between *design patents* and *regular patents*. Design patents are granted on the basis of the article's aesthetic appearance rather than on what the article does. You can get a design patent on an ashtray, a microphone, or a chair. These chairs could be the subject of design patents: not because they do anything different or because they operate any differently than any other chair, but simply because they look different than any other chair. Design patent coverage is a subclass of regular patent coverage.

There are also plant patents. You can patent an asexually reproduced plant, roses for example, or grafted fruit trees of various kinds. The life of a plant patent is the same as a regular patent. A patent has a life of seventeen years. All patent coverage is essentially the same. Other than for plant patents, significant controversy has arisen in recent years regarding whether gene-splitting and the products of bio-chemistry should be patentable. The courts have finally decided that they can be patented under the existing patent law.

The argument was made for many years that you could not patent anything living. You could patent drugs that killed germs, but you couldn't patent a germ that killed other germs, even though you discovered it. It was something that was already living and existing in nature. And when scientists learned how to generate new kinds of antibodies and new kinds of bioorganisms through gene-splitting and other methods, the question was: Should you be able to patent the results? If you changed something living, should you be able to patent it? The courts finally decided that you can patent that sort of thing. You still cannot patent a new breed of dogs,

for example. But you can patent a product of biochemistry when you produce some new organism.

Another controversy arose with the development of computer technology. You cannot patent a computer program that is nothing more than the algorithm for computing pi, for computing the ratio between the diameter and circumference of the circle. If it is a straight computation and your computer program does nothing more than put that fixed, that known algorithm into effect, it cannot be patented.

Based on that reasoning, the patent office began rejecting all computer program patents. If you sent in an application on a computer program, they'd say, "It must contain an algorithm someplace, and we won't look at it." I think the patent office was being swamped with patent applications on computer programs. They were saying, "They're too hard to examine and they take too much time." The government had cut back on the appropriation of money for operating the patent office. As a result, the commissioner of patents was looking around for a way he could get rid of some of the work so they could operate within their budget and so that they could put pressure on the government to increase the patent office budget.

The fact of the matter is that if your computer program is a new method of operating a computer, with method steps in it that are new and different, you should be able to patent it. This has always been my view and the more recent cases have held in favor of granting such patents. The computer program must actually be a patentable method that includes new and non-obvious steps.

You can also patent a specific hard-wired program as a "new and non-obvious article of manufacture" for a machine. If the program does include mechanical and physical elements that have not been used before, that are combined in a non-obvious way, then it might also be possible to patent the hardware for practicing a new program.

# Copyrights

Copyrights also derive from the Constitution. The same section of the Constitution that provides for patents gives Congress the power to *"promote the progress of science and the useful arts by securing to authors, for limited times, the exclusive right to their writings."* Copyrights constitute an entire body of law. It is interesting that these provisions in the Constitution take only four or five lines to write out. The patent and copyright law are based on these few lines but yet each one takes a book to explain. And there are shelves of legal decisions based on the patent law and the copyright law that span many years and which try to determine what the Constitutional provision means, what the law that is based on it means. This has become a very complex area of law.

Copyright law basically protects writings. It has been expanded to protect works of art, paintings and statuary. It has also been expanded to protect maps and computer programs. You can copyright photographs. You cannot copyright an idea, and you cannot patent an idea. You can patent a specific article or manufacture based on an idea. You can get a copyright on a specific rendition of an idea. You can copyright reproductions of works of art. If you could take the Mona Lisa and make a three-dimensional reproduction of it, such as a statuette, you could probably copyright that. You might even be able to copyright a rendition of the Mona Lisa on burlap.

One question that sometimes arises is, "If you can take a photograph of the Golden Gate Bridge right at sunset and copyright it, why can't you copyright the photographic mask that is used to make a computer chip?" These masks show the very complicated patterns used in creating the chip. People ask: "If I can copyright a work of art, why can't I copyright the artwork that goes into making these computer chips?" I think the law is going in that direction. Eventually the artwork that goes into making a computer chip will be copyrightable. However, an argument that they are not copyrightable still remains at this point in time.

In order to get a copyright you have to have something new; original, some degree of originality has to be introduced. You may well be able to get a copyright on your arrangement of somebody else's song—to the extent that you added something else to it. That doesn't mean that you have the right to use it.

For example, if I were to write a history of the City of San Francisco, I can copyright my book on the history of San Francisco. That would not prevent you or anyone else from writing a history of San Francisco. The facts that are involved would have to be the same. If I've written a history of San Francisco and copyrighted it, then I am protected from someone else coming in and taking my particular work, copying, publishing and selling it as their own. But I'm not protected against someone else saying, "Hey, it's a great idea to write a history of San Francisco. I think I'll write one, too," and doing their own work.

One big question, of course, is how close can someone be to a book or a computer program without infringing on it? Could someone change a few lines or have exactly the same structure and just paraphrase these sentences?

Consider for a moment, a map of San Francisco. I can copyright it, but I can't keep you from making a map of San Francisco. If I make a map of San Francisco and you make one, they've got to be the same, or very nearly the same. The streets have got to be the same. The size of it can be varied. The colors used can be varied.

Many publishers of maps will put a fictitious street in. So if a person takes that map with the fictitious street in it and copies it rather than make his own map, he's going to pick up that fictitious street.

To show copyright infringement you have to prove:

1. that the copier had access to the alleged copied material, and
2. that he copied it.

If you buy his map and find out that this second-comer, this copier, has picked up that street, you have proof.

Copyright infringement of a written history of San Francisco is a little harder to demonstrate. You'd get into looking at specific paragraphs and sentences. What you have to do is look at all the elements that make up the history and see how much of it is similar. It could be a lot like comparing the two maps, to see what's the same and what's different.

There have been a number of interesting cases. One interesting case involved the movie *Gaslight*. Bob Hope did a spoof of *Gaslight* and he put it on television. All the dialogue from *Gaslight* was the same in both productions. But, in Hope's spoof, the words and the actions didn't match. The words were the same, but they were said with different intonation and with different actions in order to make it humorous. There was a suit. And it was decided that it was a copyright infringement, since they used the same words as in the basic underlying work. Even though the net result was entirely different, that was a copyright infringement.

You get into very complicated problems when you get into music. You can copyright the underlying musical composition. You can copyright the specific printed sheet music that is sold to the public. You can copyright a record that is made of someone singing that particular song. So there are three different copyrights you can get on that one underlying composition, all of them based on specific renditions of the idea.

Ordinarily, one of the basic requirements for infringement is access to the underlying work, access to the copyrighted material. The requirement is that you must actually have registered your copyright with the copyright office before you can sue somebody for infringement.

The length of time that the work is protected depends on whether it is a "work for hire" or not. The typical length of a copyright is based on the author's life plus fifty years. When you file the application for registration, you include your birth date which becomes an essential feature of the copyright coverage. The old copyright law, that was effective until 1980, was that a work was protected for twenty-eight years and that protection was renewable for twenty-eight years. The new copyright law has given a substantial extension to the life of the copyright.

So a copyright is for the life of the author plus fifty years, unless it's a work for hire. If it's a work for hire, then the copyright is for seventy-five years from the date of publication. Work for hire is where the author is hired to produce the work. Say Walt Disney hires someone to write a story for a movie, and that work is produced as a result of their being hired. That would be a work for hire, and the life of the copyright would be seventy-five years.

In the United States, a new copyright law went into effect January 1, 1980. After many years and a lot of hearings, they finally came up with a new copyright law. Under the old copyright law, you had to publish the book, and you had to publish the song, you had to publish the written material with the copyright notice on it before you could register the copyright. If you published any number of them without the copyright notice on them, you placed them in the public domain and you could not go back and claim the copyright if you inadvertently let it out without the copyright notice on it.

One of the cases I was involved in was the "Keep on Trucking" signs. Remember that old "keep on trucking" cartoon that suddenly popped up and caught everybody's interest, and you saw it all over everywhere? It was a kind of symbol of the Sixties. The author of that eventually copyrighted it and sued a large number of people who picked it up and started using it. And he did quite well until he got into one suit in San Francisco where they were able to show he had given his marketing manager the right to put that on their cards and use it and there was no copyright notice on the cards. The court held he had lost his copyright because he had let somebody else use it without the copyright notice.

The copyright notice is a "C" in a circle—©—the name of the person claiming the copyright, and the year in which it is published. This means something different than the "R" in a circle you often see. That has to do with trademarks.

## Trademarks and Service Marks

Trademark law is entirely different thing from patent and copyright law. U.S. trademark law, for example, is not based on the Constitution. Trademarks are based on common law. Trademarks go back to the old Guilds in England and Europe. If you were a member of a guild, the silversmiths' guild for example, you would put the mark of that guild on your product when you made it to show:

1. who made it; and
2. that it was made by a person who was authorized— a member of the guild.

In later years it came to be more of an identification of source. If you find some of Paul Revere's silver products in museums, you will see his mark on the silver.

The idea of trademarks has expanded. The trademark is supposed to indicate the source of the goods. In recent years, under the U.S. trademark law, there's also a public interest involved in the trademark. In other words, the trademark is also supposed to protect the general public from confusion as to source. If you go in and buy a box of Tide laundry soap at the grocery store, the feeling is that the general public should have some assurance that if they buy Tide today and then they go back and buy Tide tomorrow, it's going to be the same product and from the same source. The idea is to avoid confusion by the general public as to what kind of products they're buying, even though the developers may be willing to let someone else make their product.

There are trademark licenses, McDonald's licenses or Kentucky Fried Chicken licenses, where somebody has established a trademark and then licenses it or franchises it and allows other people to use it. If you allow someone to use your trademark without exerting quality control, you may lose rights in it. The goal is to make sure the general public is protected, so that when they go to buy something under a given trademark, they get a given level of quality. It doesn't have to be high quality, but it has to be the *same* quality. They're not really interested in insuring high quality, but in insuring that the same quality is covered by that trademark.

A *service mark* is used when you don't have any trademarkable goods. The NLP logo, for example, is a service mark, because NLP training programs are a service. The Chevron used on the filling stations is technically a service mark. What are they doing? They are selling a fluid. You can't stamp it as it comes out of the pump. And they are offering a service, the supplying of gasoline to motorists who drive by and want to buy it. In recent years I must have seen forty different applications for registration of Chevron because they've gotten into insecticides, fertilizers, household cleaning goods, window cleaners, and what they've had to do is register that Chevron for each of these products as they've begun to sell it in interstate commerce with the trademark on it.

Trademarks are registered in some forty different categories. If you are going to register a mark you could register it in some thirty different categories for goods and then there are about five different categories for services: educational, business, and entertainment are the kinds of services. Then finally there is a miscellaneous category that covers all kinds of things.

There are three important things about trademarks:

1. the word itself;

2. the form of the word;

3. the goods on which it is used.

For example, in the U.S. there are Johnson and Johnson Baby Powder, Johnson's Floor Wax and Johnson's Outboard Motors. Three entirely different companies, all using the same or substantially the same trademark—but the goods are entirely different.

Incidentally, a trade name is not the same as a trademark. The trade name is the name of the company. The trademark is the mark that identifies the goods. For example, General Electric is the trade name of the General Electric Company. GE, the little GE with the squiggly thing around it is their trademark. And they would fight you to the death on the trademark. If you call yourself General Electronics or GE, they probably won't fight you. Everybody knows who GE is, and they know it's not you.

Mercury Outboard motors are not made by Ford Motor Company nor with Ford Motor Company's permission. As a matter of fact, Ford Motor Company sued to try to stop the people from using the name Mercury on outboard motors. The courts in that case held that people who buy outboard motors are discriminating purchasers. That is, they are not going to put that much money into a motor without knowing who built it.

People who buy automobiles know very well before they spend thousands of dollars buying a car whom they are buying it from. They are discriminating purchasers. The goods are unrelated. People who buy cars are not necessarily going to buy outboard motors and vice versa. So it's entirely possible for both companies to use the name Mercury in connection with their specific goods without there being any likelihood of confusion. "Likelihood of confusion" is the test in connection with trademarks. GE is an interesting example of that. The fact is that a lot of people have and can use GE, but they can't use it in the specific form that General Electric has.

Basically, there's two dilemmas in connection with trademarks. Everyone wants to come up with a trademark that's so good and so catchy that everybody will use it. That's all very well and good as long as it's not too good, too catchy. Then you get into the situation of names like "cellophane," "aspirin," "kleistron" or even more recently, "thermos bottle," where the product is so new and the name is so good that it becomes the generic name.

You generally always want to be sure to use the trademark as an *adjective* and not as a noun. When you start using it as a noun you have problems.

Aspirin originally was a trademark. A German company came up with it. Now it's generic: Everybody makes aspirin. Cellophane is another one. They didn't know what to call this kind of thin transparent paper. It still doesn't have another name. If you talk about "cellophane thin transparent paper," maybe it'd be all right, or "cellophane flexible wrapping paper." But cellophane was lost very quickly.

Kleistron was originally a mark of Sperry Gyroscope. Probably most of you don't know what a kleistron is. The word is Greek for a wave beating on a shore. It was an atomic particle velocity modulation device and the name was a very classy reference to ancient Greece. It turned out to be the name of an entirely new type of device and it was lost as a trademark. So choosing names that become too popular is a pitfall in the trademark field.

Xerox has fought very hard to keep from losing their name because it's almost too good. It's a coined name. It didn't mean anything until they came along and made up the name and adopted it as their trademark and started building meaning for it. It got so bad that people would say, "Make me a Xerox of this," or "I'm going to Xerox this report"; and probably people still do. Xerox has actually been trying very hard to stop it.

Kodak almost lost their name for the same reason. You lose your trademark rights in a name to the extent that you begin to use it or allow other people to use it generically. Kodak had a bunch of ads in the 20's or 30's reading, "Kodak your way across the country." A trademark should always be used as an adjective—for example, "Xerox photo copy machines." There Xerox is imaginative. Or "Kodak hand-held cameras." To use a Kodak hand-held camera is one thing. To use a Kodak is another. Does Kodak define the camera, or is it the thing that it names?

Mylar and Lucite are probably in the borderline category. The Coca Cola company spent millions to protect its trademark for the same reason.

## Copyrights versus Trademarks

Copyrights are not the same as trademarks. Its a thing that many people confuse, one of the things that most of my clients are confused about. They come in and they have a name and say, "I want to copyright this name." Or they'll say that so and so's name is copyrighted.

You cannot copyright a name or a short slogan or a trademark. You don't copyright the name. Copyright is reserved for expression of ideas. A book is copyrightable. A photograph or a drawing is copyrightable. Architects' drawings are copyrightable. Records and music are copyrightable: They are all expressions of ideas. But a name, a short name that distinguishes one company from another is not copyrightable.

You register trademark rights in a name. If it's a name you want protection for, in the U.S. you register your name as a trademark either with the state or federally. Every state in the union will register trademarks. They will register the name of your company or the name you sell a product under. In the state of California, you could claim exclusive rights in a name and you could register it with the Secretary of State. If you want to register the name federally, then you have to go to the Patent Office in Washington and register it. You cannot register a name federally until you have actually shipped goods across state lines with the trademark on it. In other words, until you actually participate in interstate commerce, you can't register the name federally.

Let's assume you start using a name for your goods, "Acme Products." Acme's going to be your trademark and you put Acme with an "R" in a circle on your goods and sell it in interstate commerce. It sounds like it should be all right. The trouble is, the "R" in the circle indicates that it is registered federally. If it's not federally registered, you put a little "TM" by it. And if you use the "R" in a circle before you've actually gotten the federal registration, you're committing a fraud. At least, the Patent and Trademark Office takes the position that that's fraudulent. If you've used the "R" in a circle with your trademark before you've actually registered it, you shouldn't be allowed to register it at a later date.

That's directly contrary to the old copyright law which said, "If you want to claim copyrights in something you've got to publish something and put the 'C' in a circle on it."

It's kind of confusing, isn't it? Copyrights and trademarks had the opposite requirements. What was right for one was wrong for the other. That, of course, is one of the classic problems with 'critics.' It's like spelling a word wrong because you are trying to forget the wrong spelling.

**RBD**: If you only had one critic to satisfy, everything would be easy. Critics usually come in clusters—and their values are not all the same.

**RWD**: One part of the United States government grants patents because the Constitution says that Congress shall have power to promote progress of science and useful arts by granting to inventors exclusive rights to their invention. What's an exclusive right? An exclusive right is a monopoly. Anytime you say "monopoly," it's like waving a red flag in front of a bull: the anti-trust division of the United States government. They don't like monopolies. But they can't attack patents, although they might like to, because patents are protected by the Constitution.

Suppose you have a company like the Aluminum Company of America. They were the first ones to come up with a practical way of extracting aluminum from ore. So they put it into practice and they organized a good management team, and a good research and development team. And they made more inventions. They invested some of the profit that they made to further perfect their refining techniques. They put some of the money that they made in buying new deposits, building new plants, staying ahead of their competition. They did such a good job that all of the patents that related to aluminum refinement were owned by the Aluminum Co. of America. They had no competition. They concentrated all the patent coverage. Any time anybody came up with a good idea that had to do with aluminum, they bought it. Any time there was a new discovery for aluminum ore, they bought it. Any time there was need for a new aluminum plant they built it. And they ended up with a monopoly. The anti-trust division of the U.S. government decided that something needed to be done about it. Nobody could get into competition with them. So they sued them for violation of the anti-trust law, and were able to make them divest themselves of some of their patent rights. It was illegal to make a "patent pool." It was held that they had done just that.

The same thing applied to RCA. RCA was established by GE, Westinghouse and Bell Telephone, pooling their radio patents into a patent pool, and establishing a corporation, namely the Radio Corporation of America, to hold them. And this patent pool was uncontested during the First World War. As a matter of fact, Franklin Delano Roosevelt suggested that it be done. The First World War had started and it turned out that Marconi had established and owned all the radio companies that were then in operation. When the war broke out in Europe, America suddenly realized that it didn't have any well-established radio companies. Therefore Radio Corporation of America was set up. There was this fantastic new development where you could speak here and it could be heard over there and there were no wires in between. All the patents that related to that were concentrated in Radio Corporation of America. That made it quite a powerful company for many years. I think IBM and some of the corporations on the West Coast of the U.S. have eclipsed RCA.

If you take these limited monopolies and you stack enough of them together, you can build a big monopoly that would violate the anti-trust laws of the United States. I don't think patents are a monopoly. They are limited in time. They have a seventeen-year life. I don't think you're really talking about a monopoly. But, as you might recall, monopoly is where the patent law started in Queen Elizabeth's time.

## Trade Secrets

In addition to patents, copyrights, and trademarks, there is another area of law that relates to ideas that we have been talking about. That is trade secrets or proprietary information.

The new copyright law and the patent law have made inroads over the years in proprietary information trade-secret type protection. The copyright law says that as soon as anything is rendered in tangible form, as soon as you've made a copy of a drawing, as soon as you've taken this idea that's existed only in your mind and put it down on paper, then it becomes subject to the federal copyright law and can no longer be handled in accordance with the state law of unfair competition. So the copyright law has taken that out of the hands of the state and put it all under the copyright law.

Trade secrets are protectable under state law in the U.S. If you've invented a new composition of matter or put together a new arrangement of chemicals that produces an item that's particularly saleable, there are two things you can do. One would be to patent it. The other would be to keep it a secret if in fact it is something that could be kept secret, something that couldn't be discovered by analysis. You make and sell the product and if it's not possible for the person who buys the product to subject it to the kind of sophisticated testing that's available to people today and determine what the materials are that make up that composition of matter, then maybe it's a good idea to keep it secret.

If you patent it, you are given limited rights, rights limited in time. In order to get a patent, you have to give sufficient information to allow anyone who has ordinary skill in the art to make and to practice your invention, to make your composition of matter or to make an article having your composition of matter. If you've done that and if it's decided that it's new and non-obvious and entitled to patent coverage by the patent examiner, the patent will be issued and you will then be protected for seventeen years. At the end of seventeen years, everything that you've taught, everything that you've set forth in your patent application becomes available to the general public for use as they see fit.

## Discussion: Examples of Copyright Protection

**Question**: I've written a novel and I've copyrighted it. But I'm starting another one, and every time I write a draft I put a little "c" in a circle and my name and a date. Does that protect it until it's published? I don't necessarily want to have to register drafts.

**RWD**: The new copyright law gives you a copyright in your work as soon as you reduce it to some concrete form. As soon as you've put the ideas down on paper, you immediately have rights in that work whether you have the copyright notice or not. If a few copies are distributed—let's say you send a few copies out to publishers to see if they're interested in publishing it—you have not lost your right to copyright it. In fact, the copyright law provides for registration of unpublished works. You could take the copy of your work and go down and make a photo-copy of it and send it to the Copyright Office and you could register it, in unpublished form. And you would have a copyright in the work. The new copyright law is more lenient with respect to allowing a limited number of the works to be published without the copyright notice. Of course, it also enables you to register it before you publish it.

Nonetheless, I think the habit of including the copyright notice on your drafts can't hurt you, and it could help you. You can't sue for infringement of copyright until you have registered the copyright with the Copyright Office. You must register the copyright before you can maintain suit against someone.

Copyright law is interesting in a couple of ways. It has a criminal section in it. If someone infringes your copyright you can always threaten to report him to the Attorney General and get him sent to jail. There can be a fine and jail sentence for copyright infringement. It has to be willful and wanton and intentional copyright infringement. But there is enough of that that goes on, that I think it's worth still having in the law. And it is sometimes enforced.

**Question**: I have a catalog that I have put the copyright notice on. I haven't registered it. And I have a trade name that I put there with a TM next to it. Is that OK?

**RWD**: That's no problem. The copyright law says that if you put the copyright notice on the work you should proceed with the registration. You probably should proceed with it in the near future. It's a fairly inexpensive process. You get the forms from the Copyright Office, you can fill them out. The difficulty with a catalog is that you've got to give the name of the people that bound it, the name of the people that produced the material, anybody who had anything to do with printing it. It still has to be put down. That's an archaic thing. The old copyright law was written in such a way as to encourage people to have their photocopying and printing done in the United States. They actually would not allow you to copyright something where the printing, lithographic things, had been done outside the United States.

At least the copyright no longer refuses protection, but it requires you to tell them who did the printing and binding. Send a ten dollar fee to the copyright office and you've got the registration.

As for the trademark, there's nothing to compel you to ever register a trademark. Using the TM is a good idea. Don't use an "R" in a circle, use the TM, use an asterisk and then someplace else put "trademark of Joe Smith" or "trademark of such and such company" until such time as you've actually completed the registration in the Patent and Trademark Office.

Rather than a trademark you may really have a service mark if you're offering a service—a mail order service in this case. The distinction is whether or not you have a trade or a service, whether you're offering goods, which this name identifies the source of the goods, or whether you're offering these people a service, and the name identifies the source of those particular services. There isn't any real distinction in the rights that are involved.

The Trademark Office has divided all the goods into thirty or forty categories. We've now got an international classification system.

**Question**: I know that if you have a song you can send a tape of it to the Copyright Office and protect it. Once you have copyrighted the tape, can someone make some sheet music of that song and use it, or is the content of the tape protected?

**RWD**: Under the new copyright law, there are two different ways you can copyright a song. One is by actually getting the written notation and registering that with the copyright office. The other is by recording it on a tape and registering the tape with the copyright office. Both cases protect the song.

**Question**: How does that apply to software?

**RWD**: You can register it by getting a print-out of your software. You can also register it by sending in the actual disc.

**Question**: Do you have to send in the source code then, or do you just register the final product?

**RWD**: You can copyright the final product.

**Question**: Let's say you did a creativity seminar. What kind of rights do you have in that?

**RWD**: In this kind of situation, you've got two things going, what's customary and what's legal.

There are the so-called performance rights. There are copyrights. There are unfair competition rights. There are all kinds of rights that you could get in a seminar.

Certainly, if it's recorded you could copyright the tape. You could prevent someone from taking the tape and presenting an essentially identical performance of the seminar. Of course, if you use that tape as the basis for a book, you could copyright the book.

Plagiarism, of course, is copyright infringement. Under the new copyright law, there is a fair use doctrine. It's always been possible to quote from somebody's copyrighted work as long as you show that it's their copyright and that you contact the copyright owner and tell them you're quoting from their book. You obviously can't take a best seller and then say, "As they said in *Gone With The Wind*..." and then repeat the entire book. But you can pick certain pieces out of a book. It's considered a fair use as long as you haven't taken the entire work and used it for your own purposes. If you are using it as an illustration of some sort, an illustration of something as part of a much larger work, it is considered a fair use.

Anybody can list anybody's books in a bibliography and say, "This paper is based in part on...." The person who has published the book under that name has no objection he can make to the fact that you have used his book in preparing your paper. Mentioning it is like mentioning the name of a public figure. Newspapers do it all the time. If you do something noteworthy, they can use your name: It's not a violation of your right of privacy to report that, in fact, you climbed the side of the Bank of America building to the top and were arrested by the police. Whenever you've done anything that's noteworthy, such as publishing a book, that item is a fact that can be used. So a bibliography is no problem so far as listing the names.

You would get into a problem if you had an appendix and in the appendix you essentially reprinted somebody's doctoral thesis or a chapter out of somebody's book without their permission. Then you're getting into copyright infringement.

In general, If you're going to make a quotation of content from somebody's work, it would be good practice to get their approval, such as a signed letter of release.

# Utilizing the Critic

What I want to emphasize is, as with all critics, the scope or the "what" of legal protection is a very narrow and limited part of creativity—but an important one nonetheless. You can get legal protection for a very small, very restricted part of creativity. It's hard to obtain legal protection for a highly creative sermon or work of art. You can copyright the architectural plans for a hotel which is an entirely new kind of building but that does not protect the idea for the building. It simply prevents someone else from buying those plans, reproducing them and selling them. It does not prevent me from buying the plans and building a $20 million building based on those plans once I've gotten them. Copyright protection does not extend to the results.

If you've gone through this creative process and come up with a new product, you don't have to get a patent on it in order to have the right to sell it. You can sell anything you want. People sell coats, suits, and pants. Ninety-nine percent of what is sold today is not patented. Most of it is staples: groceries, clothing, radios, thermos bottles, etc. These things may have been patented at one time long ago, but now are no longer patented. They're still sold in large quantities. The patent does not grant you the right to make something. It does grant you the right to exclude others from making it.

Legal protection is the epitome of the critic. Everything is cast in negative terms. Neither patents nor copyrights grant the right to use or do something. They simply grant the right to *exclude* others from using or doing a certain thing. That's a big difference.

A patent is a right to exclude others from making, using, or selling. A copyright is a right to exclude others from making, using, or selling. In both cases you still have to be concerned about whether or not someone else has a basic right. You could get into overlapping rights. One person can get a patent that has claims that are very broad, but you can find that one specific part of the area covered by the broad claim is more saleable, or more interesting.

You can claim coverage to the extent that you contributed something unusual to an existing expression of something. In the case of a patent, not only must it be new and unusual, it must also be non-obvious. So your coverage is limited to the extent that you have made a non-obvious addition to an existing item. Some people talk about them as being improvement patents. You'll hear someone say, "He has an improvement patent on something." Well, really, all patents are improvements over the prior arts. I can't think of any patents that don't include things that already existed in prior art; or any invention that doesn't have something about it that's drawn out of prior art. So to that extent, all inventions are improvements on prior art.

In order to get a copyright, all you have to do is do something that is new and original, has some degree of originality. Just like patents you'll find overlapping coverage. In the case of a musical composition, for example, one arrangement of the song might be more appealing than all the others.

The Patent Office doesn't make any value judgments on an invention. The patent law of today says, "Whoever invents a new and useful article of manufacture is entitled to a patent for it." And almost anything is considered useful. A toy sword you stab someone with which squirts red ink out the end because it collapses is considered useful and patentable, and it has been patented. As long as an invention is new and useful, it is patentable, unless it would have been obvious to one having ordinary skill and art at the time the invention was made. This non-obvious requirement makes inventions a lot like jokes. What is it that makes a joke funny? It's that twist at the end. It is the unexpected, the non-obvious statement that makes the joke funny and it is the same thing that makes an invention possible. It is the non-obvious unexpected feature of the device that makes it patentable.

I may want to build an automobile using all left-handed threads. Nobody has ever done that before. Automobiles today have right-handed threads. I'm going to do it with all left-handed threads. That's new and it is useful. An automobile is useful. I could argue at least that using left-handed threads makes it easier for left-handed people to work on their car. So it's new and it's useful. But is it obvious? The answer is yes. If you can do it with all right-handed threads, you can do it with all left-handed threads. Where there's no non-obvious feature, perhaps the least obvious aspect of the invention is the ingenious argument for why it would be useful. There are a lot of patents granted on that.

In order to get patent coverage, you must look for the non-obvious, the unexpected. Quite often, inventors will come to my office and disclose the invention to me, and I'll laugh. I am laughing because I had expected the obvious. The inventor will show me the problem he faced and the unexpected solution he came up with.

I remember a patent attorney I met when I first started out. Ever since I met him, I've avoided saying that you cannot patent something. He said, "I can patent anything. I'll patent horseshit if you want me to. What you do is, you press it into pots and you sell it as a combination pot and fertilizer. That get's you a patent on horseshit." Of course, he's not actually patenting it. He's patenting a specific kind of pot and fertilizer.

The only thing I know of that the Patent Office ever rejected as not useful is the perpetual motion machine. The Patent Office will reject any invention where the candidate produced a perpetual motion device. One of these days I think somebody's going to do it.

The Patent Office keeps telling you you can't do it. And inventors are notable for saying, "If you tell me I can't, I'm going to do it." As a matter of fact, I had that experience in telling an inventor he couldn't patent a perpetual motion device. It didn't bother him. He came to me with this invention that was a complicated pump. It supposedly used a heat cycle—it isn't worth going into all the details of what it was—but I finally managed to get a patent issued for him. We had to cut the claims down, and we had to claim a very specific part of it to finally get the patent issued. But we finally got the patent issued and I sent him a copy of it. And he sent a letter back to me thanking me for my help in getting a patent on his perpetual motion machine. This pump was an essential part of a larger system which we were never able to patent. It was a complicated system, and if you went through the whole system including that pump it was a perpetual motion system. He carefully concealed this and said, "All I want is coverage for that pump device." And we did get some coverage for it.

The point is, the patent office doesn't make any decisions about whether an invention is good or bad, the question is, "Is it new and is it useful?" As long as you can show a use for it they don't make a value judgment.

The judgment they make is, "Is it non-obvious?" "Would it be obvious to 'one having ordinary skill in the art at the time the invention was made?'"

An American politician made the remark one time that he thought there were an awful lot of useless patents granted. He said he remembered reading that someone patented tetraethyl lead. Someone got a patent for putting tetraethyl lead in gasoline to cut down on knocking—which, incidentally, is considered a bad invention today because it pollutes the environment. It was considered a good invention when it was made, but today it's bad. The politician's comment was, "What's patentable about that? What else can you do with tetraethyl lead? You can't put it in coffee." To him it was an obvious thing. Obviously, you put it in gasoline. You can't put it in coffee.

Of course, this is a classic case of "20-20 hindsight." A lot of things seem obvious after someone has done them. The less knowledgeable a person is about a particular area, the more likely it is he will fail to see anything non-obvious about an invention. After all, if you don't know anything about a certain area, anti-knock formulas for gasoline, for instance, the more obvious anything you learn about it becomes—because it is the only thing you do know about it. This is another feature of many critics.

So you have critics of other critics. That's part of what makes patent law interesting. In the U.S., patent examiners in recent years have latched on to this notion that there are too many useless patents being granted and they reject a great number of patent applications on the grounds that they are obvious. The first action of an examiner, nine times out of ten, is a rejection because he wants to make you argue, to clarify the situation.

I had an old patent attorney as a teacher who expressed the attitude of a classic critic (and a good patent attorney). He said, "I never took any pleasure in getting a patent allowed on first action or on winning an appeal. Because if I got the patent on first action, it meant I didn't claim it broadly enough to get into any argument with the examiner. If I won an appeal, it meant I should have won it in the first place and I didn't present it right or I wouldn't have had to go to appeal." So what you want to do it present your claims broadly enough that the examiner will have to reject it, but then you go in and argue with him in order to tailor the claims to the right size.

The examiners will often use obviousness as an objection. One way to respond to that is by showing commercial success. It isn't enough to argue, "If my idea's so obvious why hasn't it been done before." The examiner will say, "Well, it's new, and I can't find anything that's exactly like it, but I think it's obvious." You say again, "Well, if it's so damned obvious, why didn't somebody do it?" And his response to that is, "Well, if nobody did it, it's because it wasn't worth doing." So if you can go in and show commercial success, you can overcome the obviousness rejection.

It is clear that if you can show that in a prior argument the examiner said, "You can't do what you've done, you can't connect A to B and then add C," you should be able to get a patent on A connecting to B and adding C. If you can show that it is in fact useful and if you can convince the examiner that you have in fact done it you ought to be able to patent it.

Most inventors who come to me are very concerned that someone is going to steal their idea. They think that their big problem is going to be to protect themselves from having their ideas stolen. In my experience, the inventor's problem is exactly the opposite. His big problem is to get someone sufficiently interested in his invention that they will invest in it. There are all kinds of people out there who'll say, "Oh, that's a great idea. That's a tremendous idea. You ought to do something with it." They're all anxious to encourage you to do something with your invention, but when it comes time for them to invest in somebody else's idea, they find it hard to do.

The inventor's big problem is not so much theft of the idea as it is getting people to invest in the idea. This is particularly true if you've taken the minimum steps to provide protection for your idea.

## Preparing for the Critic: Taking Steps to Protect Your Ideas

What are some of the minimum steps to provide protection for your ideas?

One would be keeping engineering notebooks. If you're planning on doing something creative, it'd be a heck of a good idea to get a notebook—a bound book with numbered pages, preferably. It's a good idea to get one that has quarter inch squares in it so you can make notes and little drawings and sketches on it—kind of like Leonardo da Vinci. Write down your ideas. You don't know which ones are good. A lot of them are answers to future problems. Maybe they don't work for what you're working on today, but you've made a note of them. At least you have them written down. Sign and date each page. Periodically, have someone else take a look through the notebook and sign and date it. Have them write "witnessed and understood"—preferably on each page. You can paste in newspaper articles, photographs and other papers. Try to sign partly over the photographs and partly over the page. Have the witness sign across it too, so that you have some proof that the photograph was signed by the witness.

The Patent Office and the courts generally will never listen to the inventor, although there is some talk about trying to change that. You always have to have a corroborating witness or witnesses. So it's a good idea to have one or two people sign your notebook.

You don't have to keep a notebook. You could simply keep a written record of any idea that you think is particularly good and have it witnessed, signed and dated. Sign and date it yourself, and have the witness sign and date it.

Notes sent to yourself by registered mail don't do you any good. To prove that an envelope went through the mail registered doesn't necessarily prove that you had anything in it when it went through the mail. There's all kinds of ways of opening envelopes and putting something else in it. It's far better to draw it out on a piece of paper, and have someone that you expect to be in contact with over a period of time sign it and date it. (*See* Appendix G for more suggestions on keeping a laboratory notebook.)

Of course, even this will not necessarily insure protection. The Patent Law says, "That person who is the first, to conceive an idea, to think of it, and with diligence carry it to an actual or constructive reduction to practice is entitled to patent for it." The documents, the engineering notebooks, the paper I'm talking about preparing is proof of conception. If you keep a notebook and you keep notes in it as to what you've been doing to try to carry that idea to an actual reduction to practice, that helps you prove diligence. You do have to do something with your idea. Once you've gotten it written down, you have to proceed with it, with all deliberate speed. It doesn't mean to be diligent you have to give up everything else you're doing in life in order to carry that idea to an actual reduction to practice, but you do have to do what would be reasonable for a person to do who had an idea of that kind.

RCA, General Electric or General Motors would have to proceed a heck of a lot faster than you do as a private individual—particularly if the invention is something that would be of interest to a corporation. The corporation must proceed more rapidly to be diligent than an individual would have to who had limited means. So proceeding diligently to an actual reduction to practice is another important thing to do to insure protection—but it is open to interpretation.

One constructive reduction to practice is buying a patent application. There are a lot of inventions that might be too expensive for the individual to actually reduce to practice, so the next step would be to file a patent application within a reasonable time.

## The Dedicated Advocate and the Creative Critic

One of the pitfalls of creativity is falling in love with your invention. And I think that's a problem in a couple of ways, but it also has its positive side. That fact that inventors have a tendency to fall in love with their inventions powers a lot of creativity. I was talking to someone recently about the amount of creativity that has been required for inventors to tailor their pet idea to fit within a government-funded research program. Back in the days when the government was putting out a lot of money to fund research programs, there were inventors all over the country who could figure out one way or another to make their idea applicable to a particular government contract and thereby be able to finance the research involved in developing it.

The danger in falling in love with your idea is characterized by the invention developers, who flourished for many years. What the invention developer would do was offer to develop your invention for a fee. And if they could get you to sign up, they'd say, "This is a very touchy business. I'll need to be out contacting people all day and I'll call you if I'm able to do anything. You realize of course that I can't guarantee you success, but I'll be out there doing what I can. So don't call me, I'll call you if I get anything." So you give them your money and that's the last you hear of them.

After a while they had to get a little more crafty than that. They'd say, "Oh, a thousand dollars is too much. I'll tell you what I'll do. If you'll give me a fifty percent interest in your invention, I'll do it for five hundred dollars." That sounds pretty good. The only trouble is they don't intend to do anything. All they want is the five hundred dollars. If they can find some way to convince you that you should invest in your invention with them, they're willing to give you all kinds of encouragement—especially if you're willing to pay for it.

Obviously, having multiple developers of an idea presents its own problems even when it is valid. This issue comes up especially in companies. I worked for a time at the electronics firm EIMAC. Jack McCullough (who was MAC of EIMAC) didn't believe in buying inventions from outside the company. And furthermore, he didn't believe in investing in ideas unless he could identify the "dedicated applicant." To make an idea successful you need to be dedicated enough to face the critic and not buckle under—it doesn't really help to pay someone for encouragement.

Joint inventorship can be a real problem. You quite often have the problem in universities or in industry where a man will have a number of people working for him, and this manager has a way of adopting the inventions of the people who work for him as his own. I've run into that quite a bit in my own work.

In order to file the patent application and get a patent, I've got to know as much as I can about the invention. So nine times out of ten I will criticize the invention. I'll be pretty hard on the invention when I'm talking to the inventor to try to find out where the invention is, and, in the case of joint inventions, to find out who the real inventor is.

It's a little bit like Solomon and the two women who each claim that the baby is theirs. Solomon decides to cut the baby in two so they can each have a half. One of the mothers is willing to go along with it, but the other would rather give up the baby than have it killed. At that point, Solomon knows who the baby's real mother is. If you criticize the invention, the one who's not the inventor will say, "Well, I never thought of that," and be ready to give in to you. The one who is the inventor will say, "Wait a minute. There's got to be some way we can get around that objection. Oh, yeah, here's a way to do it." He'll figure out some way to make it work. He's dedicated to making the invention work no matter what obstacle he's going to run into.

I think that's why stubbornness is one of the hallmarks of the inventor. I've learned over many years that it's the dedicated advocate who makes the invention go—no matter how long it takes, or how much money. Eventually, if it's possible to make it go, he'll make it go. If you put the same idea in the hands of people who are not the dedicated advocates, it'll fail every time.

**RBD**: It is important to know how others are going to view your ideas. One of the functions of the critic is to tighten up your own thinking process.

**RWD**: Another way of saying this is that a lot of creativity goes into being a critic, responding to a critic, and in figuring out what kind of legal protection you can get for an idea. Maybe you can't protect the whole thing but there's some part of it you can protect. For instance, maybe you find that you can't protect the basic idea of some game, maybe you can't copyright the game board—but maybe you can get trademark rights to the name it's sold under.

Scrabble is an example of that. Scrabble is a word game that was popular for a while. Shortly after it came out, somebody wanted to compete with them and sold a game called "Skip-across." I don't think Skip-across even exists any more. But is was basically the same game as Scrabble. I remember one night we invited some people to our house to play Scrabble and got out the Skip-across game, and they said, "We came to play Scrabble. This isn't Scrabble, it's Skip-across." They didn't want to play it even though it was exactly the same game.

You never know what might be the thing that protects or sells your idea. That's why a dedicated advocate and creative critic is so important.

**RBD**: The pet rock didn't make it because it was a better idea than anything else. It was something that could be protected and marketed in a viable way.

I read recently that the old 'flying wing' was supposedly a much more economical and elegant way of designing an aircraft. But it kind of slipped through the cracks as a product. It was only years later that they began to realize that it could save a lot of money and fuel, etc. Nobody ever followed through with the development of the flying wing even though it was potentially a much better way of engineering a flying craft because it didn't have a dedicated advocate.

# 6

---

# Coordinating the Dreamer,
# the Realist and the Critic

**RBD**: The point that we have been making throughout the book is that the feedback loop between goals, evidence and operations, and between dreamer, realist and critic is the essence of effective creativity. Without this loop, even the most exciting ideas will fail or turn sour.

In fact, some of the most innovative people I have met are hospitalized or are on the drug Thorazine used to treat schizophrenia. They are examples of people who are incredibly creative but who have no way of filtering their ideas. They are consumed by the dreamer but have no realist, no critic, no balance.

I worked with one young man who had been labeled schizophrenic who had a very simple, but powerful, creativity strategy that made him an excellent dreamer—but not much else. He would sit around all day and take pictures of objects— say a coat rack, a television set and a microphone, for example.

He would make a picture of each of these objects as if they were on a clear plastic transparency and then overlap them on top of one another. He brought them together and tried to make something out of the synthesis of all these objects.

Try it for a moment. How would you bring together a coat rack, a television set, and a microphone? Maybe when you hang your coat on the hat rack at a restaurant, a little voice would ask for your name and then it would tell you where to sit.

Maybe when you talk into the microphone, your coat would come out from the coat rack and you would simply put it on. Instead of having a person there checking your hat, you would mention your name and see where it was located on the television screen.

This was a great strategy for generating ideas. I'm sure you could use this overlapping picture strategy and innovate a million things a day. You could come up an idea a minute— and one or two of them might even be good. Try it out if you ever get bored. Take a couple of things and see what you can make out of them. Take the sprinkler system, a radio and a chair. Overlap them and bring them together into one image. In fact, there's no need to stop with three images. This young man claimed he could overlap as many as thirty-two pictures at a time, but that if he got more than that his skull would crack.

He actually came up with some interesting inventions. He came up with an idea for a bathtub where you would run the hot water pipes around the outside of the tub so it would heat up the cold porcelain while you were running your bath. Then when you sat in the tub there wouldn't be such an uncomfortable differential between the temperature of the water and the tub against your back. There may be some potential in that idea. He also invented things that were not that useful like "anti-gravity foot warmers."

Like most creative people, he had a sense of humor about it at least. He once told me he spent most of his time "thinking about shit." He was actually looking for ways to take horse manure and use it for an alternative energy source. It generates a significant amount of methane gas. He had enough information to develop some interesting ideas about it.

The point is, this young man was constantly constructing pictures and overlapping them. But he had never related the pictures to anything concrete or to any meaningful action. One of his main problems was that he was very out of touch with his body. He was always in outer space. He was so out of touch with his body that he was constantly having accidents; he accidentally burned down his house, he'd had numerous accidents on his motorcycle. He once told me, "I'm very accident prone. The accidents aren't usually very serious, but the proneness sure is!"

I wanted to to help him become more of a realist by enriching the kind of evidence procedures he used to evaluate his ideas so they could enter a more useful, and less dangerous, feedback loop with the other aspects of his experience.

One of his main problems was that he linked his ability to creatively come up with ideas to the identity of being "a schizophrenic." He was afraid he would lose his creativity if he got well. One of the things I wanted to do was to help him break that link, or at least have more choices about it, so he could enrich his creativity and his perception of himself. I questioned him about his strategy until I could do it myself (without having to be a schizophrenic, of course). I told him about the process of bissociation and how I believed his thought process was actually more like Gutenberg or Leonardo than a schizophrenic. I pointed out that his process wasn't crazy, it was just incomplete.

When I came back the next day, I had used the strategy to come up with a bunch of ideas that were as bizarre and innovative as his own. Some were as useful and some were as improbable. For example, I designed a car that was a perpetual motion machine. It was simple: I put bigger wheels on the back, smaller wheels on the front so that it would always be going downhill. But I also came up with the idea to use computer programs to treat schizophrenia (I overlapped a picture of him with a computer game I was playing). This idea actually led to others that proved to be valuable and I have ended up building a whole software company around it.

I had a computer game that would draw a maze that you were supposed to find your way through. It would show you the maze from a top or 'God's eye' view in which you were disassociated and looking down on it—the way this young man typically viewed the world. Then it would put you inside the maze so that all you saw was a single hallway with doors going off in different directions. In the course of the game the player switches back and forth between the disassociated top view and the associated inside view. The more you can remember and relate the two views together, the easier it is to get through the maze. This was a skill he did not have. He began playing the game and became pretty good at it. I think he actually enjoyed the metaphor of "getting through the maze," It was probably a lot like his life.

Using this and other computer games that required the development of certain kinds of strategies, we assisted him in developing new ways of thinking about things. He typically never saw himself implementing any of his ideas. I had him visualizing himself actually completing one of his projects using the New Behavior Generator Strategy. I asked him, "What would you need to do? What is your evidence for progress? Where are the holes? Can you see all the steps?" After combining this approach with other therapeutic techniques he began to improve.

He learned to take an idea—not necessarily the first one he came up with—and refine it to make it more and more realistic. He actually helped me design the picture that is on the cover of this book, which we have used as the logo for our creativity program. (You can see the reference to his strategy.) I had him contributing ideas to the initial program design, and marketing and implementation. He helped out quite a bit and learned to think more realistically in the process.

# Exercise: Design Grid

**RBD**: In the next exercise we'd like to put all of the various aspects of creativity that we've been exploring into a single strategy. While this exercise may be done either individually or in teams, we are going to present the exercise in the context of a team project.

The goal of the exercise is to come up with an idea in a design team that you would present to a larger group for evaluation. The group will evaluate the idea from two points of view: protection and marketing.

To make a creative idea successful you've got to be able to evaluate it and articulate it in a way that gives the appropriate balance of protection and marketability.

The format for this exercise is one that you can use to generate ideas in many different areas. It's what I call the "Chinese Menu" approach to creativity—where you get to choose one item from column A, one from column B, etc.

As you look over the grid on the following page you will see that it involves the definition and interplay of three elements of creativity that we've been dealing with throughout the course of this book: variables, outcomes, and criteria. Variables are the components or elements that you will be combining together to generate ideas. Outcomes are the goals that provide the direction and purpose for the ideas. Criteria are the evidence that is used to filter the ideas and determine which are to be kept or discarded.

The order in which you fill out the grid is important. First fill in the "General Goal" statement. This is basically a statement of your overall purpose for the team. It could be any number of things, depending on the kind of team and team members. If you are a group of musicians, it could be to create a piece of music. If you are entrepreneurs, it could be to develop a new product or company. If you are a sales team, it could be to develop an innovative marketing plan. If you are a group of trainers or teachers, it could be to design a course. The goal could even be to come up with exercises for a seminar or book on creativity.

Next, as a team, fill in the criteria section. The criteria you specify will define the basis on which ideas will be judged and evaluated. When you form your design team the first question to address is, "What are the minimum criteria our idea has to satisfy?" At this point you have no idea of what kinds of ideas you will be generating, and that's good. You don't want to bias your core criteria by gearing them toward any particular idea. At this stage, you don't know what ideas might come up, but you know that whatever they are, they will have to satisfy these particular criteria. One obvious suggestion is to start with the NLP well-formedness conditions for outcomes that we mentioned earlier and then add whatever other criteria might be relevant to your general goal. (Appendix G reviews well formedness conditions which apply to various stages of creativity.)

For instance, your group may decide an idea has to be financially profitable, or it has to make X amount of dollars in order to be accepted. Maybe it has to take advantage of certain resources. Maybe it has to occur within a particular time limit. In other words, what are the things that your idea has to do, even though you don't know what it is yet?

**TE**: It could be something off the wall, such as that it makes you "feel good." That could be a criterion.

**General Goal:** _____

| *What criteria does your idea have to satisfy?* |
|---|
|  |

*List the categories of basic elements you will be combining.*

| A | B | C | D | E |
|---|---|---|---|---|
|   |   |   |   |   |

| *Outcomes* |
|---|
|  |

**Figure 6.1. Brainstorming Grid.**

**RBD**: If you try to figure out what you're going to invent before you invent it, you're automatically going to limit your potential range of innovation. Criteria are very general filters. You want them to be for the overall goals or outcomes of your ideas.

For example, Chester Carlson, the guy who invented the Xerox machine, didn't just sit down and say, "Gee, I guess I'll invent the Xerox machine today." He was a lawyer and had to deal with tons of paperwork and records. He was constantly finding himself in a situation where he'd have someone type something up, make carbon copies for everyone who needed them and send them out—and sure enough someone would need one more. He'd have to have the whole thing re-typed. His first thought was, "Wouldn't it be nice if I had something that would sit on a table top and could make exact copies of things?" He wanted something that would give him that flexibility. The value of the Xerox machine is that if someone wants one more copy you don't have to redo the whole thing. The overall goal was increased flexibility. The criteria were set in terms of size and performance, not in terms of the specifics of the machine's design.

So the first step is to make a list of the essential criteria your idea has to meet. Does it have to make you money? Does it have to help other people? Does it have to be fun?

At the bottom of the grid, you will notice another box labeled "Outcomes." Fill this in next by answering the question, "What are some specific goals that you could accomplish with the ideas you will generate?" Unlike your core criteria, these are things you don't *have* to achieve with the idea, but they are possible goals that might be met by the ideas. They're not something that each idea has to accomplish. They're desired outcomes relating to the team members' interests.

The difference between a criterion and an outcome is that a criterion is something the idea **has to** satisfy, an outcome is something that relates to your team's interests that the idea could help with.

If your design team was a group of teachers and your general goal was to design a course to teach language skills, you might say, "Our criteria are that the idea has to be an activity that engages everybody in the class, and it has to be something that can be done within an hour time limit." In other words, those are the constraints the idea has to fit inside. On the other hand, possible outcomes might be, "We could teach the class about spelling. We could teach them about grammar. We could teach them creative writing skills." In other words, those aren't things it has to do; those are possible goals of the activity of teaching.

The distinction is not in the kinds of words you use. It is between what you select as a constraint that it has to meet versus a potential direction or result. One team may have profit as a criterion; another may have it as a possible goal. This will greatly influence the role that profit plays in the idea.

Sandwiched in between your criteria and your outcomes are five columns in which to list your "operators"—the things you will be varying in order to generate ideas and achieve outcomes. The headings for these columns of variables are up to the individual team members to decide upon. They will depend upon the background, the focus and expertise of the various team members.

Each column represents a particular class of key tools or variables that you have to work with or work around.

For example, if you wanted to use this grid to come up with exercises to develop creativity, you might list headings related to the elements which determine the structure of an exercise, such as: A) *Contexts for exercises,* B) *teaching equipment or instruments,* C) *number of people in a group,* D) *time frames* and E) *types of activities.* This is a potential set of parameters that could be varied to create different exercises and achieve different training outcomes.

If you're a group of musicians with the general goal of composing a piece of music, you would put in different column headings such as: A) *type of audience,* B) *musical instruments,* C) *styles of music,* D) *number of performers* and E) *types of musical compositions.*

If you're a team of entrepreneurs with the general goal of creating a new product or company, you might put in headings like: A) *new technologies,* B) *product types,* C) *market trends,* D) *time frames* and E) *funding sources.*

If you're a group of video game designers designing an innovative video game, you might select headings like: A) *types of computers,* B) *types of user interfaces,* C) *popular movies,* D) *previous best-selling games* and E) *types of special effects.*

If you're a sales team making a marketing plan, you might choose headings like: A) *geographic locations,* B) *distribution channels,* C) *key market segments,* D) *product features* and E) *needs to be filled.*

Basically, you want to put down a set of headings that represents the relevant kinds of tools your team has available and kinds of parameters you have to work with. Obviously, there is no right set of variables for any one group. On another level, in fact, the headings you choose for the columns are a variable themselves.

Once you have your headings, the next step is to make a list of the individual elements in each category. For instance, if you're a group of musicians and you've chosen *musical instruments* as a heading, you want to list a number of possible musical instruments underneath that heading—say, *piano, guitar, drums, saxophone,* etc. In essence you are "chunking down" each of the headings into a list of possible expressions of that category of variables.

At this point, you don't know, nor should you care, how these elements are going to fit together. All you are trying to do is list some of the variables that you have to work with.

**TE**: So, if you are a communications group, perhaps one of the variables you might want to explore would be the different channels you could communicate through and list them: television, newspapers, radio, letters, face-to-face discussions, etc. You might also want to have a heading for different groups of people, and list them: ministers, entrepreneurs, college students, bankers, etc.

**RBD**: The column headings are like Lowell's knobs. The list beneath each heading represents the possible values you could adjust the knob to.

The example on the following page shows a sample of what the grid might look like fully filled out for a training team designing creativity exercises.

Clearly, this is only one possible way to fill it out. A different team working with the same goal of designing creativity exercises might fill the grid out completely differently. This is just one possibility.

**TE**: Each individual team will define their own "knobs" by determining what they would like to have as variables, or believe are necessary to have as variables—like Lowell did in his strategy. You don't know ahead of time what the knobs are going to produce. You're not defining them by what you're planning to end up with specifically. You're just asking, "What kinds of knobs would we like to have here?" Who knows what it'll do when we put it with the other knobs? We don't have the slightest idea yet. Let's define our knobs first and then find out what they produce as we begin to adjust them.

## Phase 1—The Dreamer

**RBD**: This is the fun part. Once you have got the grid filled in, you simply have each team member choose one item from column A, one from column B, one from column C and so on. As I said earlier, this is the "Chinese menu" method of brainstorming. Each team member chooses one variable from

**General Goal:**     Design Creativity Exercises

| *What criteria does your idea have to satisfy?* |
|---|
| Develops a practical skill        Relevant to a range of professional backgrounds |
| Enjoyable                         All group members benefit in some way |
| Fits with other activities        Builds on existing competency |
| Involves physical activity        Unique/Novel |

*List the categories of basic elements you will be combining.*

| A | B | C | D | E |
|---|---|---|---|---|
| **Contexts** | **Equipment** | **Number of People in a group** | **Time Frames** | **Activities** |
| | | | | Questionnaire and Discussion |
| Classroom | Computer | 2 | 5 min. | Case Example and Discussion |
| Hotel | Musical Instruments | 3 | 10 min. | Demonstration |
| Downtown | Video | 4 | 20 min. | Role Play |
| Restaurant | Useless Objects | 5 | 30 min. | Simulation |
| Home | Flashcards | | | Conversation |
| | Book | 6 | 1 hr. | Games |
| Office | | | | Sports |
| | Blackboard | Whole Group | Full Day | Dance |

| *Outcomes* |
|---|
| Increase Observational Skill        Develop Synesthesias |
| Learn Sub-Modalities |
| Enhance Memory        Expand Behavioral Flexibility |

**Figure 6.2. Example Brainstorming Grid Filled Out.**

each column and writes them down, so that each team member will have written five items on his own piece of paper, chosen at random from each column. Each team member randomly sets each one of the "knobs" to a single value.

**TE**: For instance, in our creativity exercise example, I might choose: A=downtown, B= musical instruments, C= four people, D=forty-five minutes, and E=dance. I write down one item from each column.

**RBD**: As another member of our team, I might instead select: A=home, B= computer, C= three people, D=thirty minutes, and E=case example and discussion. I end up with a different set of "menu items." I've ordered a different meal from the menu.

**RWD**: As a third team member, I might pick: A=office, B= book, C= two people, D=one hour, and E=conversation.

**RBD**: After we have each randomly selected our group of items, the task of the team is to consider each grouping and come up with as many ideas as possible that combine those things together into a single product—an exercise, in our example.

Specifically, we start with Todd's grouping of items and ask, "How could you combine downtown, musical instruments and dance for forty-five minutes with four people to make an exercise in creativity?" This is where you all get to be like Gutenberg, da Vinci, or my so-called "schizophrenic" client, and overlap, synthesize and "bissociate" these elements into a single thing. Obviously, you can incorporate any of the 'Dreamer' strategies we've presented in this book.

This is also where your list of outcomes enters into the process. As you are thinking of how to combine these elements, look over the list of outcomes at the bottom of the grid and see if any of them help to focus the particular components you are playing with into a particular synthesis. Maybe you begin to wonder how you could develop representational system flexibility in the context of the downtown area of, say, Santa Cruz, utilizing musical instruments within the activity of dance.

At some point, someone will start the brainstorming process by proposing an idea. At first, the ideas will probably not seem that great or that creative. But that's OK. That's the way it's supposed to be. This is only the first stage of the whole process. In fact, it is the job of all of the group members to help support and stimulate each other. Your first task is to help draw out ideas from each other. You are all being 'Dreamers' together—at the same time.

Let's say, for example, that one of us suggests that we assign people to form groups of four and give them the task to go downtown and perform a dance on the walking mall. Another one of us might go, "Great idea! And in order to promote representational system flexibility, we'll have them compose a piece of music, using Michael Colgrass' strategy, and score it as a painting." Another one of us then suggests that for the dance, one group member will do the actual dancing, two will play the music on their instruments, and the fourth will display the painting and direct the music and dancing from the painting.

Somebody else might then propose an altogether different idea. For instance, he suggests that we could have the group perform a dance together as a team. Instead of using real musical instruments, they are to mime that they are playing certain musical instruments in order to help develop auditory and kinesthetic synesthesias.

And we go on like this, proposing ideas for synthesizing Todd's group of items.

Of course, at some point we need to have a way of ending our brainstorming on Todd's menu items so that we can move on to the other team members' items. This can be done in one of three ways:

1. Set a time limit. You might decide as a team to spend 10 or 15 minutes on each person's group of items, for example.
2. Set an "idea quota." The team could decide to keep brainstorming until you have 3 ideas, or 5 ideas or $x$ ideas for each person's set of items.
3. Require a proposal from each member of the team. The team could decide that each member should make at least one proposed synthesis for each cluster of items.

Whichever your method your team selects, the mission of the team is to end up with a set of ideas for each team member's cluster of items. In our example, our team would end up with a set of ideas for Todd's group of items, a set of ideas for my group of items and a set of ideas for my father's group of items. At that point we have completed the "Dreamer" phase of the exercise.

## Phase 2—The Realist

Once we have our group of ideas, we want to hand them over to the "Realist." The goal of the realist phase of this exercise is to make these dreams fit our core criteria. I want to make it clear that it is not the job of the realist to decide if the idea is good or not. The job of the realist is to refine or fine-tune the ideas to fit the constraints imposed by the criteria that the team set at the very beginning of the process.

Specifically, as a group, we need to review each of the ideas that we've come up with during the brainstorming phase, look at each of our criteria, and find out if the idea satisfies that criterion. If it does, great, we move on the next criterion. If it does not satisfy a particular criterion we do not throw the idea out. Remember this is the realist phase, not the critic phase. Instead we try to figure out what we have to add or change about the idea to make it fit those criteria.

For example, our creativity exercise team would take the first idea we came up with about composing a piece of music and performing a dance on the walking mall and ask, "Does this exercise provide sensory-based evidence that the group is developing representational system flexibility?" Well, that is definitely something that you ought to be able to see, hear, or feel in this exercise. That appears to be built into the structure of the exercise. So, we all say, "Good, let's move on to another criterion."

"Does it draw out unconscious competencies? Does the structure of this exercise automatically draw out abilities from each member without them having to consciously concentrate on it?" That seems to be built into the exercise pretty well. "Good. Does it use all participants?" Definitely.

"Is this self-corrective? If the group runs into a problem, is there something built into the exercise to help them recognize what is causing it and how to correct it?" The way the exercise is structured right now, it is not obvious that it would be self-correcting. There's no process designed into it that says, "If one of them makes a mistake, here's what they can do amongst themselves to help correct it."

So, we've found a criterion that our first idea doesn't fulfill. Rather than reject the idea, however, the team asks, "How could we adjust this exercise in order to make it self-corrective?" Now the task of the team is find ways to get the exercise to accomplish that criterion. Somebody might say, "In order to identify and correct problems you need feedback between the different members of the performance group. Since we already have a conductor or director for the performance maybe that could be one of his functions: to direct feedback between group members." Another team member might add, "Since they have a score for their musical performance, maybe they can make a score for their performance as a group."

The point is that the team begins to incrementally modify that initial idea in order to make it fit with the criterion it did not satisfy. You keep checking each of the ideas you've come up with against your criteria until you've adjusted them all to satisfy each of the core criteria.

If you are really having trouble getting one of the ideas to fit all of the criteria, you don't throw it out. Instead, begin to change one of the variables. Let's say you can't make your downtown dance performance idea fit the self-correcting criterion. Then change one of the variables. That is, instead of doing it downtown, change the context to a classroom or a home. Or, change the activity to sports or a role play instead of a dance. Perhaps I change the group number, so I send two groups of four people downtown. One of the groups of four serves as a coach for the other group of four. Changing one of the variables can open up a lot of new possibilities.

Let's review some of the key elements to the exercise so far. 1) You don't know what the ideas are going to be before you start brainstorming. It might be that you come up with hundreds of ideas that have never been thought of before. 2) You don't apply the criteria until *after* you've come up with the ideas. The initial set of ideas is like a first draft. You finish the first draft before you start checking for spelling and grammar. One of the most common problems in creativity is that people start mixing together the dreamer, realist and critic in a way that brings them all to a standstill.

You start by setting a general goal as a team and then picking the criteria that you want your ideas to satisfy, even though you don't know what they are going to be yet. And then go through, identify your basic categories of variables, and fill in specific examples of each variable category.

Then each member picks one item from each column.

**TE**: You could do it with your eyes closed.

**RBD**: Throw darts.

**TE**: You just go: Here, one of these, one of those, one of these and one of those, and somebody writes it down—Chinese menu style. This first step is not goal-oriented. I don't know what's going to happen when I put this one with that one and this one and this one. All I know is, "Now I've got this group of things that we're going to try to put together into an idea." At this stage we are truly beginning to engage in "not knowing."

**RBD**: So, in phase one, the team just wants to come up with an idea that puts together the set of variables that we are being presented by a fellow team member. You might not even like the ideas you first come up with—even if it is your own idea. Its purpose is just to give you a starting place. This first step is intended to be a mind-broadening experience. You are supposed to expand the ideas first and filter them later.

At phase two we go back and look at each idea and ask, "Does it check out with all our criteria? If it doesn't, what do I have to change about it to make it fit?" If it doesn't fit the criteria, you don't throw the idea out, you try to incrementally adjust or modify the idea so that it does fit. If that doesn't work, you ask, "Which one of the variables could I change to help make this idea fit that criterion?"

If you still find that you are not getting anywhere with the sets of variables you've chosen, then make up another variable heading and add that in, or change one to something else. For instance, you could change "number of people in a group" to "types of professional backgrounds" or something like that.

**TE**: Now that we've chosen these variables and put them together, we've got to run back over to our criteria and ask, "Does it meet all the criteria?" If it doesn't meet the criteria, you've got three choices. You can either:

    1. adjust or modify the idea in some way,

2. go back and pick another variable that will adjust it to meet the criteria, or

3. you can make a new variable up.

Just don't give up. Be tenacious. Be outrageous!

**RBD**: Ideas evolve through this kind of feedback loop. What you come up with when you start this exercise isn't going to be what you end up with. It's a bit like panning for gold. You pour a bunch of variables into these columns and variables. Then you turn it over and you shake it around and see what falls through the filter of your criteria and what doesn't. When you get one idea through and it satisfies all of them, you write it down and you do another one.

**TE**: We'd like to ask you to suspend the way you normally create ideas. Use this model only as a place to start from. It's just a place to begin. It by no means defines the end product. But it is a way to start, especially when you have a group of people who've never worked together before. Everybody in the group has the opportunity to offer input and participate.

**RBD**: The first two phases of this exercise are about the interaction between the dreamer and the realist—a very essential feedback loop in creativity.

In fact, a great majority of practical creative activity happens this way.

Chester Carlson began his invention of the Xerox machine by starting with a set of criteria. It had to  eliminate the retyping problem, it had to be small enough to fit in someone's office, and it had to cost under $100,000, or something like that. Those were the criteria. He knew it had to satisfy those basic constraints. That was the starting point. He didn't know what the specific expression was going to look like or sound like or feel like. He just knew that it had to accomplish those things. Whatever the idea was, if it didn't accomplish those things, then it was outside his mission.

Once those are defined, he asks, "What do I have to work with?" "Well, there's different types of photographic processes." Carlson actually made a study and a list of every kind of photographic process that had been developed since the time of the Greeks. "There are also different kinds of documents I've got to be able to copy." "There's different kinds of professions and offices: lawyers, managers, doctors, etc. There are people I can go to for money." And so on. Once he collected all the information together he said, "Now that I have all these things, I have to come up with some way of putting it all together somehow." He had to start somewhere. In fact, Carlson actually said, "I had to make something that I knew ahead of time wasn't going to work. But I had to make it in order to get the feedback I needed to know where to go next."

In other words, he had to make a first draft or prototype in order to be able to take his next step. That starts the feedback loop between dreamer and realist. So let's say he comes up with an idea and makes a device that copies everything, no matter what size the document is, the only problem is that the machine is the size of the Empire State Building. So he says, "That doesn't fit my criteria. It's got to fit on somebody's desk, and this machine won't—unless they're a very big person. So now I've got to go back and change something about it. Refine it or modify it until it fits that criterion."

I heard of a fascinating example of a group of scientists who were trying to invent a device that filtered molecules. Talk about chunking down! They were trying to come up with a way of filtering specific molecules out of a substance. They could identify the shapes of the molecules, but they couldn't figure how to make the holes small enough to filter individual molecules. Finally they said, "We'll make the holes big at first, and then shrink everything. If we can find a substance in which we can make the holes and then dehydrate it, we make it shrink." And that worked. They found certain substances that they could cut these specially shaped holes in and then shrink it and make a membrane that would actually be small enough to act as a filter for molecules.

If it doesn't work, you don't throw it out; you try something different. You try another way of doing it. You change one of your variables.

The same kind of process can be just as effective in situations involving communication, like sales. If you're in real estate and a customer comes in and says, "I want a house with a big backyard," and you don't have any houses with big backyards, you don't have to say, "I'm sorry I can't help you." If you can't achieve the goal then find the criteria. You can ask, "What do you want a big backyard for?" The customer may say, "Well, I want a big backyard because I have five kids and I need a lot of space for them to play." Now you have opened up some flexibility because you have the criterion behind the outcome. You might say, "Well, I don't have any places with a big backyard, but I have a place that's only three blocks from the park. There's a lot of space for the kids to play—and think what you'd save in property taxes." If the customer says, "I want a big backyard because I want to raise Arabian horses." You can ask, "What do you want to raise Arabian horses for?" "Well, I want to make some money." "Oh, so you're looking for an investment..."

If you can identify the criteria, you can enter into a feedback loop to attempt to satisfy it in different ways, by changing other variables. The customer might be just as satisfied with the house that is three blocks from the park.

In fact, my wife, Anita, did a research study on innovation in companies in the Silicon Valley area of California. Her findings were that the vast majority of product innovations came from the feedback loop between companies and their customers.

Before going on to the next section of the book you may want to get together with other people of similar interests and come up with some ideas using this method.

Creativity is largely an incremental, iterative process that is incessantly improving the initial idea—kind of like the process of evolution. The trick is to have a goal, an outcome that is neither stated too generally so that anything can fit through, nor too refined so that nothing can fit through.

# Phase 3—The Critic

The next phase of the exercise, we hand our ideas over to the "Critic." The job of the critic is find out whether the idea is protectable and marketable. Is it really a good enough idea to proceed with? What would you have to do to make it protectable? Is it really marketable?

In our seminar we had four teams: Business, Computers, Ministry, and Engineering. We asked a spokesperson from each group to present their idea and asked them questions to determine the viability of each idea. Here are some of the ideas that people in our seminar came up with.

As you read over their ideas, keep in mind that this material comes from early 1983. Many of the ideas they came up with independently are an ongoing part of today's reality. For instance, this first idea is a definition of today's Macintosh computers (remember there was no Macintosh in 1983).

How about the computer group?

**Woman**: We came up with computer "picture processor" or "color processor," It would work like a "word processor" except instead of text, it would edit pictures and colors. In addition to the function keys you would use something like a light pen (this was before the advent of the "mouse"—RBD), and you'd have more functions. The product would be both software and hardware and would allow you to do things like overlay and mix different colors. For instance you could draw something with the light pen, then hit the yellow function key so it was colored yellow. Then you make another object that was blue. You could either overlay the blue object or mix it and make green. You could make a whole picture that way.

This product is mainly for artists and word processors. You're able to draft a picture on the screen with the light pen and then you can edit colors from a menu at the bottom of the screen. You can process any dimension of the picture—all the submodalities. You could change the picture, store it, and then you could come back the next day, load it again and work with it some more.

We interfaced a video camera, so you could bring it downtown and do a portrait of people. Take a picture of them, take the frame on the screen and add to the drawing.

**TE**: Put little mustaches on it.

**RBD**: I've heard of a person who developed a device for hairstylists that did something like that. It had a video that would show the customer's face and then you could draw the hairstyle over the image. And you could know what it was going to look like before you got your hair fixed.

**TE**: With your idea you could do the same thing, or show clothes for that matter, whatever you could draw on.

**Woman**: Our picture processor would be portable, so you can take it with you on your vacation and take a picture of a scene and make a computer postcard or a slide. You could also change it or modify it.

**TE**: That's for when you go to Washington or Oregon in the winter and you want to say you went on a sunny vacation. I think you could sell that to the chamber of commerce in Portland, no problem.

**RWD**: I would say you have both patentable and copyrightable matter, although I don't know if there's any new hardware that would be required.

**Woman**: I don't know that there is either. I think a lot of it already exists. I know that there are already some types of video editor equipment.

**RWD**: You might have to put some additional keys on the device to control the color. There might be some additional keys and there certainly would be additional software. So the software would be copyrightable. I suspect, as a matter of fact, if it's a method, there's some possibility of getting a method coverage.

The difficulty is obviousness. You wouldn't really be doing anything different than is being done now with the hardware. As I understand it, you can control color with existing hardware. So I think obviousness might be the one thing that would keep you from getting a broad method patent.

I would try to claim, "the method of producing color pictures on a CRT comprising the steps of controlling the pen so you could first produce one color and then produce a second color."

Most CRT's have 3 dots, red, blue, and green, in a very small area. You excite one or another. I think in order for your editing pen to be able to only excite the red one, or excite the red/blue just the right amount, you'd like to be able to control how much each pixel is excited. I assume you don't want just solid red colors, solid blue colors, etc.

**Man**: Well, you can get different ranges of colors.

**RWD**: But can you edit them with pen?

**Man**: I don't think so. You just select a color. The pen just turns pixels on and off. You can select color "medium blue/green," color number 159. If you put the pen on there, all you do is excite that particular color.

**RWD**: I think it is possible to come up with a way that would dynamically combine and mix colors on a CRT. I think there would probably be patentable subject matter in the solution— once you've gotten a device where you could, by operating the keyboard, select any color you want, paint with the pen that color at that location, and then go back and paint another color with the pen. I would expect that you're going to run into a number of mechanical problems. The solution to those problems would probably be patentable. You may very well end up with it being a software problem. Maybe it's possible with the equipment you have now and what you have to do is come up with some software.

**RBD**: So there's bad news and good news from the critic. The bad news is you can't do it. The good news is if you can invent the thing, you can patent it.

Let's go to another group. What did the ministers' team come up with?

**J**: We did not get a patentable thing.

**RBD**: Wait a minute, it's our job to be the critics. You've got to at least give us the dream first. Besides our purpose isn't to reject any ideas. If you come up with the idea, we'll say, "If you want to get this thing protected or marketed, this is what you'll need to do." And maybe you'll find there is a way to patent it. I think it would be useful to at least present the idea.

**J**: O.K. Our goal was to contribute something to the planetary movement for global unity. One of the elements we incorporated was the feast of "agape"—which is a Greek word for love, brotherly love. The feast of agape was a common meal of fellowship that was started by the early Christians and included prayers, songs, readings of the Scripture and offerings for the poor. Under the guise of a feast, all the community would get together and do things to support each other.

**RBD**: So you'd go into a community and organize a feast that all the people would come to. Do they pay to come there or is it free?

**J**: Most people would pay. It makes money. But some of the people won't have money.

**RBD**: How would this be different from a dinner, like a campaign dinner that someone would put on for a candidate?

**J**: It's called a "People's Support Community" which means that if I have an idea or a challenge that I need to communicate, there are people there to communicate with that could be a resource.

**RBD**: So it's a giant design team, doing a creativity exercise— while they're eating.

**J**: Eating together gives them something to do in common.

**RBD**: Automatic pacing, automatic rapport.

**TE**: Yes, eating is a fairly common experience. Of course, you'd have be careful of going into a town that has a lot of anorexics.

**RBD**: Their problem is that they'd eat too much.

**TE**: "Let's have something to eat and talk about our weight problems."

**RBD**: So, the idea is that these people are going to get together and communicate ideas. How are they going to do it? Are you looking to get fifty people together, or five hundred?

**J**: Everyone in the community.

**RBD**: You'd get the whole community together?

**J**: Right. We're talking about farmers, townspeople, children, etc.

**RBD**: All from within a specific geographic area. So you're talking about a lot of people.

**RWD**: With a lot of different backgrounds.

**J**: Right.

**RBD**: How would they go about communicating? If I am a person who comes to this feast, and I say, "I have such and such a problem," what would happen?

**TE**: In other words, what would be the forum by which you'd get to express your idea?

**RBD**: Would I have a microphone?

**J**: No, everyone is communicating at the same time. There's no particular forum.

**RWD**: Your idea is that they're all gathered there for a common purpose, namely eating, and they're going to talk while they're eating, so they exchange ideas unconsciously. Since there's no profit motive, legal protection really doesn't enter in.

I'd mention one thing. You're going to have to put out a lot of posters and ads, so you're going to have to call it something.

Also you'll have to be careful of people who might try to take advantage of the situation. Let's say I'm a con man and I come into this community, and I see that these people are putting on this very big feast. And they've got to get food for the feast. I decide to go around and knock on people's doors and tell them I'm associated with the feast. I collect money and I disappear with it. You might need some kind of registration, some sort of protection of that name to prevent others from misusing it. That's one thing you might consider.

**RBD**: Of course, that's something you could turn into opportunity. If you can create a service mark for your feast, then people are going to start to identify it with your idea. If you come up with something catchy, people are going to see it and say, "I wonder what that's all about." Not only does it protect you from someone illegitimately saying, "I'm involved with this group," it also begins to create a way of identifying you as part of something special. So you wear a little badge that says FA or something like that and people go, "What's that?" It helps to create community awareness and interest.

**Lady**: Can you copyright a procedure for doing it? There could be a specific procedure for moving in and setting everything up in different communities.

**TE**: You mean for the organization?

**RWD**: I'm afraid it's kind of like "bank night at the movies." When I was younger, they used to have "bank night at the movies." Somebody came up with the idea of fostering attendance at the movie theaters by having everybody who bought a ticket put them into a barrel. At the end of the movie you drew one out and whoever's ticket was drawn got ten percent of the proceeds for that night. It started at one theater somewhere in the country and eventually spread all over the country.

Not copyrightable! Not protectable! It is an idea. It's a method of doing business. Your procedure for handling this feast would be a method of doing business. It would not be something that could be copyrighted.

On the other hand, if you wrote a booklet and distributed it and this booklet described the purposes behind the feast and what you wanted to accomplish, a certain expression of the idea: That could be copyrighted. If you decided that you wanted to have an illustration that was going to be the symbol of this event, that could be a trademark and could be copyrighted, depending on what its artistic content was. So there are things you could get that would protect your identity as the source of the idea and method.

**RBD**: There's something else I can think of, too. Let's say you've got all these people from this community together, and I'm a participant along with hundreds or thousands of other people. I don't know who's who, how do I find people who might be resources for me? Now, let's say that everybody that comes in checks in at a computer terminal used as a data base. So they say, "I'm Joe Schmoe, I'm a banker. And my interests are blah blah blah. My particular issue is such and such." This information is keyed into the computer and it tells you the table numbers of people with like professions, interests or issues. So now you have access to those people.

Instead of having to have the community get a computer system, you have a feast of agape. Maybe there's ten thousand people in this community. How are they going to get to know other people of similar interests or complementary needs? You might supply the computer and develop the software for this community information network. In addition to connecting people together you automatically build a mailing list at the same time.

**RWD**: And of course the mailing list is protectable.

**RBD**: And then you sell the mailing list. (Laughter.)

**RWD**: It's saleable and it's also protectable from misuse.

**TE**: You order the mailing list on your way out of the feast.

**RBD**: So someone comes in and they're interested in learning disabilities. They give you a list of the programs they have available, you supply them with a list of people that they could get in touch with, and BAM, you've got information flowing. The Holy Spirit enters the information age. I'm sure Jesus would have loved to have had such a system for the Sermon on the Mount. The "meek" could locate the "peace-makers" and the "poor of spirit" could find "those who hunger and thirst for justice" and so on.

**TE**: What about the engineering group?

**Man**: We started working on parking.

**TE**: I'm glad somebody has. Thank you very much.

**Man**: We came up with a prefabricated, movable sort of a ferris wheel kind of thing, where you drive your car in and it moves up, another car moves in. And cars move out on the top level.

**RBD**: And if you washed them at the same time, you could have them come around like clothes at the dry cleaners, you know, put cellophane over them.

**RWD**: I think you'd better have a patent search, because I think you might infringe on issued patents. I think in San

Francisco there is a parking lot where you drive in, up on a ramp, and then your car is raised and held. They are stacked two high.

**Man**: O.K., we had another variation. I know I've seen it in Switzerland. We could go underground and hollow out the hills. You could maintain the existing structures and you could prefabricate them. Another idea we had was the idea of building them on the sides of existing buildings. You could stack them up against existing buildings.

**TE**: Not only that, you could have the people who work in those buildings park on the right floor.

**RWD**: I don't quite understand the mechanism. Do I understand that you are going to have some kind of belt arrangement, perhaps not circular?

**Woman**: We haven't agreed on the final design.

**RWD**: You will run into a lot of prior attempts to do the same thing. You would be amazed. When I have clients who come into my office, they'll describe to me an invention and say, "I've been in this business fifty years and I've never seen anything like it. I've looked everywhere for it, in the catalogs and can't find it." The first thing I recommend to them is that we have a patent search made. At least half the time the patent search turns up things that were done, perhaps back in the 1930's, sometimes earlier, that would make it impossible to get patent coverage. It's amazing what's in the prior patent art. I don't know what all you'd find. The device you're talking about is patentable subject matter.

Of course, even if there were patents that went back into the '30's that would prevent you from getting a patent, those patents would have expired and would not inhibit you from building or selling such a structure. You could certainly trademark your service.

**RBD**: You could call it "Car Carousel."

**RWD**: Yeah, car carousel. If you come up with a good catchy name for it, you could certainly trademark it. I don't see copyright coverage as being of importance, but I do see trademark or service mark as important. I do think you could probably find something in it that you could patent or copyright. Maybe there would be some computer hardware or software required to operate it, or perhaps the structural features would be unique.

When you try to do it, you undoubtedly are going to run into problems. As I said with the picture processor device, if you run into problems you don't know the answer to and you can't find the answer to it in books, then you probably have something patentable if you can find a solution.

**RBD**: What about our team of business executives?

**Man**: We were working on a a special pencil. A regular pen or pencil is too slow. One of our criteria was to save time—to get more free time. We came up with the idea of a laser pen or pencil, that would write very rapidly. The idea was to use some substance like charcoal or carbon, and shoot it onto the page.

**RWD**: So it is some kind of hand-held pneumatic device where you're blowing charcoal particles on a piece of paper and then you're hitting them with the laser beam as they reach the page? So that you're coalescing them in some way, or fixing them on the paper?

**Man**: Yes, that would make it so you could write faster. The tip would never have to touch the page.

**TE**: Would this have some device on it to turn it on and off?

**Man**: Yes, some sort of trigger.

**RBD**: Do you actually need the carbon? I was thinking that you could have it so the pen just emits a laser beam. You could shine it on chemically treated paper and, as in the Xerographic process, it would alter the chemicals and turn them dark.

**RWD**: Let me say that there's one problem in a device of that kind. One of the things that has worried people about working with lasers is the potential damage they could cause. You walk into a lab where they're working on lasers and all of a sudden you go blind because somebody moved the laser—it hit the doorknob, it went from there up to a light fixture and came down into the retina. If your laser beam is going to be powerful enough to melt carbon, remember, the body is made mostly of carbon.

**RBD**: So make it a tattoo pencil.

**Man**: We were quite excited about this. What we managed to do in that short space of time was to take ten-cent item, alter the function of it, and turn it into something that costs twenty-five thousand dollars.

**TE**: Like the guy who's selling pencils on the corner. Somebody comes up and asks him, "How much for the pencils?" "Twenty-five thousand dollars." "You must not sell many pencils at that price, do you?" "No, but I only have to sell one a year." (Laughter.)

**RWD**: I assume that your group knows that the reverse of your invention has already been done—the laser eraser. There is a patent on it. They actually came up with this device and it was marketed, based on the use of a laser. If you made a mistake typing, this device would erase it by burning the carbon off the paper. The pencil was worth ten cents, and an eraser about a nickel—this device about $25,000.

I assume your group is also aware of the modern printers that shoot a jet of ink. What they do is charge the ink electrically and then deflect it to make the letter. But I think your pen is patentable. If you came up with your device, I'm sure it could be patented. But I think you'd want to look into whether you'd actually increase speed. I don't think using a laser would necessarily mean you could print faster than they do with their jet of ink.

**RBD**: If the pencil idea doesn't work, or you think it's too expensive to produce to make it marketable, you might try making it bigger. Make a laser cannon. It could be a way to write messages in the sky, perhaps on clouds, or on the sides of buildings.

Or make it smaller. There is a movie called *Blade Runner* that's set in the future. People have learned how to genetically engineer things, so they make fish and they make snakes and all kinds of cloned creatures. The genetic designers sign their names with a little laser beam. If someone made a fish, they'd have their own tiny, tiny marker on each scale.

The advantage of having a laser type device is you could write really big things or you could write very little things.

**RWD**: Or maybe it produces some more permanent form of writing rapidly. Maybe you could engrave as fast as you could write.

**RBD**: How do you think they made the Ten Commandments?

# Discussion: Process versus Content

**Man**: I was very interested in the process. It kind of underlined everything that you had presented. We were all such different people. I'm sure that it would have been very easy to waste a lot of time in arguments or disagreements if it hadn't been for the process.

**RBD**: It is always much easier to get people to agree on a process for reaching a result than to get them to agree on a particular result. In other words, it is easier to get people to accept form than to accept content. I learned that from a politics class I took in college. Actually, I didn't learn much from the class itself, but getting into the class was real interesting. It was required for politics majors and there were sixty people trying to get in, but the professor said he could only accept twenty. He said, "I don't care who gets in, all I care is that everybody agrees unanimously about who is getting in." This first class session was supposed to be an hour and a half, and two hours later, people were still fighting over who should get in. The longer people waited and "invested" time, the more adamant they became about getting in—so they wouldn't feel that they'd wasted their time.

It was incredible. The teacher let the bickering go on and on. The seniors were saying, "This is our last chance to get this class." The younger politics majors were saying, "Well, I don't really know if I want to go on with this major if I can't qualify right now." Everyone had a reason for why they should get in to the class. Every time someone would give a reason, the teacher would ask, "Does everyone agree to that?" and of course, not everyone would. So they'd start all over again.

As long as everyone was trying to argue for their own position, they couldn't do it. There was always a counter argument. After two and a half hours they'd lost about a third of the people due to attrition or frustration, but there was still twice as many people as could fit in the class. Finally people began proposing *processes* for deciding who should get in. In other words, instead of each individual stating their case and the whole group trying to decide, "You can go in, and you can't," on an individual basis, they tried to come up with a process for making the decision that the whole group could agree upon.

First, they set a few basic criteria like, "If it's your last quarter and you're a senior and you have to have the class to graduate then we all concede that you should get in." They then selected certain categories of people and figured what percentage of each category should get to get into the class. A certain number of politics majors, a certain number of people who are interested, but aren't seeking the major, etc. They had to represent each group of people that were there somehow or there wouldn't be unanimous agreement. Beyond that, the only process everyone could agree upon as being "fair" was randomly drawing names out of a hat. So in the end they all agreed to pull a certain number of names from each group out of a hat. I don't know whether I was lucky or unlucky to have my name drawn.

But what I did learn was that in order to get to a consensus in a system of very diverse people, you had to focus on the strategy, the process for making the decision, not the result. To reach a unanimous agreement, they had to define the process and not know what the final result was going to be for any individual. The amazing thing was, once that was done, people that had been vehemently fighting for hours accepted the results without conflict, even though the results weren't in their favor.

# 7

---

# Conclusion:
# Using the Other 90%

**RBD**: The ability to intentionally direct the creative process
has always separated human beings from other animals.
One of my favorite quotes is by Jacob Bronowski, the author
of *The Ascent of Man*. He said, "Every animal leaves traces of
what it was. Human beings alone leave traces of what they
created." Human beings are distinguished from other animals by the depth of their ability to make maps and use tools
to turn those maps into reality. Ants can leave a trail, bees can
do dances and make complex hives, but neither can draw
something that only exists in their imagination.

I remember having a discussion once with John Grinder.
We both agreed that the ability to choose was at the root of
evolution. That the process of evolution was the process of
gaining more and more choices. Choice requires 1) having a
richer and wider model of the world and 2) the ability to
disassociate yourself from an immediate reflex. John felt

that the ability to make a disassociated image of yourself doing something, before you do it, as in the New Behavior Generator, may well be one of the major evolutionary distinctions between human beings and animals. I do not know if a dog can visualize itself when Pavlov rings the bell, and think, "What am I going to do next?" What distinguishes human beings is the degree to which they can step back and make a map of something in their brains. Evolution is a function of increasing that ability.

It is estimated that your brain has the hardware potential of ten million computers the way it's wired up; and that most people only use about 5–10% of that capacity. Creativity is not a function of how much space you have. You have plenty of it. We have quite a few years before we use up all those billions of cells up there. Creativity is a function of how you use that capacity.

Human beings also have a unique capacity for developing and using tools—tools that extend their capabilities even beyond the ten million computers they come with. Some tools allow us to extend our own individual bodies and nervous systems, others allow us to link our nervous systems with other people and other systems around us to add potentially millions, even billions more computers to our creative capacity. Our goal in this book has been to offer you some tools to release more of the immense capacity that is your birthright as a human being, and to connect this capacity more fully to your interactions with others—tools for the dreamer, tools for the realist, tools for the critic.

We have presented conceptual tools in the form of the R.O.L.E. Model, the T.O.T.E. Model, Meta Program patterns, Logical Level distinctions, outcome Well-Formedness Conditions, and an understanding of the tools of patent and copyright law. We have offered you a number of operational tools in the form of techniques and formats to apply those conceptual tools as individuals and teams, to a variety of contexts requiring creativity. These operational tools include strategy elicitation procedures and the B.A.G.E.L. distinctions, the T.O.T.E. and R.O.L.E. utilization processes, the New Behavior Generator, the S.C.O.R.E. Model and the Design Grid.

In summary, the key points of this book have been:

1. You think with your brain. Your brain operates by processing sensory representations and impressions. Those sensory impressions are the meat of what makes a human being "human" and of what makes creativity "creative."

2. The way in which you link those representations together as you build your model of the world determines the kinds of choices you perceive as available to you. The more rich and robust your model of the world is, the more rich and creative a life you will experience. Our models of the world are a function of the links that we establish between our perception of the environment, our behavioral actions, our internal plans and strategies, our beliefs and values, and our sense of self.

3. The process of building our model of the world involves a feedback loop, or T.O.T.E., composed of internally generated goals, operations with which to implement those goals, and evidence procedures with which to evaluate our progress towards those goals.

4. The basic function of this feedback loop is to generate and filter experiences. We are bombarded with so much information that we end up needing to filter much of it out. The way in which we adjust and utilize our perceptual filters determines what we do with the information that is available to us.

5. Our inner representational and neural processes are supported and manifested through physical and behavioral activities in the form of accessing cues and physiological states.

6. Creativity involves the constant incremental updating and changing of goals, evidence procedures and operations. Different types of creativity derive from changing different fundamental parts of the feedback loop through which we interact with the world:

   *Innovation* is a function of generating new goals and visions.

   *Discovery* is a function of changing perceptual filters and evidence procedures.

   *Invention* is a function of applying and varying the operations with which we manifest and achieve goals within the constraints of our environment.

7. Creativity is a reiterative process that involves a constant cycle of macro programs in the form of dreamer, realist and critic.

8. The total process of creativity not only involves our own mental activity, but our interface with the brains and nervous systems of other people. Creativity is influenced and expressed through our interaction and communication with others in a system wider than ourselves.

We hope that you have discovered and developed some more tools for setting filters, using your brain, and balancing your dreamer, realist and critic. The paradox of creativity is that the majority of it is actually a highly reiterative incremental process based on feedback. If you try something and it doesn't work, go back and try something different. Instead of giving up, or throwing ideas away, or trying the same thing one more time just to make sure, change it a little bit and try it again. You are constantly piling up the little changes and suddenly, BAM, it appears that you've made a quantum leap. The 99% perspiration produces the 1% inspiration.

Sometimes people think of perspiration as a negative thing. But whenever I think of it I remember something my junior high school basketball coach said. We had just finished an intense practice session. As we were all leaving the court, dripping with perspiration, I said something about how much we were sweating. He winked at me and replied, "That ain't sweat. That's satisfaction." And he was right.

**TE**: I want to remind you that these tools are not just for making money or inventing things that can be patented or marketed. The thing I hope you take with you from this book is a rekindling of the childlike attitude of being curious, not worrying about failing, and doing things because each thing you do represents a success of some kind. So whether you're going to use these tools to make money, or to be able to communicate with somebody you care about better, or just to make yourself feel better all by yourself in a room somewhere, remember that whatever you do counts. And it counts all the more if you do it with childlike curiosity and fascination. If you follow these kinds of techniques with that in mind, the chances are you're going to come up with something worthwhile for yourself and those people around you.

**RWD**: Patents, copyrights and trademarks cover only a very small portion of human creativity. But the thing that I've always enjoyed about the patent field is that being around the process of inventing and creating is a joyful thing no matter what form it takes and regardless of whether you're a dreamer, a realist or a critic. The more we can be creative in communications, creative in art, creative in music, creative in coming up with new ideas whether protectable or not, the more possibilities we will have to experience joy and to experience being human. I believe that's going to be the savior of society and the earth.

**RBD**: Over the years I've heard NLP described as many things: a set of communication skills, a collection of quick fix techniques, a model of behavior, a type of psychotherapy, and on and on. But to me what NLP has always really been is "tools for dreamers." The tools for those of us who wish to make dreams come true. We hope you will find these tools of some assistance in making your own dreams a reality.

# Afterword

Now that you have experienced the map, we invite you to explore the territory. We are sure you will find that these tools will have many practical applications in your daily lives.

As we mentioned in the book, effective performance requires constant practice and feedback in order to maintain the experience curve necessary for behavioral competence. Seminars and workshops, such as the one that serves as the basis for this book, are one effective way to acquire the skills and practice to use the tools we have presented here in the most successful and comprehensive manner.

The *Dynamic Learning Center for Neuro-Linguistic Programming* provides consulting and training services for both professionals and lay people in the applications of NLP. In addition to Creativity and Innovation, the Dynamic Learning Center provides trainings, tapes, books and interventions in the areas of Health, Leadership, Education, Psychotherapy and Modeling as well as certification courses for NLP Practitioners, Master Practitioners and Trainers.

For further information contact:

**Dynamic Learning Center
for Neuro-Linguistic Programming**
P.O. Box 1112
Ben Lomond, California 95005
Phone: (408) 336-3457
Fax: (408) 336-5854

# Bibliography

*Neuro-Linguistic Programming Vol. I,* Dilts, R., Grinder, J., Bandler, R., DeLozier, J.; Meta Publications, Cupertino, California, 1980.

*Plans and the Structure of Behavior,* Miller, G., Galanter, E., and Pribram, K., Henry Holt & Co., Inc., 1960.

*Principles of Psychology,* William James, *Britannica Great Books,* Encyclopedia Britannica Inc., Chicago Ill., 1979.

*Using Your Brain,* Bandler, Richard; Real People Press, Moab, Utah,1984.

*Walt Disney: The Dreamer, The Realist and The Critic,* Dilts, R., Dynamic Learning Publications, Ben Lomond, CA, 1990.

*Albert Einstein: Neuro-Linguistic Analysis of a Genius,* Dilts, R., Dynamic Learning Publications, Ben Lomond, CA, 1990.

*NLP In Training Groups,* Dilts, R. and Epstein, T., Dynamic Learning Publications, Santa Cruz, CA, 1989.

*The Structure of Magic Vol. I & II,* Grinder, J. and Bandler, R.; Science and Behavior Books, Palo Alto, California, 1975.

*Frogs into Princes,* Bandler, R. and Grinder, J.; Real People Press, Moab, Utah, 1979.

*Applications of Neuro-Linguistic Programming,* Dilts, R.; Meta Publications, Cupertino, California, 1983.

***Changing Beliefs With NLP,*** Dilts, R.; Meta Publications, Cupertino, California, 1990.

***Beliefs; Pathways to Health and Well-Being,*** Dilts, R., Halbom, T. Smith, S.; Metamorphous Press, Portland, OR, 1990


The following booklets are available from:
  Superintendent of Documents
  U.S. Government Patent Office
  Washington, D.C. 20402
  General Information Concerning Patents
Patents and Inventions: An Informative Aid for Inventors
General Information Concerning Trademarks
Questions and Answers About Patents
Questions and Answers About Trademarks

*Introduction to Patents,*
  SBA, P.O. Box 15434, Ft. Worth, TX 76119.

# Appendix A

## Strategies Overview

### I. Definition of *"Strategy"*

A. From the Greek word *"strategos"* meaning *"general."*

B. *A detailed plan for reaching a goal or advantage."* (Random House Dictionary)

C. In NLP, the term *"strategy"* is used to mean the steps of a mental process or program (in the sense of a computer program) that leads to a particular goal or outcome. Each step in the strategy is characterized by the use of one of the five senses or *"representational systems."*

### II. Classes of Strategies

A. Memory

B. Decision Making

C. Learning

D. Creativity

E. Motivation

F. Reality

G. Belief (or Convincer)

# III. Structure of a Strategy

A. General Systems Model

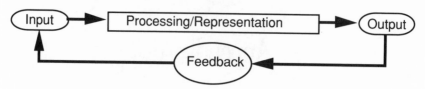

B. **T.O.T.E.** Model—
Stands for **T**est-**O**perate-**T**est-**E**xit

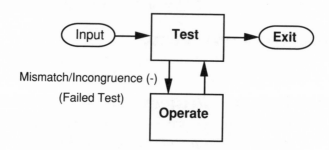

C. NLP Strategy Structure

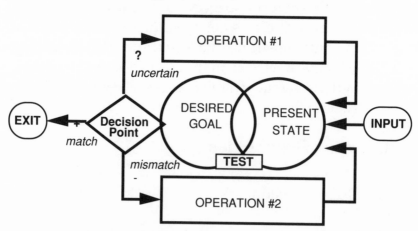

# IV. Strategy Procedures

A. Elicitation
B. Utilization
C. Design
D. Installation

# Appendix B

## R.O.L.E. Model Overview

The **R.O.L.E. Model**™is a simple but effective way of organizing information about how someone is thinking. The distinctions indicated by the R.O.L.E. model should be identified for each significant step in the thinking strategy you are modeling. The letters stand for the following fundamental elements:

1. **Representational System.** Which of the five senses is most dominant for the particular mental step in the strategy: **V**isual (sight), **A**uditory (sound), **K**inesthetic (feeling), **O**lfactory (smell), **G**ustatory (taste).

   a. **Sub-Modalities.** Each sense perceives a special set of qualities that can also be a critical factor in the thought process. For example:

| Visual | Auditory | Kinesthetic |
|--------|----------|-------------|
| BRIGHTNESS (dim-bright) | VOLUME (loud-soft) | INTENSITY (strong-weak) |
| SIZE (large-small) | TONE (bass-treble | AREA (large-small) |
| COLOR (black & white-color) | PITCH (high-low) | TEXTURE (rough-smooth) |
| MOVEMENT (fast-slow-still) | TEMPO (fast-slow) | DURATION (constant-intermittent) |
| DISTANCE (near-far) | DISTANCE (close-far) | TEMPERATURE (hot-cold) |
| FOCUS (clear-fuzzy ) | RHYTHM | WEIGHT (heavy-light) |
| LOCATION | LOCATION | LOCATION |

2. **Orientation.** Is the sensory system oriented (**e**)xternally toward the outside world or (**i**)nternally toward either (**r**)emembered or (**c**)onstructed experiences?

3. **Linkage.** How is a particular step or sense linked to the others?

    For instance, is it part of an overlap or **"synesthesia"** as in a *"see-feel"* "(V->K), *"hear-see"* (A->V), *"feel-see"* (K->V), *"hear-feel"* (A->K), etc.

    a. If the linkage is not an automatic synesthesia, is it a *congruent response, polarity response* or *meta response* (a response about something) to the previous step?

4. **Effect.** What is the result, effect or purpose of the step? It could be to either (a) *access* (b) *organize* or (c) *evaluate or judge* information. So the function of the step could be to

test information from the senses or to operate to change some part of the ongoing experience.

   a. Making the R.O.L.E. into a **B.A.G.E.L.** Once the above information is elicited, it can be confirmed or put into play through the following physiological processes:

      1. **B**ody Posture;
      2. **A**ccessing Cues—breathing rate, noises, facial expression, etc.;
      3. **G**estures;
      4. **E**ye Movements;
      5. **L**anguage Patterns.

# Appendix C

## The R.O.L.E. Model

The purpose of modeling is to create a pragmatic map or "model" of some particular phenomenon that can be used to reproduce that phenomenon by anyone who is motivated to do so.

### A. Representational System

Representational systems are the brain structures which operate the five senses—*Visual (sight)*, *Auditory (sound)*, *Kinesthetic (feeling)*, *Olfactory (smell)* and *Gustatory (taste)*. Based on the fact that the brain stores and processes information from the five senses, NLP considers each step in a mental program to be a reactivation of some sensory processes— i.e., that "thinking" is the combining and sequencing of mental images, sounds, feelings, etc. Whether the thought process is one of memory, decision making, learning, motivation, creativity or belief it will involve sensory experience. The way in which we combine and sequence our mental representations during thinking will to a great extent determine the accuracy and impact of the information we are considering.

The sensory system(s) someone uses to carry out a particular mental task can make a significant difference in their effectiveness. For instance, some tasks are more visual in nature (proofreading, for example) and require the ability to visualize. Other behaviors are more dependent on one of the other senses, such as playing a musical instrument (auditory) or performing gymnastics (kinesthetic).

## 1. Language as a Representational System

While the spoken word is part of the auditory system, its function is to organize and connect information from the other senses as opposed to simply register qualities of an experience as the more purely tonal elements of the auditory system. Since language is actually represented differently in the brain than pure sounds, NLP considers language to function as another representational system. Thus NLP distinguishes between the linguistic and the tonal functions of the auditory system by designating pure sounds as $A_t$ for (**A**)uditory (**t**)onal, and words as $A_d$ for (**A**)uditory (**d**)igital (the term "digital" is used since words are discrete verbal symbols or digits).

## 2. Sub-Modalities

Each representational system is designed to perceive certain basic qualities of the experiences it senses. These include characteristics such as: color, brightness, tone, loudness, temperature, pressure, etc. These qualities are called *sub-modalities* in NLP since they are sub-components of each of the representational systems.

People will differ in their abilities to detect and manipulate these sensory characteristics which can be an important determining factor in the ability to perform particular mental tasks. It is the information about sensory qualities of things that are most important to our minds, not the things themselves. In fact, a number of the techniques of NLP are based on having the subject consciously change the submodality qualities of their mental representations in order to change their reactions to particular memory or thought.

The table below lists the various sub-modalities of the senses.

| Visual | Auditory | Kinesthetic |
|---|---|---|
| BRIGHTNESS (dim-bright) | VOLUME (loud-soft) | INTENSITY (strong-weak) |
| SIZE (large-small) | TONE (bass-treble) | AREA (large-small) |
| COLOR (black & white-color) | PITCH (high-low) | TEXTURE (rough-smooth) |
| MOVEMENT (fast-slow-still) | TEMPO (fast-slow) | DURATION (constant-intermittent) |
| DISTANCE (near-far) | DISTANCE (close-far) | TEMPERATURE (hot-cold) |
| FOCUS (clear-fuzzy ) | RHYTHM | WEIGHT (heavy-light) |
| LOCATION | LOCATION | LOCATION |

## B. Orientation

There are three basic ways we can orient the use of our senses: (1) to take in information from the *external world,* (2) to *remember* or *recall* information that has already been taken in by the brain, and (3) to *construct,* imagine or piece together new information that has not ever previously been sensed.

Clearly, we guide our lives based on how we piece together our memories and constructs of the future to respond to what we are able to perceive in the ongoing external environment. The emphasis placed on these various functions, the order in which they are balanced and combined together, how much information is brought in through each, etc., will influence the success or failure of a particular thought process.

In NLP we use the abbreviations **e, r,** and **c** to show when the orientation of a representational system is (**e**)xternal, (**r**)emembering, or (**c**)onstructing. If it is unclear or unimportant whether the orientation is constructed or remembered we simply use the abbreviation **i** for (**i**)nternal orientation.

## C. Links

The sequence and manner in which each sensory step is linked to the step that comes before it and the one which comes after it is another important feature of thought. There are two basic types of linkage: *analog* and *digital*.

### 1. Sequential or Digital Links

Digital linkages are links which basically function as a trigger or a switch. They turn a particular process on or off. There is no overlap between the representation that serves as the stimulus or trigger and the one that occurs as the response. Most *verbal* and *symbolic* cues form *digital* linkages. For example, the word *"cat"* does not physically sound like a cat, feel furry, nor do the sounds or letters attempt to indicate four legs, whiskers, a tail, etc. The word is simply a cue for us to access a particular class of mental pictures, sounds, feelings, etc. In NLP notation, digital links are shown as an arrow connecting the two experiences that have been linked. The arrow points from the trigger representation to the response. So $A_d$->$V^r$ would indicate a word which triggers a remembered mental image. The abbreviation $V^e$->$K^e$ would indicate an external visual cue (like the red light on a traffic signal) that cues an external movement.

### 2. Simultaneous or Analog Links

With analog linkages there is an overlap between the mental processes that are linked together. Unlike a digital link, two representations which are linked together analogically vary in proportion to each other (as to either being on or off). For example, some people experience an overlap between what they see and what they feel. Dancers, for instance, sometimes report actually feeling the movements of someone they are watching perform. Furthermore, if the movements they see are more intense, their feeling response is more intense. In NLP this connection would be called a *"see-feel"* overlap. We will notate this type of analog linkage as $V^e=>K^i$. A musician may have the same kind of overlapping link between tones and images. Such a linkage would be called a *"hear-feel"* overlap ($A_t=>V^i$).

The particular sequence of the steps that linked together is a very influential factor in the effectiveness of the strategy. For example, a see-feel link might be better for evaluative functions like art criticism or copy editing, while a feel-see link might be better for productive functions like creating a piece of art or brainstorming.

### a. Synesthesia

In NLP the term *synesthesia* is often used to refer to the process of overlapping the information coming from one sense to information in a different modality. The term literally means "a synthesizing of the senses." Two experiences become so overlapped together that it is difficult to distinguish or separate them. Synesthesia patterns can be a very important factor in determining the ease or effectiveness with which certain mental functions are performed. As with the other distinctions we have made, the strength of the various synesthesia relationships vary for different people. In many ways these are very primary neurological functions and will determine a person's innate capabilities, and form the fundamental building blocks of intelligence and personality.

### b. Synesthesias between Sub-modalities

It should also be noted that these synesthesia links may occur between the sub-modality qualities of the various representational systems as well. For example, in a $V=>K^i$ synesthesia some people may feel relaxed when they see the color blue and irritated when they see red, while others may have little response to color but feel relaxed when they see slow movement and irritation when the movement is too fast. For others, the intensity of feeling may be linked to brightness, and so on.

For example, sub-modalities may be used to change the reaction associated with a particular memory or thought. To try this out, think of a pleasant meal and an unpleasant trip to the dentist. Which qualities of sight, sound, feeling, smell and taste make the one pleasant and the other unpleasant? As an experiment, change some of the dimensions of the sensory qualities of your memories. Alter the mental image you have of the pleasant meal by making it dimmer and then brighter. Make the size of the image bigger than life and then make it smaller and further away. Make the sounds you have associated with the experience louder and then softer. Raise and lower the pitch of the voices and other sounds. Notice how these affect the degree or quality of the feelings of pleasantness associated with the experience.

Now do the same thing with the unpleasant experience of the dentist's office. For instance, make any pictures you have associated with the experience dim and far away. Try viewing your memory of the experiences from a disassociated point of view-as if you were sitting in a theater watching yourself as a movie character. Reduce the volume of any of the sounds associated with it, lower the pitch of the drill to low, slow drone. Most likely you will find that altering the qualities of the experience in this way will significantly change the degree of unpleasantness you experience in connection with the memory at the moment.

Your ability to make these manipulations will give you some information about your own most highly developed, most valued and most conscious representational systems.

## D. Effect

The function or purpose that each particular mental step or linkage plays in the overall program is another important influence of the effectiveness of a strategy. The effect of a particular step in the thought sequence is a function of how it is used and what it is used for.

## 1. The T.O.T.E. Structure

*The pursuance of future ends and the choice
of means for their attainment are the mark and
criterion of the presence of mentality in a phenomenon.*
—William James, *Principles of Psychology*

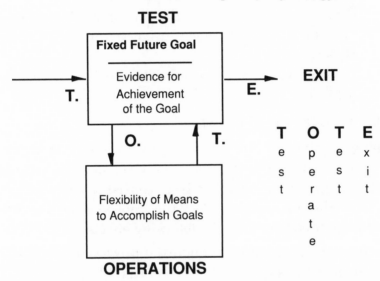

A mental strategy is typically organized into a basic feedback loop called a T.O.T.E. (Miller, et al, 1960). The letters **T.O.T.E.** stand for ***Test-Operate-Test-Exit***. The T.O.T.E. concept maintains that all mental and behavioral programs revolve around having a *fixed goal* and a *variable means to achieve that goal*. This model indicates that, as we think, we set goals in our mind (consciously or unconsciously) and develop a TEST for when that goal has been achieved. If that goal is not achieved we OPERATE to change something or do something to get closer to our goal. When our TEST criteria have been satisfied, we then EXIT on to the next step. So the function of any particular part of a behavioral program could be to (**T**)est information from the senses in order to check progress towards the goal or to (**O**)perate to change some part of the ongoing experience so that it can satisfy the (**T**)est and (**E**)xit on to the next part of the program.

In order to have the minimum information about how someone thinks we must identify:

1. the person's goals;
2. the evidence used by the person to determine progress toward the goal;
3. the sets of choices used by the person to get to the goal and the specific behaviors used to implement these choices; and
4. the way the person responds if the goal is not initially achieved.

## 2. The AEIOU of Effects

In detailing the effects of the steps in a strategy it is helpful to remember that Operations usually consist of *accessing* or *utilization* procedures; and Tests consist of *organization* and *evaluative* procedures. Thus, the steps in a strategy will most likely produce one of the following effects:

(**a**)ccess information through the process of association and the application of perceptual filters.

(**e**)valuate or judge information by comparing it or testing it against some standard or criteria.

(**i**)nput information from the external environment.

(**o**)rganize information by arranging it in a certain structure.

(**u**)tilize some aspect of the external environment in order to express or change something.

The typical sequence of these functions would be:

(**i**)nput from environment->(**a**)ccess other relevant information associated with the input -> (**o**)rganize the information into an appropriate structure->(**e**)valuate the information according to priorities of criteria -> (**u**)tilize something in the external environment in response to the evaluation (which creates new input).

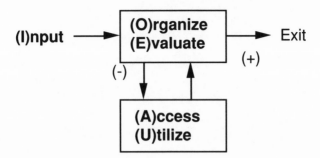

According to NLP, of course, it is the type of representational systems, sub-modalities, orientations, linkages, etc., that a person uses to carry out these various tests and operations that will determine their degree of success.

# Appendix D

## Meta Program Patterns

**1. Approach To Problems**
   a. Towards the Positive—Proactive
   b. Away From the Negative—Reactive

**2. Chunk Size**
   a. Large Chunks—Generalities
   b. Small Chunks—Details

**3. Time Frame**
   a. Short Term—Long Term
   b. Past—Present—Future

**4. Approach to Problem Solving**
   a. Task (Achievement)
      1. Choices—Goals
      2. Procedures—Operations
   b. Relationship (Power; Affiliation)
      1. Self—*My, I, Me*
      2. Other—*You, His, Their*
      3. Context—*We, The Company, The Market*

5.   **Mode of Comparison**
     a.  Match (*Similarities*)—Consensus
     b.  Mismatch (*Differences*)—Confrontation

6.   **Thinking Style**
     a.  Vision
     b.  Action
     c.  Logic
     d.  Emotion

# Appendix E

## Strategy Elicitation Procedure

### I. Preparation

**A.** Be clear about your purpose for eliciting the strategy. The goal or outcome you have for getting the strategy will determine how much detail you will need about the strategy.

    **1.** Establish your criteria for selecting who you will use as models, the chunk size of the strategy, the number of people you will sample, manageable length of time, etc. For example, if you are trying to help someone solve a personal problem you will operate very differently than if you are designing a reading course or hiring a new executive.

**B.** Remember to start with the most general patterns (like *primary representational system*, most obvious *accessing cue*, etc.) first and then move to the specifics. Once you have a thumbnail sketch of the basic strategy structure, you can begin to fill in the details with a lot less chance of becoming lost or confused.

**C.** Remember that it is always better to get *BEHAVIORAL EXAMPLES* of the strategy than it is to *talk about* the strategy.

**D.** Remember that some (and occasionally many) steps of the strategy may be outside of the conscious awareness of your subject so (1) *rely on your sensory observations* of accessing cues and other minimal cues and (2) *be patient* —the information will sometimes surface after a few repetitions. Often you will find that the finer the details you are going for, the more chance that the information will be out of awareness.

**E.** Timing is very important. The subject will often answer your question immediately with an unconscious behavioral cue long before they begin to say anything about it.

**F.** *If the information is important it will repeat itself.* If you missed observing a particular step or are unsure about one, just reaccess the strategy— if it is an essential piece of the strategy sequence it **WILL** repeat.

## II.  Procedure

### A.  General Elicitation Procedures
1. Access **specific examples** of success and failure. That is, if you are eliciting a creativity strategy, elicit examples of being stuck as well as being creative. If you are exploring memory, get behavioral demonstrations where the subject cannot remember in addition to when they can.
2. In some cases it is too difficult to set up and elicit ongoing behavioral demonstrations. In these cases remember to:

    **a.** Orient the subject to specific past instances and examples.

        **1.** Say, *"Think of a specific time you were really able to be creative (or wanted to be creative but got stuck)*, rather than something too general like *"How are you creative?"*

    **b.** Filter out any pieces of the memory strategy your subject is using to initially recover the instances you are asking for.

    **c.** Sort by the **PROCESS** rather than the content or the event.

    **d.** Make sure your subject has chosen a manageable length of time; i.e., if the subject is thinking of an experience that took several weeks or months it will be very difficult to get specific details. You are looking for a mental program (that usually only takes a few seconds total) that cycles over and over again.

    **e.** Associate your subject back into the experience. Say, *"Put yourself **fully** back INTO that instance and re-experience again exactly what you were doing. Go through it and relive it again right now."*

## B.  Contrast Method of Elicitation.

    **1.** Contrast two examples that are as SIMILAR as possible in content but differ only in that one was a success and the other was a failure.

        **a.** For example, say, *"Think of a phone number that is so easy to recall that you know you'll never forget it... Now try to remember a phone number that you know you should remember but that you still have a hard time with."*

    **2.** Find out what is **DIFFERENT** between the two experiences. This will bring out immediately what is essential to success or failure in the strategy.

### C.  Comparison Method of Elicitation

1.  Compare three examples that are as DIFFERENT in CONTENT as possible but are each examples of the SAME PROCESS (i.e., memory, creativity, etc.).

    a.  For example, say, *"Think of a specific time you wrote something you consider to be very creative... Think of an instance you made a creative move or play in your favorite sport... Think of a specific example of when you came up with a creative solution to a problem you were working out in your business."*

2.  Find out what is **SIMILAR** about the thought process and physiology used in each of these different instances.

### D.  Sequential Method of Elicitation

1.  Find the beginning of the strategy and ask, *"What happened next?"* until you reach the endpoint of the strategy.

2.  Identify the end of the strategy by asking *"How did you know you were done?"* And then continue to ask *"And what happened just before that?"* until you reach the beginning.

### E.  Elicitation of T.O.T.E. Functions

Elicitation Questions for Behavior "**X**." (eg., *Be Creative, Remember Something, Make a Decision, Motivate Yourself, Learn Something, Convince Yourself.*)

1.  Elicitation of the **Decision Point**.
    *Response to a Satisfactory Test.*

    a.  How do you know when you've been able to satisfactorily **X**?

    b.  When you are able to **X**, what lets you know you are done?

    c. Think of what it is like to be absolutely sure you've been able to **X**.

*Response to an Inconclusive Test.*

    a. What lets you know you are not yet finished with your strategy to **X**?

    b. What lets you know you are not ready to move on to something else yet?

    c. When you are not sure that you have successfully been able to **X**, what lets you know?

**2.** Elicitation of the **Test**.

    a. What is a demonstration that you have successfully been able to **X**?

    b. What kind of comparison do you use to know you have succeeded to **X**?

    c. How do you know whether or not you have been able to **X**?

    d. How do you know whether you have done well or poorly when you **X**?

**3.** Elicitation of the **Operation**.

    a. What specifically do you do as you are preparing to **X**?

    b. What do you do when you are not sure you have successfully been able to **X**?

    c. What specific steps do/did you take to **X**?

    d. What procedure do you go through to make sure you are ready to **X**?

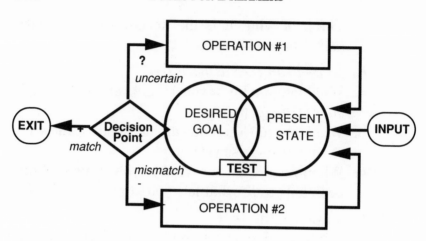

# Appendix F

## The S.C.O.R.E. Model™ for Change

**A.** The S.C.O.R.E. Model™ identifies the primary components necessary for effectively organizing information
about any goal or change. The letters stand for Symptoms, Causes, Outcome, Resources, and Effect. These
elements represent the minimum amount of information that needs to be gathered to create changes.

   1. **Symptoms** are typically the most noticeable and
   conscious aspects of the *presenting problem* or *present
   state*.

   2. **Causes** are the underlying elements responsible for
   *creating* and *maintaining* the symptoms. They are
   usually less obvious than the symptoms themselves.

   3. The **Outcome** is the actual *goal* or *desired state* that
   would take the place of the symptoms.

   4. **Resources** are the underlying elements responsible
   for creating and maintaining the outcome.

      **a.** Techniques, such as *reframing, change history,
      anchoring,* etc., are structures for applying
      particular resources.

   5. **Effects** are the results of, or responses to, the
   achievement of a particular outcome. Often the

desired effect of achieving an outcome is mistaken for
the outcome itself.

   **a.** Positive effects are often the reason or motivation
   for wanting the outcome to begin with.

   **b.** Negative effects can create resistance or ecological problems.

**B.** **Vital Signs** are the specific characteristics or features
that are associated with each of the elements identified
above. In NLP these vital signs are:

   Accessing Cues
   Predicates
   Meta Model Patterns
   Body Posture and Gestures
   Critical Sub-Modalities
   Meta Program Patterns
   Criteria
   Beliefs

**C.** **Behavioral Demonstrations** are specific, observable,
ongoing examples of these vital signs. A behavioral demonstration should be elicited for each of the S.C.O.R.E.
elements.

**D.** **Levels of Change** are organized into the following
hierarchy:

   Specific Behaviors
   Capabilities
   Beliefs
   Identity

Each level is progressively more encompassing and impactful.
It is thus important to know at which level each of the
S.C.O.R.E. elements is occurring.

| Causes<br>*Problem State* | Symptoms<br>*Present State* | Techniques<br>**Resources** | Outcome<br>*Desired State* | Effect<br>*Ecology/Result* |
|---|---|---|---|---|
| Vital Signs | Vital Signs | Vital Signs | Vital Signs | Vital Signs |
| Behavioral<br>Demonstration | Behavioral<br>Demonstration | Behavioral<br>Demonstration | Behavioral<br>Demonstration | Behavioral<br>Demonstration |
| Level of<br>Change | Level of<br>Change | Level of<br>Change | Level of<br>Change | Level of<br>Change |

# Appendix G

## Suggestions for Keeping Laboratory Notebooks

Whether you are developing a physical product or working with some less tangible expression of creativity it is valuable to keep a record of your work in a laboratory notebook. When properly kept, a laboratory notebook is important because it establishes a permanent record which can be referred to in the future to prove what was done during the course of a project, and particularly what inventions were made and when. Below are specific instructions designed to provide the best possible legal protection for your inventions:

1. **INK.** While records in pencil are better than no records, entries should be made in ink. (Never erase anything; cross out if necessary.)

2. **SPACE.** Do not leave blank space above, below or between entries. Close each entry with a horizontal pen line immediately following the last line of writing and begin the next entry immediately below this line.

3. **SKETCHES.** Include and explain sketches and diagrams whenever possible. In general, fragmentary

sketches or diagrams, and sketches or diagrams without explanation should be avoided

4.  **INSERTIONS.** Sketches, photographs, blueprints and other material on separate paper should be securely glued (avoid rubber cement or scotch tape) to a page of the notebook. Each insertion should be identified with a suitable caption or number, and reference should be made to it at the appropriate place in the notebook.

5.  **SUBJECT.** Whenever possible, the subject of each entry should be written at the left of the page at the beginning of the entry.

6.  **DATE.** Each entry should be dated at the right of the page immediately following the last line of the entry or the signature, if it is signed.

7.  **SIGNATURE.** Each entry which you think has possible significance should be signed and dated by you.

8.  **WITNESS.** Each significant entry should also be read and understood by two other competent engineers and, immediately following your signature and date, each should write "Witnessed and Understood" and write his or her signature and the witnessing date. If a model is built and tested it should also be similarly witnessed.

# Appendix H

## Well-Formedness Conditions for Evaluating New Ideas

### "WANT TO" Phase—Dreamer

Establish the payoffs of the idea.

> **Why** are you doing this?
> **What** is the purpose?
> **What** are the payoffs?
> **How** will you know that you have them?
> **When** can you expect to get them?
> **Where** do you want to be in the future?
> **Who** do you want to be or be like?

### "HOW TO" Phase—Realist

State the specific goal in positive terms;
Establish time frames and milestones for progress;
Make sure it can be initiated and maintained by the appropriate person or group and, that progress is testable through sensory experience.

> **What** will *we be doing?*
>> (As opposed to what will we *stop* doing, *avoid* or *quit*.)

**How** specifically will the idea be implemented?
**How** will you know if the goal is achieved?
**How** will the performance criteria be tested?
**Who** *will do it?*
(Assign responsibility and secure commitment from the people who will be carrying out.)
**When** will each phase be implemented?
**When** will the overall goal be completed?
**Where** will each phase be carried out?
**Why** is each step necessary?

## "CHANCE TO" Phase—Critic

Make sure it is ecologically sound and preserves any positive by-products of the current way(s) of achieving the goal.

**Why** might someone object to this new idea?
**Who** will this new idea effect and who will make or break the effectiveness of the idea and what are their needs and payoffs?
**What** positive things do you get out of our current way(s) of doing things?
**How** can you keep those things when you implement the new idea?
**When** *and* **where** *would you* not *want to implement this new idea?*